Global James Bond

Global James Bond

(Re)Imagining and Transplanting a Popular Culture Icon

Edited by

Lisa Funnell and Klaus Dodds
Foreword by Monica Germanà
Afterword by James Page

LEXINGTON BOOKS
Lanham • Boulder • New York • London

Published by Lexington Books
An imprint of The Rowman & Littlefield Publishing Group, Inc.
4501 Forbes Boulevard, Suite 200, Lanham, Maryland 20706
www.rowman.com

86-90 Paul Street, London EC2A 4NE

British Library Cataloguing in Publication Information Available

Library of Congress Cataloging-in-Publication Data

Names: Funnell, Lisa, 1980- editor. | Dodds, Klaus, editor. | Germanà, Monica, writer of foreword. | Page, James (James Bond expert), writer of afterword..
Title: Global James Bond : (re)imagining and transplanting a popular culture icon / edited by Lisa Funnell and Klaus Dodds ; foreword by Monica Germanà ; afterword by James Page.
Description: Lanham : Lexington Books, [2024]. | Includes bibliographical references and index.
Identifiers: LCCN 2023048894 (print) | LCCN 2023048895 (ebook) | ISBN 9781666905328 (cloth) | ISBN 9781666905335 (ebook)
Subjects: LCSH: James Bond films--History and criticism. | James Bond films--Cross-cultural studies.
Classification: LCC PN1995.9.J3 G66 2024 (print) | LCC PN1995.9.J3 (ebook) | DDC 791.43/75–dc23/eng/20231107
LC record available at https://lccn.loc.gov/2023048894
LC ebook record available at https://lccn.loc.gov/2023048895

This book is dedicated to my dad and the many others who lost their lives during the COVID-19 pandemic. While the depth of loss is immeasurable, the love my father had for James Bond lives on in me and the work that I do.—Lisa

Contents

List of Figures

Foreword

Is the World Enough for James Bond?

Monica Germanà

The 2012 release of James Bond's twenty-third outing, *Skyfall* (Mendes), was accompanied by a host of events that marked a significant moment in the life span of the world's most iconic secret agent. On 27 July 2012 almost a billion people watched a tuxedoed Daniel Craig as he appeared to escort Elizabeth II to the opening ceremony of the London 2012 Olympics by helicopter, before Her Majesty the Queen parachuted herself onto her seat at Stratford Olympic Stadium. A few weeks earlier, the *Designing 007* exhibition curated by former British *Vogue* editor Bronwyn Cosgrave and Bond costume designer Lindy Hemming was inaugurated at the Barbican Museum on 6 July 2012. With highlights such as Ken Adam's set designs, Jaws (Richard Kiel)'s prosthetic steel teeth used in *The Spy who Loved Me* (Gilbert 1977) and *Moonraker* (Gilbert 1979), and Honey Ryder's iconic white bikini fashioned for Ursula Andress's memorable scene in *Dr. No* (Young 1962), *Designing 007* went on a tour around some of the world's most glamorous galleries in Shanghai, Moscow, Melbourne, and Dubai among others.

The climax of such preliminary events was 5 October 2012, named Global James Bond Day, to celebrate the fiftieth anniversary of the longest-lasting film franchise in cinema history on the day the first Bond film, *Dr. No*, was released in 1962. Bond euphoria spread infectiously across the globe, with a host of official events including a film retrospective screened at New York's MoMA and a Music of Bond night at LA's Academy of Motion Picture Arts and Sciences. Stevan Riley's documentary *Everything or Nothing: The Untold Story of 007* (2012) was simultaneously released at movie theaters in four continents, while, back in Bond's homeland, London's prestigious auction house, Christie's, sold a cornucopia of memorabilia including a fiberglass shotgun from Tiger Tanaka's ninja training school in *You Only Live Twice* (Gilbert 1967), the scorecard used in the card game at the Fontainebleau Hotel in Miami Beach in *Goldfinger* (Hamilton 1964), and Solitaire (Jane Seymour)'s tarot pack from *Live and Let Die* (Hamilton 1973) (Brown 2012).

If the price tag of some of the official events might have been restricted to an exclusive clique of connoisseurs and collectors, a much larger crowd of Bond fans were invited to partake in the worldwide Bondmania. From Belgium to South Africa office workers ended their ordinary working weeks with Bond-themed Casual Fridays, while radio stations around the world added iconic Bond theme songs to their playlists (*PR NEWS* 2012); Global James Bond Day was embraced as a large-scale worldwide phenomenon, with a kind of enthusiasm that did not seem to fade with time: "wherever you are in the world and whatever you are doing," quoted Bond blogger David Leigh on the tenth anniversary of Global James Bond Day, "today is the day to raise a vodka martini and celebrate the James Bond phenomenon in all its glory" (2022). Even dissenting voices—"It's a chance for fans around the world to revel in cinema's most beloved alcoholic aristocratic borderline-misogynist state-sponsored murderer," wrote Stuart Heritage provokingly in *The Guardian*—are further proof of the wide popularity, if not appeal, of Bond. With fan clubs and communities scattered across the globe since the James Bond International Fan Club was established in 1979 (following the earlier American James Bond Fan Club founded by Richard Scheckman and Bob Forlini in 1974) (Rye 2004), after *Skyfall*, the most recent films have been rising in popularity outside the British and American contexts (Jones and Higson 2020).

While Bond's golden anniversary brought home the knowledge that the fan community had grown as international in range as the geographical settings of the franchise's films, it is also true that the Bond phenomenon was, arguably, global from the start. Penned at Goldeneye (Jamaica), by a Scottish writer on the back of his British naval intelligence work during World War II, *Casino Royale*'s successful recipe of visceral realism and escapist fantasy owed much to Fleming's experience of world politics at its best and worst. Although Fleming had attempted to secure film rights for his novels earlier, it was not until March 1961, when *Life* Magazine cited *From Russia with Love* (1957) as one of John Fitzgerald Kennedy's favourite novels, that Canadian producer Harry Saltzman signed an agreement with Fleming's agents for the filming rights of the Bond novels (all except for *Casino Royale* [1953] and *Thunderball* [1961]). It was the Jamaican setting of *Dr. No*, however, that featured in Bond's first cinematic outing, the treatment for which, drafted in September 1961, displayed the transnational scope that would become the trademark of subsequent installments in the franchise. The glamour of foreign locations met with an international plot that, whilst remaining fictitious, resonated with current affairs; foreshadowing the Cuban missile crisis, the villain of the original draft, Paul Duncan remembers, "plans to stuff a ship full of explosives and blow it up in the Panama Canal under the Cuban flag" (Duncan 2012, 31).

It was also in 1961, with the publication of the eighth Bond novel, *Thunderball*, that the Soviet counterintelligence agency SMERSH was replaced by SPECTRE "as an international crime organization which contained elements of SMERSH and the Gestapo and the Mafia" (Fleming 1964, 106), in answer to a shifting political climate that complicated the East/West divide of the earlier novels. Around the same time, censorship of Fleming's *Dr. No* (1958) under Francisco Franco's dictatorship in Spain was equally telling of Bond's international appeal and the subversive threat it posed to oppressive regimes. In more recent times, while Bond's dubbed voice in countries such as France, Spain, and Italy suggests a level of adjustment "to suit local preferences" (Jones and Higson 2020, 112), China's censorship of *Skyfall*'s references to torture practices in Chinese security services and Macau's sex trade has perhaps cast a shadow on the global appeal of Bond films. Indeed, just as *Skyfall* celebrated Bond's global outreach, the spectacular destruction of both Bond's "spiritual" and ancestral homes, MI6's London Headquarters and Skyfall lodge in Scotland, also undermined the foundations of Bond's heroism in nationhood and empire.

The global breadth of Bond studies, which now includes the *International Journal of James Bond Studies*, has recently started to investigate the centrifugal forces that have, arguably, always been driving the colonial politics of 007 away from the center. Works such as Lisa Funnell and Klaus Dodds's coauthored *Geographies, Genders and Geopolitics of James Bond* (2017) and Ian Kinane's *Ian Fleming and The Politics of Ambivalence* (2021) have, among others, convincingly challenged monolithic readings of gender, race, and colonialism within the Bond canon. Emerging from this growing scholarship, *Global James Bond: (Re)Imagining and Transplanting a Popular Icon* explores the local ripples that the global swell of the Bond phenomenon has generated over the last seventy years. While reinforcing the global popularity of the British cultural icon, the collection also draws attention to the problematic sets of "foreignness" the novels and the films juxtapose to Bond's (white) Britishness. *Global James Bond* is the timeliest and most comprehensive act of "decolonization" of James Bond.

Bibliography

BBC NEWS. 2012. "Daniel Craig's James Bond trunks fetch £44,450 at auction."
6 October 2012. Available at: https://www.bbc.co.uk/news/uk-19857385.

Brown, Mark. 2012. "Daniel Craig's *Casino Royale* trunks in Bond memorabilia charity auction." *The Guardian*, 6 September. https://www.theguardian.com/film/2012/sep/06/james-bond-charity-sale.

Duncan, Paul. ed. 2012. *The James Bond Archives*. London: Taschen.

Fleming, Ian. 1964. "Playboy Interview: Ian Fleming." *Playboy*. December: 97–106.

Funnell, Lisa, and Klaus Dodds. 2017. *Geographies, Genders and Geopolitics of James Bond*. London: Palgrave.

Heritage, Stuart. 2012. "Buy Me Another Day." *The Guardian*, 30 August. https://www.theguardian.com/film/filmblog/2012/aug/30/james-bond-day-budget-celebration.

Jones, Huw D., and Andrew Higson. 2020. "Bond Rebooted: The Transnational Appeal of the Daniel Craig James Bond Films." *The Cultural Life of James Bond: Spectre of 007*, edited by J. Verheul. Amsterdam: Amsterdam University Press. 103–22. https://doi.org/10.1515/9789048532117-007.

Kinane. Ian. 2021. *Ian Fleming and The Politics of Ambivalence*. London: Bloomsbury.

Leigh, David. 2022. "Global James Bond Day." 5 October. https://www.thejamesbonddossier.com/content/global-james-bond-day.htm#:~:text=On%205th%20October%201962%20Dr,as%20Global%20James%20Bond%20Day.

PR NEWS. 2012 "Celebrate The 50th Anniversary of James Bond on Friday, October 5." 3 October. https://www.prnewswire.com/news-releases/celebrate-the-50th-anniversary-of-james-bond-on-friday-october-5-172444721.html.

Pulver, Andrew. 2013. "James Bond outflanked by Chinese authorities as *Skyfall* is censored." *The Guardian*, 17 January. https://www.theguardian.com/film/2013/jan/17/james-bond-chinese-authorities-skyfall.

Rye, Graham. 2004. "Adventures in the Fan Trade." *Double-O-Seven Magazine* 43, June: 32–43.

University of Bangor. 2012. "Censorship under Franco's Dictatorship Still Casts a Shadow over Literature in Spain." https://www.bangor.ac.uk/news/archive/censorship-under-franco-s-dictatorship-still-casts-a-shadow-over-literature-in-spain-10029.

Acknowledgments

Lisa Funnell: Thank you to my father, Lorne, for instilling in me a love for James Bond and encouraging my curiosity about the world. Thank you to my family for your never-ending support and belief in my work. I am deeply grateful to my mom Mary, as well as my brother Dave, sister-in-law Caren, and their three children Tailor, Harrison, and Daniel for encouraging me to publish this book during a challenging time in our lives. I am also eternally grateful to my sweet pup Justice for keeping me company as I edited multiple drafts of each chapter. I simply adore you, my Puppy Galore.

In addition, I deeply appreciate the support I have received from the Bond scholarly and fan communities. In particular, I need to thank Klaus Dodds, Christoph Lindner, and Tyler Johnson for your willingness to collaborate on innovative and interdisciplinary Bond projects. I am also immensely grateful to James Page, Phil Nobile Jr., and Ben Williams for your friendship and encouragement over the past few years.

Klaus Dodds: I would like to thank most sincerely the leadership and support of Lisa Funnell in our joint work together including this edited collection.

We extend our deepest gratitude to our contributors, whose thoughtful work features throughout this book. It was a privilege and a pleasure to engage so actively with your research as you developed and refined your ideas. Thank you for contributing so thoughtfully to this project's shared dialogue and for being open to our comments and suggestions.

We also want to acknowledge a number of scholars who were interested in contributing work to this volume but ultimately could not. The pandemic has had a strong impact on the academic community and many people's ability to produce work under such difficult conditions. We support your decision to prioritize your physical, emotional, and/or mental health, and look forward to engaging with you and your work in the future.

Introduction

Global James Bond

Lisa Funnell and Klaus Dodds

According to David Bordwell in *Planet Hong Kong* (2000), "a truly global cinema is one that claims significant space" in film markets around the world (82) beyond a film series (e.g., *IP Man*), cycle (e.g., kung fu craze of the 1970s), or era (e.g., "golden age" of Hong Kong cinema in the 1980s and 1990s). Although Hollywood is the only industry that meets this narrow definition (while recognizing the scholarship on global Bollywood such as Gehlawat 2015), we question if a partial exception or even expanded demarcation could be made for the James Bond franchise—as say, a *minor global cinema*—given its long-term popularity, international revenue generation, and cultural viability for nearly six decades or *half* of cinematic history (Black 2021).

The series has not only influenced the direction of spy and action filmmaking, but the so-called Bond formula itself has been replicated and reimagined across various spin-offs and parodies worldwide often tailored to local film markets, including the highly successful *Austin Powers* and *Johnny English* series which grossed nearly $650 million and $500 million USD worldwide, respectively, over three films each (Box Office Mojo 2023). As Roger Moore noted in *Bond on Bond* (2013), it has been estimated that anywhere up to half of the world's population have watched at least one James Bond film either at the cinema, on television, or via video/DVD, and much of this exposure predates the advent of the internet and streaming services as well as social media.

Our suggestion of James Bond as a minor global cinema should not obscure the cosmopolitan encounters and academic exchanges between Bond, the cinematic figure, and a diverse array of cipher-spies and spin-offs/parodies. Some of these encounters were deliberately intended to engage James Bond as a form of popular geopolitical competition. In the 1970s, for example, the East German media authorities introduced their own spy, Alexander, as part of the television series *Das Unsichtbare Visier*. Alexander proved as adept as James Bond at foiling CIA-backed plans and those of the allies of the United States. The genesis of the show itself lay in mounting concerns east of the Iron Curtain that James Bond might be proving popular with those who were able to secretly watch Sean Connery assume the mantle of 007. In an incredible Cold War plot twist, the actor who played Alexander (Armin Mueller-Stahl) later fled East Germany and escaped westward in 1980 (and enjoyed considerable creative success in Hollywood and elsewhere) after protesting about the denaturalization of an East German dissident (Amar 2023). In South Vietnam, Ian Fleming's novels appeared to inspire Bùi Anh Tuấn to write his *Specter over Red Square* (*Bóng Ma trên Công Trường Đỏ*), which reflected on how a local Vietnamese spy negotiated the problematic role of the United States as occupier, aid giver, and protector-nation (Nguyen 2018). It offers a noticeable contrast with the way in which Bond's personal relationship with his American counterpart Felix Leiter was depicted on the big screen. The Bond films rarely reflect on how that "special relationship" with the United States was not replicated elsewhere in the world with nominal US allies. In other Bond films, in places as diverse as Greece and India, Bond either learns of others working covertly either as British spies (with accompanying cover stories) and/or depends on local representatives associated directly with the British secret service.

In our reading of James Bond, the franchise is simultaneously shaped by the individual and collective agency of film directors, screenplay writers, producers, set design and costume artists, and "star actors" as well as the structural forces of imperialism, racism, Cold War geopolitics, and the political economy of film and other media industries. This has in turn generated a great deal of reflection from scholars in a suite of disciplines including business and management and consumer psychology as to how the Bond "brand" has managed to endure as long as it has (Price and Coulter 2019). While structural factors and creative opportunities should be part of that assessment, there are other considerations at stake. Fleming's best-selling novels provided a rich starting point but so did an approach to the franchise which did not take commercial risks—Sean Connery's Bond was carefully calibrated to appeal to Anglo-American markets in particular. As Camille Alexander notes with reference to Bond in the early 1970s, the Bond of the 1960s was not going to "cut it" with more diverse American and Western audiences. In *Live and Let Die* (Hamilton 1973), the producers appropriate Afro-Caribbean locations and cultures alongside the genre of blaxploitation to re-present Bond as working with a host of Black actors including CIA operative Rosie Carver, played by the American actor Gloria Hendry. But it did so knowing that there was a prevailing "industry lore," interrogated by Timothy Havens, that assumed that

Black actors would not perform well in international markets (Havens 2014). It was not until the Daniel Craig era that Black American Jeffrey Wright, was cast as the new Felix Leiter. And in the post-Craig era, it was now finally possible, especially for many Bond fans, to imagine Bond as being played by the Black British actor Idris Elba (Hines 2016, but see the cautionary analysis by Johnson and Funnell 2022).

Despite the commercial success of the Bond franchise, the filming and the global consumption of the films have not always proven straightforward. Bond was subject to restricted viewing in the former Soviet Union and censored in China. In other countries, the franchise has not been able either to film in particular locations and/or provoked outrage at the way it depicts those countries apparently represented in particular films. The most notable example was the release of *Die Another Day* (Tahamori 2002), which appeared to unite South and North Korean commentators in critical judgments about the manner in which Korean characters and locations were depicted (Lee 2007). Overall, however, the Bond series has nonetheless proven highly adaptable over many decades and has been adopted by multiple audiences. Bond is now very much part of the viewing portfolio of audiences in places where it was previously banned and censored. All of which serves as a reminder that the production and consumption of James Bond has never been uniform.

Over the six decades, however, the James Bond films center on a globe-trotting British superspy who is sent out on missions aimed at ensuring the physical safety and resource security of the UK and its core allies, mainly the United States (Funnell and Dodds 2017). Bond crossed international borders with an ease that would have not been possible for members of the Cold War–era audiences, especially in the 1960s. The films, much like their novel counterparts written by Ian Fleming, were thrilling in the way that they stirred political anxieties, animated local and regional concerns, and trafficked in colonial and Cold War contexts. The first Bond film, *Dr. No* (Young 1962), coincided with Jamaica's independence, and EON Productions benefited from the so-called Eady subsidy (financial support given to the British film industry working in "British territories" because the filming work was completed just before formal independence) due to the fact that filming occurred in a pre-independence era (Dodds 2005, Parker 2014).

In both novels and films, Bond's overseas adventures trade in the depiction of unfamiliar and often inaccessible places—prior to the development of mass airline transit all of this served as a source of exotic escapism for many viewers (Chevrier and Huvet 2018). Bond was also stylish in both clothing and his conspicuous consumption of food, wine, and leisure pursuits such as skiing and diving (Chapman 2021). Ian Fleming's multiple professions included that of journalist, and in his book *Thrilling Cities* (1963) we find evidence of this passion for reporting on places that Fleming himself thought were exotic and risqué. Of Fleming's thirteen such cities, the cinematic Bond at least was later to visit Los Angeles, Hong Kong, Macau, Beirut, Las Vegas, New York, Hamburg, Berlin, Vienna, and Monte Carlo. These locations have since become tourist sites, with the Bond films putting these places on the global tourist map and thus imprinting the legacy of Britain and its Empire, as represented by Bond, in new and arguably neocolonial consumptive contexts (Denning 2003). Visitors to Istanbul, for example, can book walking 007 tours of the city and enjoy a Bosporus cruise while Black Tomato has recently partnered with EON Productions to launch a series of curated (read: expensive!) "behind-the-scenes" Bond "experiences" to such locations as England, France, Monaco, Italy, and Austria.

While James Bond frequently "goes global" for business and sometimes pleasure, the films present the world of/in Bond through a very distinctive lens. Bond often works with and battles against transnational figures and criminal enterprises (Earnest and Rosenau 2000), but it was not uncommon for non-Anglophone actors to have their voices dubbed in postproduction in the inaugural films of the 1960s:

> Bond Girls Pussy Galore (1964) and Tracy DiVicenzo (1969) utilize the natural voices of their English actors Honor Blackman and Diana Rigg. In contrast, the voices of Honey Ryder (1962), Domino Derval (1965), and Kissy Suzuki (1967) were replaced in post-production by that of English actor Monica van der Zyl. . . . Although the Bond Girl might initially appear "exotic" on screen, the purposeful alteration of the Bond Girl's voice in the 1960s works to align her with English culture and present her as an [Anglicized] protagonist working alongside Bond. (Funnell 2008, 64–66)

Moreover, from the outset, the Bond films were Anglo-American (or transnational) coproductions aimed at appealing to the British *and* American film markets. They have long relied on American creative film and screenplay talent such as Richard Maibaum, American characters and intelligence agencies (like the CIA), and the geopolitical standing of the United States to help bolster the position of Bond/MI6 in the postwar world, through the foregrounding of their special relationship with CIA operative Felix Leiter and a series of American Bond girls (see Funnell and Dodds 2017, 45–76).

As a result, the viewpoint forwarded in the films is more often than not actually a white, masculine, heteronormative, Western, and imperialist Cold War perspective. But this has not stopped the films from attracting global market shares. While the Bond films initially had transnational appeal in North America and Europe, they took South, East, and Southeast Asia by storm soon after. *You Only Live Twice* (Gilbert 1967) was very popular in Japan in large part because it featured a well-known and highly popular actor in Japan and other Asian markets, Mie Hama, as Kizzy Suzuki. This pattern of strategic casting was a recurring feature of James Bond films that featured substantial periods of filmic action in particularly large markets. In *Octopussy* (Glen 1983) the Indian tennis star Vijay Amritraj played a local operative who supports Bond while he is based in India on a mission. In *Tomorrow Never Dies* (Spottiswoode 1997), the Malaysian actor Michelle Yeoh, who was already a well-known action superstar in Hong Kong, played Chinese secret agent, Wai Lin, who eventually ends up working with (and arguably outshining!) 007. These casting choices among others across various films have helped to transform the reach, creative endurance, and, in the end, overall profitability of the franchise.

Currently, the franchise relies on the worldwide box office for nearly 70 percent of its revenue, and its global appeal remains strong after nearly sixty years. The first film, *Dr. No*, (Young 1962) did not accumulate large box office receipts beyond North America and Europe. The latest film, *No Time To Die* (Fukanaga 2021), by way of contrast, was popular in China and Japan, and earned $613 million in international box office receipts (and $160 million domestically) (see boxofficemogo.com). This was after a nearly two-year delay in release due to the coronavirus pandemic with audiences weighing the risks of seeing the film as cinemas began reopening. In fact, the release of the film was accompanied by sentiments that "Bond could save cinema just like the character in the film saves the world of imminent destruction" (see Johnson and Funnell 2022) thereby encouraging fans to participate in "saving" the film industry from collapsing. It is hard not to conclude that Bond is likely to remain the most successful and enduring cinema franchise.

The reception of the Bond films worldwide and their influence on local filmmaking is of particular interest to this volume. The Bond films have long been considered problematic texts that have been criticized for being sexist, racist, heterosexist, imperialist, xenophobic, and jingoistic, among other things (Chapman 2007, 13). And yet, these texts have captured the popular imagination of distinct and widespread local audiences, some of whom might be underrepresented or misrepresented by the franchise itself. *Dr. No* (1962), for example, as James Robertson (2015) notes, was surprisingly popular with Jamaican audiences on viewing. Using different lenses and often limited resources, filmmakers have reinterpreted and reimagined the figure of Bond, combining elements of the Bond film with local cinematic traditions. This has spurred a series of James Bond offshoots in cinemas around the world and captures something of the "politics of ambivalence" that Ian Kinane (2021) has recently identified in Ian Fleming's novels and filmic translation.

Our book, *Global James Bond: (Re)Imagining and Transplanting a Popular Culture Icon*, focuses on the ambivalent yet fascinating interplay between the global and the local in the longest-running film franchise in history. It explores how James Bond established itself as a global standard for action-spy filmmaking and even as a minor global cinema (i.e., imagining), and subsequently inspired a series of genre bending, blending, and breaking in local visual and some literary contexts (i.e., reimagining and transplanting). In some cases, spin-off creations of the superspy were simply used to promote products that Bond himself would never consume until *Skyfall* (2012) attracted sponsorship from Heineken. The most notable example would be the decision by the Guinness company to launch its own Bond-inspired advertising character, Michael Power (Cleveland Mitchell), as a deliberate attempt to cultivate enthusiasm for the famous Irish stout. Between 1999 and 2006, African audiences were treated to various spy adventures including the feature-length film *Critical Assignment* (Xenopoulos 2004) and "Africa's own James Bond" appeared to resonate with viewers as sales of Guinness improved markedly (Diageo 2021). Our authors also consider how the world is envisaged in the official series and subsequently reinterpreted on local and regional levels, and invested with alterative meanings which might run counter to the dominant representational and geopolitical logics of the novels and filmic texts.

On the one hand, our scholars explore the interplay between the global and the local as both the James Bond/007 figure and genre are blurred, bended, and parodied across various and largely cinematic industries. David Wilt discusses the rise of Mexican Bond films (1965–1969) which were inspired by the immense popularity of the Bond films starring Sean Connery in the local market. Wilt argues that such series as "Alex Dinamo" and "Tigresas" were not simply cheap imitations of the original but rather were infused with cultural and sociopolitical content directly related to the country of origin and pertinent to the primary viewing audience. Here it was not possible to imagine a Spanish-speaking cipher of James Bond, who defends the political status quo and the imperial legacy of the United Kingdom. Swarnavel Eswaran explores the "Bond of the Tamil Screen" aka Thennagathu James Bond (South Indian James Bond) focusing specifically on the seminal film, *Vallavan Oruvan* (The Skilled One, 1966). Eswaran argues that while the film serves as an extension of Bond generic tradition, it can also be understood as a local (re)iteration of a transnational hero through the figure of CID Shankar, who ensures the safety of people and security of resources in South India. Jessica Siu-yin Yeung considers the cultural legacy of Hong Kong *Bondpin* or "Bond films" of the 1960s and their comedy remakes in the 1990s. Focusing on two trilogies featuring the archetypal Cantonese Jane Bond character, Black Rose in Chor Yuen's *Black Rose* Trilogy (1965–1967) and Jeff Lau's *La Rose Noire* Trilogy (1992–1997), Yeung argues that nostalgia and humor are key to understanding the encoded memory archive of the Cantonese cinematic canon featured within them, which speaks to locals about the 1997 handover and the end of British colonial rule. Finally, Aaron D. Horton explores the popularity of James Bond in Japan as reflected in the manga series *Golgo 13*. While featuring many Bond-like elements, the Golgo stories reflect distinctly Japanese sensibilities and were primarily intended for an adult male Japanese audience, which arguably helps to explain their lack of success among Western anime and manga fans.

On the other hand, our scholars consider the creative and consumptive geographies of the Bond series and the messages being sent about the geopolitical standing of the UK and its relation to our nations especially in colonial and Cold War contexts. Antti Korpisaari discusses the depiction of Cuba in both the Ian Fleming novels and early James Bond films, arguing that Cuba has consistently been cast in the role of "other," thereby influencing audience perceptions of Cuba as an enemy of the Western capitalist world. Korpisaari contends that this problematic and dehumanizing depiction of Cuba continues into the Brosnan-era Bond films (1995–2002) long after the Cold War has ended. Rea Amit explores the fluctuating reception of the 1960s Bond franchise in Japan with a particular focus on *Thunderball* (Young 1965) and *You Only Live Twice* (Gilbert 1967), the latter of which was set and filmed in Japan. Amit argues their reception is indicative of what Roland Robertson has termed "glocalism," and the prevailing tensions of global, local, and even national factors in the "transnational" film market structure. Lisa Funnell examines how Bond's "sampling" of the "international buffet of women" in *On Her Majesty's Secret Service* (Hunt 1969) relays a Eurocentric impression of "the world" which overemphasizes whiteness, oversimplifies other racial identities, and overlooks the Global South. Moreover, Funnell argues that Bond's consumptive practices are couched in a narrative that emphasizes the superiority of Britain through the positioning of Bond as the colonial/universal expert/export who defeats Blofeld and his henchpeople in a series of physical feats inspired by the Winter Olympics. Finally, Paul Michael Johnson considers the overt Eurocentrism featured in *For Your Eyes Only* (Glen 1983) through the depiction of the societies surrounding the Mediterranean Sea as Europe's "global south." Johnson argues that the film leverages visual scenery, music, supporting characters, and other details to forward a stereotypical depiction of the Mediterranean that is marked by underdeveloped infrastructure, lawlessness, and passionate, irrational individuals thereby re-creating the global, and often colonial, dynamic of the franchise, without traveling outside Europe or breaking the bank.

Global James Bond is a starting point for further conversation and exchange over an extraordinary film franchise. For some media producers and viewers, the endurance of James Bond might be seen as a neocolonial artifice that sits uneasily in a world that is increasingly less likely to be dominated by Western media and cultural forms. But even within dominant Western markets,

James Bond has been consumed and engaged with in a multiplicity of ways. Alternatively, there has been no shortage of evidence—both in the Cold War era and beyond—of James Bond being a useful base material for an array of spy characters who rival or even exceed the exploits of the British superspy.

Bibliography

Alexander, Camille. 2020. "Cultural Appropriation and Capitalism: Co-opting Blaxploitation in the Filmic *Live and Let Die.*" *International Journal of James Bond Studies* 3 (1) https://doi.org/10.24877/jbs.55.

Amar, Tarik. 2023. "*Das unsichtbare Visier*—A 1970s Cold War Intelligence TV Series as a Fantasy of International and Intranational Empowerment; or, How East Germany Saved the World and West Germans Too." *Global Storytelling: Journal of Digital and Moving Images* 2 (2): 6.

Black, Jeremy. 2021. *The World of James Bond: The Lives and Times of 007.* Lanham, MD: Rowman & Littlefield.

Bordwell, David. 2000. *Planet Hong Kong: Popular Cinema and the Art of Entertainment.* Cambridge, MA: Harvard University Press.

Chapman, James. 2007. *Licence to Thrill: A Cultural History of the James Bond Films.* 2nd ed. London: I. B. Tauris.

Chapman, Llewella. 2021. *Fashioning James Bond: Costume, Gender and Identity in the World of 007.* London: Bloomsbury.

Chevrier, Marie-Hélène, and Chloé Huvet. 2018. "From James Bond with Love: Tourism and Tourists in the James Bond Saga." *Tourism Review* 73 (3): 386–401 (2018) https://journals.openedition.org/viatourism/3083.

Denning, Michael. 2003. "Licensed to Look: James Bond and the Heroics of Consumption." In *The James Bond Phenomenon: A Critical Reader*, edited by Christoph Lindner. Manchester: Manchester University Press.

Diageo. 2021. "Celebrating Guinness in Africa this International Stout Day." 3 November https://www.diageo.com/en/news-and-media/stories/2021/celebrating-guinness-in-africa-this-international-stout-day.

Dodds, Klaus. 2005. "Screening Geopolitics: James Bond and the Early Cold War films (1962–1967)." *Geopolitics* 10: 266–89.

Earnest, David, and James Rosenau. 2000. "The Spy Who Loved Globalization." *Foreign Policy* 120: 88–90.

Fleming, Ian. 1963. *Thrilling Cities.* London: Jonathan Cape.

Funnell, Lisa. 2008. "From English Partner to American Action Hero: The Heroic Identity and Transnational Appeal of the Bond Girl." In *Heroes and Heroines: Embodiment, Symbolism, Narratives, and Identity*, edited by Christopher Hart, 62–80. Kingswinford: Midrash.

Funnell, Lisa, and Klaus Dodds. 2017. *Geographies, Genders and Geopolitics of James Bond.* London: Palgrave Macmillan.

Gehlawat, Ajay. 2015. *Twenty-First Century Bollywood.* London: Routledge.

———. 2022. "Female Bonds in Bollywood." *International Journal of James Bond Studies* 5 (1) https://doi.org/10.24877/jbs.76.

Havens, Timothy. 2014. *Black Television Travels*. New York: New York University Press.

Hines, Claire. Ed. 2016. *Fan Phenomena*. London: Intellect Books.

Johnson, Tyler, and Lisa Funnell. 2022. "No Time to Die—Literally: Risk, Fandom, and Theatergoing during the COVID-19 Pandemic." *Popular Culture Review* 33 (2): 41–75.

Lee, Jamie Shinhee. 2007. "North Korea, South Korea, and *007 Die Another Day*." *Critical Discourse Studies* 4: 207–35.

Moore, Roger. 2013. *Bond on Bond: Reflections on 50 Years of James Bond Movies*. Essex, CT: Lyons Press.

Nguyen, Duy Lap. 2018. "Sovereignty, Surveillance, and Spectacle in South Vietnamese Spy Fiction." *Positions: Asia Critique* 26: 111–50.

Parker, Matthew. 2014. *Goldeneye: Where Bond Was Born: Ian Fleming's Jamaica*. London: Hutchinson.

Price, Linda, and Robin Coulter. 2019. "Crossing Bridges: Assembling Culture into Brands and Brands into Consumers' Global Local Cultural Lives." *Journal of Consumer Psychology* 29: 545–54.

Robertson, James. 2015. "Rewriting *Dr. No* in 1962: James Bond and the End of the British Empire in Jamaica." *Small Axe* 19: 56–76.

Chapter 1

James Bond à la Mexicana

David Wilt

The 1960s was a transitional period in Mexican cinema, between the "Golden Age" of the 1940s–1950s and the government-sponsored "quality cinema" of the 1970s. The film industry of the 1960s strongly relied on domestic and international trends to appeal to local audiences, such as *lucha libre* (Mexican wrestling) and rock and roll (US music) respectively, in addition to popular film genres like spaghetti westerns, horror movies, and spy action films. Mash-ups of multiple trends were also common: for instance, *Cazadores de espías* (Baledón 1968) and *Blue Demon vs. los cerebros infernales* (Urueta 1966) combined lucha libre, spy action, science fiction, and rock and roll.

The James Bond films starring Sean Connery were particularly popular with Mexican audiences. *Dr. No* (Young 1962) premiered in Mexico in February 1964, followed by *From Russia with Love* (Young 1963) in July 1965, *Goldfinger* (Hamilton 1964) in May 1966, *Thunderball* (Young 1965) in April 1967, and *You Only Live Twice* (Gilbert 1967) in October 1968. All had very successful theater runs, with *You Only Live Twice* playing fourteen straight weeks in its premiere engagement (Amador 1986, 372). In addition to the five original Bond films shown in Mexican cinemas in 1964–1968, at least fifty-nine non-Mexican spy-genre films—many of them imitative of the Bond pictures—were released theatrically in Mexico in this period (Amador 1986, 227–381). For several years, Mexican audiences were inundated with Bondian movies.[1]

The response of the Mexican cinema industry to the popularity of Bond was swift. Nearly two dozen Mexican films produced from 1965 to 1969 were directly inspired by the Bond series. Mexican filmmakers frequently inserted local cultural elements into "borrowed genres" thereby creating unique outputs: Mexican westerns, for example, often incorporated aspects of the *ranchera* genre. The same is true with the adaptation of the Bond genre. As noted

11

by James Chapman, the Bond series "is . . . unique in that there is nothing quite like it in cinema history. In this sense it might be argued that the Bond series is a genre (or at the very least a sub-genre) in its own right" (2007, 18). Moreover, Funnell argues that the "Bond franchise is defined by its own, highly specific system of narrative codes and stock characters" (2011, 210). Prior to the 1960s, Mexico did not have a significant tradition of spy films; consequently, Mexican filmmakers had only the Bond films (and their imitators) as a frame of reference.

The "Bondian" formula encompasses the "narrative ideologies of the films, their visual style, their representation of genre and their construction of national identity" (Chapman 2007, 20). The Mexican film industry adapted this formula to local circumstances—economic, geographical, political, cultural—making films on a lower budget, in Latin American locations, featuring local performers, and reflecting the sociocultural environment in which they were being made and would, for the most part, be consumed.[2] Most of these films are stripped of the specific British aspects of the original series, while still mostly eschewing overt Mexican or Latin American sociocultural attributes.[3]

The Mexican Bond films, if one knows where to look, do contain both overt and indirect ideological content. There is a long-standing tradition in Mexican popular culture of the cinematic foreign "Exploiter" character that sees Mexico specifically and Latin America more generally as a resource to be ruthlessly exploited (Wilt 1991, 298–302). The specific plots unveiled in Mexican Bond films reflect this: ruining a national petroleum industry, destabilizing a nation's currency, and looting archaeological treasures, among others. The evil organizations behind these schemes are identified as multinational (i.e., non-state organizations), and virtually all of the primary villains have "foreign" (i.e., non-Latin names): Dr. Sanders, Dr. Randall, Ruth Taylor, Miss Bristol, Hans, Dr. Klux, Iván, Garrick, Dr. Marcus, Solva, Dr. Kadar, Hugo Ulrich, Dr. Williams, etc. In *S.O.S. conspiración bikini* (Cardona Jr. 1966), for instance, the criminal group includes Anglo-Saxon, French, Italian, Asian, and unspecified Latin American members.

The Mexican Bond films also deliberately imitate the mise-en-scène of the original series—exotic locations, visions of upper-class lifestyles, technological gadgetry, spectacular action sequences, and even certain character types—and were marketed using various Bondian images and catchphrases.[4] However, in this chapter we shall focus on Mexican cinema's treatment of two key attributes that defined the Bond film formula: the protagonist (i.e., the James Bond character) and the representation of women (i.e., the Bond girl figure). These are the aspects most significantly altered from the original Bond films and illustrate how the formula could be locally modified and yet still capitalize on Bond's popularity.

James Bond Figures in Mexican Cinema

At the center of the Bond film is an iconic hero around which the action, narrative, and other characters are oriented. Mexican filmmakers used the original series as a creative template, but the James Bond persona was significantly altered in the Mexican versions. However, rather counterintuitively, the protagonists of these films are not overtly "localized," that is, given specific Mexican attributes or allegiances. Instead, they are set within a broad but recognizable Latin American context—a sort of Pan-Americanization.

Setting aside Mexican Bond films that only peripherally relate to the Bond phenomenon, we are left with fifteen titles (in order of production): *Machuchal agente 0 en Nueva York* (Cortés 1966); *Operación 67* (Cardona Jr. and Cardona 1967); *El tesoro de Moctezuma* (Cardona Jr. and Cardona 1968); *S.O.S. conspiración bikini* (Cardona Jr. 1967); *Blue Demon destructor de espías* (Gómez Muriel 1967); *Pasaporte a la muerte* (Gómez Muriel 1967); *La Mujer Murciélago* (Cardona 1967); *Peligro . . . ! Mujeres en acción* (Cardona Jr. 1967); *Operación Carambola* (Zacarías 1967); *Con licencia para matar* (Baledón 1967); *Cuatro contra el crimen* (Véjar 1967); *Muñecas peligrosas* (Baledón 1967); *Alerta, alta tensión* (Corona Blake 1967); *Cazadores de espías*; and *Santo contra Blue Demon en la Atlántida* (Soler 1969).[5] Seven of these have a primary (singular) man as protagonist, one has a primary woman as protagonist, and seven have dual or group protagonists (including two with multiple women protagonists). Thus, over half of the films do not meet the fundamental James Bond premise of an individual man as secret agent and hero. Moreover, even those which do have a "solo" man as protagonist do not strictly follow the formulaic Bond characterization.

James Bond is an agent of MI6, the United Kingdom's foreign intelligence service; in other words, he is an employee of a national government and sent out on state-sanctioned missions. One might reasonably expect a Bondian film made in another country to substitute a corresponding local/national institution for MI6—in the United States, for instance, the CIA or FBI. However, the majority of the Mexican Bond films deviate from the Bond employment model. In only one film, *Cuatro contra el crimen*, are the protagonists specifically identified as agents of a Mexican governmental agency.[6] Otherwise, the protagonists in Mexican Bond films take orders from multinational organizations, both real (Interpol) and fictitious such as "Bureau Internacional de Inteligencia," "Seguridad Lationamericana," "Seguridad de Estados Americanos," and "JUS." In several of these films the organization is specifically headquartered outside Latin America (New York and Paris, for example).

There are several possible reasons for this somewhat Euro-American and even global focus. A hero not identified as an agent of a specific government might allow for wider audience identification across Latin America and beyond. This is in keeping with some of other non-Mexican Bondian efforts. For example the television series *The Man from U.N.C.L.E.* (1964–1968) pitted good and evil multinational organizations (U.N.C.L.E. and THRUSH) against each other.[7] This denationalization trend also appears in the Bond films proper: although James Bond is an agent of the British secret service, "the films were deliberately de-politicized and detached from the Cold War background of the novels" (Chapman, 2007, 60), with the non-state organization SPECTRE supplanting the Soviet SMERSH as the antagonist across the 1960s.

It's also possible Mexican filmmakers deliberately eschewed portraying their heroes as government agents because the terms "secret police" and "secret service" had a somewhat pejorative connotation (i.e., as agencies used for internal political purposes that were often nefarious). Few Mexican spy films were made prior to the 1960s, and those that did exist often substituted amateurs for intelligence agents. For example, *Soy puro mexicano* (Fernández 1942) and *Espionaje en el Golfo* (Aguilar 1942), deal with Axis spy activity in Mexico during World War II (1939–1945). The protagonists of these films are Mexican *bandido* Lupe and intrepid reporter Luis, respectively; the non-villainous professional secret agents in each film are specifically identified as representing the United States and the Spanish Republican cause. In *Las aventuras de Carlos Lacroix* (Gómez Urquiza 1958), rocket scientists are murdered to steal scientific secrets for a foreign power, and it is private detective Carlos Lacroix who foils the plot.

The seamy side of the Mexican *policía secreto* is illustrated in *El complot Mongol*, a 1969 novel by Rafael Bernal adapted to the screen in 1977 and 2018. Filiberto García is a pistolero working for the Mexican secret police. Filberto's superior tells him of an alleged Communist Chinese plot to assassinate the President of the United States on his visit to Mexico City. While Filiberto himself is a relatively sympathetic character (although he does commit various murders and other crimes as the story unfolds), he's the pawn of a corrupt political machine rather than an autonomous professional, and his disposability is seen as a virtue by his masters. It's therefore not surprising to find the Bond surrogates in Mexican cinema are not Mexican government agents, but they are overtly identified as working for agencies which presumably have a somewhat altruistic global, or at least Western, orientation.

Alex Dinamo

The cinematic James Bond has often been described as "an iconic representation of modern masculinity"; he has a "take-charge playboy mentality [and] exudes charm, sophistication, vigor, and wit while living a life of elegance and danger . . . his gender is male; his class—wealthy/upper; nationality—Anglo-Saxon; and ethnicity—white" (Hoxha 2011, 198). Perhaps the most overt Mexican imitations are the films featuring Alex Dinamo: *S.O.S. conspiración bikini* and *Peligro . . . ! Mujeres en acción.*[8] Dinamo was played by Julio Alemán, an all-purpose leading man of the era. Alemán and the other actors who portrayed Mexican Bonds in multiple films—Jorge Rivero and Carlos East—are all *güeros* (fair-skinned).[9] This allows them to visually resemble the Anglo-Saxon James Bond, but in the context of the films they also represent Latin America in general—Dinamo was specifically called "the first Latin American secret agent" in publicity for film[10]—for Latin American audiences, but also be ethnically and nationally "neutral" when the films were exported. While "Alex" is a fairly common nickname for "Alejandro," "Alex Dinamo" is neither a clearly Latin name nor an overtly foreign one, a more "neutral" identifier than Jorge Rivero's recurring character of "Jorge Rubio" and Carlos East's Bondian roles as "Julio" and "Ricardo," respectively.

In *S.O.S. conspiración bikini*, Dinamo possesses many of the cinematic Bond attributes: he's a member of an intelligence agency, he's well-dressed (sometimes wearing a Bond-ish tuxedo), drives a sports car, uses various spy gadgets, is competent at hand-to-hand combat and gunplay, and is an inveterate womanizer. After a brief pre-credits sequence, Dinamo first appears in a long fight sequence on a banana barge, defeating a gang of drug smugglers. He tells an Ecuadorian police inspector that he has a date in Quito. "Watch out for the skirts," the Inspector says. "They cause trouble." "You think?"

Figure 1.1. Secret agent Alex Dinamo with an ally (Sonia Infante) and an enemy (Lorraine Chanel) in *S.O.S. conspiración bikini*.

Source: Productora Fílmica Nacional & Filmadora Ecuatoriana, 1967. Screenshot by author.

Dinamo replies. The viewer is thus introduced to Dinamo as a man of action with a soft spot for the ladies. Throughout the rest of the film, Dinamo engages in numerous physical altercations with the villains, and repeatedly flirts with women (despite the fact that he has a preexisting relationship with Adriana), telling the Inspector: "You know, where there are beautiful women, I'll always be there."

But in a twist on the Bond formula, while Dinamo is reasonably competent at his job (although he functions more as a detective than a secret agent), he is rudely rejected by virtually all of his would-be feminine conquests, apparently sleeping with only one. This directly contradicts some basic aspects of the original James Bond series, in which "Bond is a successful seducer, attractive to women 'good' and 'bad," and to both major and minor characters . . . his successful sexuality is . . . an important source of humor, and sometimes pathos, and a crucial support to the notion of his competence" (Black 2001, 108–9). Consequently, Dinamo in *S.O.S. conspiración bikini* fails to fully emulate James Bond despite outward appearances. The fact that the second Dinamo film—made a year later—corrects the "flaws" in the protagonist's character, suggests audiences did not respond favorably to a Latin man who was not successful with women, particularly "foreign" women, who in Mexican cinema are almost always attracted to Mexican men.

Peligro . . . ! Mujeres en acción adheres even more closely to the Bond formula, particularly in Alex Dinamo's character but also in other aspects of plot and setting. This may be one reason why the film achieved some success in the international market: an English-dubbed version (*Danger Girls*) was produced, and the film was released in Italy, Egypt, Greece, Brazil, South Africa, and Yugoslavia (at least), in addition to the usual Spanish-speaking markets. While *S.O.S. conspiración bikini* was a largely tongue-in-cheek action film, *Peligro . . . !* is more serious in tone. The surface Bond attributes are also stronger this time: Dinamo is a well-dressed secret agent involved in various action sequences in a plot that spans three different Spanish-speaking and Anglo-Spanish-speaking locations (Ecuador, Puerto Rico, and the United States); he uses high-tech gadgets and has frequent interactions with attractive women. Dinamo seems much more ruthless, competent, and serious than he did in his initial adventure; he's wounded multiple times in the line of duty, and doesn't hesitate to kill his enemies, even shooting them in the back.

Unlike the first Dinamo film, women in *Peligro . . . !* are attracted to the protagonist—although a number of them have an ulterior motive as agents of S.O.S. In his first scene, Dinamo visits the dressing room of Samantha, an exotic dancer and informant; they kiss, but it's a ruse to distract the secret agent so an assassin can shoot him in the back.[11] Instead, Dinamo spins around and Samantha is the one who is killed (Dinamo then shoots the assassin). Later, S.O.S. agent Monique lures Dinamo to her hotel room and attempts to stab him; after a brief tussle, he pins her down and kisses her, and she's later discovered, bound and gagged in the closet. Cristal, a double agent, gives Dinamo valuable information, kisses him, and promises they'll "have fun" when he returns to Puerto Rico. Thus, in this film Dinamo successfully imitates Bond's "male virility [that] highlights the importance of sexually conquering all women, especially those deemed as femme fatal" (Hoxha 2011, 193). More closely adhering to the overall Bond formula, and portraying Dinamo as Bond's equal in both spycraft action and romantic prowess, *Peligro . . . ! mujeres en acción* is the more successful and "serious" of the two Dinamo films. Largely eliminating the spoof aspects of the plot and protagonist's persona may well have contributed to the film's increased international exposure and popularity, compared to its predecessor.

The Alex Dinamo films were popular enough in Mexico to warrant the publication of a comic book between 1967 and 1969, a rare Mexican example of a preexisting movie character receiving a comic book series.[12] The Dinamo character and the films have something of a cult following even today. 2012 obituaries for Julio Alemán almost always mentioned the actor's Bondian role, and Mexican commentators still fondly comment on the character: "the great Julio Alemán, who gave a Latin face to the James Bond dress suit, with his [Anglo-]Saxon characteristics but with Latin American spirit; Alex Dinamo is the king of Mexican secret agents" (Trejo 2018).

S.O.S. conspiración bikini and *Peligro . . . ! mujeres en acción* are perhaps the purest of the Mexican Bond films. They aren't diluted by association with another genre (*lucha libre*, comedy), nor by casting a star with a preexisting screen persona (such as comedian Capulina[13] or *luchador* El Santo), nor by gender-switching the protagonist (the Tigresas series). Dinamo is the Mexican James Bond and was is appreciated as such.

Lucha Libre

While Alex Dinamo was featured in more spy action films, there was another group of non-comedy Mexican Bond films emerging at the time that were hybrids of the Bond formula and the Mexican *lucha libre* genre.[14] *Lucha libre* refers to professional wrestling, but *lucha libre* films are not "sports" movies which just happen to deal with professional wrestlers; they are action films featuring a protagonist who is a masked professional wrestler battling criminals or fantastic villains such as monsters or aliens. In the strictest interpretation, the protagonist should be played by an actual, real-life wrestler, not an actor cast in the role, and the film should include wrestling scenes which may or may not be relevant to the plot. The *lucha libre* genre began in the late 1950s with El Santo as the chief protagonist, and became quite popular in the 1960s, with wrestlers such as Blue Demon and Mil Máscaras also starring in movies. All five *lucha*-Bond films have a dual-hero premise, four of them pairing a masked superhero with a more conventional Bondian character, and one (*Santo contra Blue Demon en la Atlántida*) featuring two wrestlers, although Santo is the primary Bondian protagonist.

The four films in which Santo and Blue Demon are teamed with non-wrestling secret agents give both parties various Bondian attributes. Santo appears twice with actor Jorge Rivero (*Operación 67, El tesoro de Moctezuma*). True to the *lucha libre* genre, Santo and Jorge are both depicted as professional wrestlers, but they are also secret agents (and are billed that way in the credits) for Interpol. Both men participate in the film's action sequences, drive expensive sports cars, and use advanced spy technology. Although both protagonists are introduced in the first film in the company of bikini-clad women, it's Jorge who chiefly fulfills the Bondian role as the suave womanizer. This may be attributed, at least in part, to Santo's screen persona—he's frequently given a romantic interest in his films, but is not promiscuous.[15] In both films it is Jorge who has Bondian sexual encounters with enemy agents who try to kill him, as well as with nonaligned women characters, and with a fellow Interpol agent (in *El tesoro de Moctezuma*).

Figure 1.2.   Secret agents El Santo (center) and Jorge Rivero (right) in *El tesoro de Moctezuma*.

Source: Cima Films, 1966. Screenshot by author.

Alerta, alta tensión! brings Jorge Rivero back as secret agent "Jorge Rubio." This may or may not be the same character Rivero played in *Operación 67* and *El tesoro de Moctezuma*, since he's now working for SEA (Seguridad de los Estados Americanos) rather than Interpol. Jorge is once again characterized as a Bondian secret agent who's an inveterate womanizer: the fact that his personal assistants, many of the employees of SEA, and various members of villain Cero's group are all sexy women certainly does not help him conquer his excessive lechery. A significant portion of the film is like a fetish video showing Jorge being tortured by and/or seducing/being seduced by women.

Santo went solo as a secret agent in *Santo contra Blue Demon en la Atlántida*. This film retains Bondian plot elements, including several double agent characters, high technology, and a global menace, but Santo functions as more of an action superhero than secret agent (similar to Blue Demon in *Pasaporte a la muerte*, the science-fiction sequel to *Blue Demon, destructor de espías*) in a film which is more science fiction than spy adventure. Blue Demon spends a large portion of the film brainwashed into villainy, leaving Santo with the primary hero's role.

The two films in which Blue Demon is teamed with a non-wrestling secret agent follow the Santo/Rivero movies blueprint rather closely, especially *Blue Demon, destructor de espías*. Wrestler Blue Demon and sportswriter Julio (Carlos East) are, jointly, "Agent Zero" of the international Counter Espionage organization. Each of the heroes has a romantic interest, Julio with fellow agent Nora and Blue Demon with double agent Marcia (during one wrestling match, Blue repeatedly maneuvers his opponent to the side of the ring where Marcia is sitting, so he can flirt with her). Bondian gadgets abound, including a flamethrower ring and a trumpet that shoots poison darts.

Although 1969's *Santo contra Blue Demon en la Atlántida* marked the effective end of overt Mexican imitations of Bond films, the *lucha libre* genre flourished throughout much of the next decade. Some Seventies *lucha* films dealt with international intrigue, such as *Misión suicida* (Curiel 1971) in which Santo—working for Interpol again—battles Soviet agents training women spies and saboteurs in the Dominican Republic. By the late 1970s the *lucha* genre was passé, although random examples continue to appear from time to time.

The *lucha libre* genre was often combined with elements of other genres, including horror, science fiction, comedy, sport dramas, crime/mystery, jungle adventure, and even westerns. Each genre allowed the protagonist to demonstrate a different facet of their ability, in addition to simple athletic prowess. The Mexican Bond *lucha* films gave the masked heroes a chance to play a suave international agent caught up in international intrigue, enhancing their prestige with their audiences.

Representation of Women in Mexican Bond Films

The representation of women in the James Bond films has been the subject of considerable study and a fair amount of controversy. The term Bond girl "has conventionally been used to describe every woman appearing in the Bond franchise, including 'Bad Girls' (i.e., villains), and 'Secondary Girls' (i.e., relatively unimportant characters in the narrative)" (Mills 2015, 111). While most agree "Bond has historically been defined by his relationships with women and particularly through heterosexual romantic conquest" (Funnell 2015, 1), critical evaluation of the Bond girls varies, from writing them off as sexy window dressing with limited narrative value (see Funnell 2008), to assigning them crucial functions. For example, compare Timothy Hoxha's argument that "female characters are crafted as the femme fatale, vamps, exotic foreign seductress and appendages to masculinity" (2011, 193), with Tom McNeely's assertion that "the women of Bond films are usually strong, intelligent, skilled, and—to put it quite literally—more than meets the eye" (2011, 178).

Mexican Bond films recognized the important role women played in defining the world of James Bond across the films of the 1960s. In fact, women were featured as primary protagonists in three films, primary or co-primary villains in five films, and in major supporting roles in virtually all the other films. While the first five Bond films present villainous women in key positions within the SPECTRE organization—Rosa Klebb (#3) in *From Russia with Love*, Fiona Volpe as assistant to Emilio Largo (#2) in *Thunderball*, and Helga Brant as (#11) in *You Only Live Twice*—the criminal masterminds in each film including the overarching SPECTRE villain Ernst Stavro Blofeld (#1) are all men (played by different actors). In comparison, *S.O.S. Conspiración bikini, Peligro . . . ! Mujeres en acción,* and *Operación 67* each feature different criminal organizations led by women. In *Con licencia para matar*, there is competition for some stolen gold between two sinister organizations, one led by Adrián, a woman leading a group of foreign revolutionaries; a similar situation exists in *Cazadores de espías,* in which the leader of one of two rival spy gangs is a woman. As with men villains in other Mexican Bond films (and the original Bond pictures), the women villains are frequently depicted as "foreigners," either implicitly by their name, appearance, or accent, or, less frequently, explicitly. Women protagonists in the Mexican Bond films and those presented as allies to the primary protagonist are less often identifiably non-Latin.

This multinationalism may have been inspired by two preexisting character types in Mexican popular culture and especially films—the blonde and the foreign exploiter (mentioned above). "Blondes" in Mexican cinema are non-Mexicans (generally non-Latins as well) who are notably attractive, independent, and assertive, attributes which are often depicted negatively or at least ambivalently (Wilt 1991, 245–51). This is illustrated by the two types of women in the Mexican Bond films, villains and sympathetic characters, who are often—but not always—respectively characterized as foreign (non-Latin) and Mexican/Latin American.

Women villains in Mexican Bond films with non-Latin identities include Miss Bristol and Madame Rapiere (Anglo-Saxon, French) in *S.O.S. conspiración bikini*; Solva, Monique, Natasha, and Ingrid (indeterminate nationality except Monique, who is French) in *Peligro . . . ! Mujeres en acción*; Silvana (Italian) in *Cazadores de espías*; and Ruth Taylor and an unnamed dancer (Anglo-Saxon, Asian) in *Operación 67*. In contrast, there is only one clearly non-Latin woman agent with a significant sympathetic role, Estela in *El tesoro de Moctezuma*. The majority of the women villains (and Estela) die in the course of their films. Women villains in Mexican Bond films suffered double jeopardy, as foreigners and as assertive, sexually liberated women. Their status as foreign villains—the preexisting Mexican exploiter trope—marks them as dangerous enemies (of, simultaneously, Latin America, democracy, Western values) and subject to the supreme penalty for their murderous actions. Furthermore, as femme fatales their demise fits the Bond formula elucidated in Funnell's comment: "In the 1960s, then, the Bond franchise uses the figure of the sexually liberated female villain to illuminate the new freedoms that feminism has accorded to women; while it does this, however, it also positions this woman as a locus for social anxieties about these freedoms—anxieties which are invariably borne out in her violent punishment and death" (Funnell 2011, 199).

In contrast, the favorable women in Mexican Bond films are almost entirely portrayed as Latin American (although this national identity is chiefly achieved by the absence of a foreign name or accent, rather than specific labeling), and are generally competent and active participants in the narrative's action. This is not necessarily to suggest the Mexican Bond films are an unsung treasure trove of feminism—they often use women as sex objects in the manner of the authorized Bond movies—but the overall representation of women presents them in a more assertive and competent light than one might reasonably expect. For example, although *S.O.S. conspiración bikini* and *Peligro . . . Mujeres en acción!* are full of attractive young women in bikinis, and protagonist Alex Dinamo is presented as a Bond-ish womanizer, the films aren't as sexist as one might expect.[16] S.O.S. in each film is depicted as a powerful international organization under the direction of a woman (Miss

Bristol is ruthless, and Solva is austere and dominating, respectively), with men and women serving as members.[17] Virtually all the women—on both sides of the conflict—are shown to be assertive and physically and mentally capable; they are not simply sex objects or victims. In *Peligro. . . .* Maura, Dinamo's aide, is a competent secret agent in her own right (she and Alex take turns rescuing each other). Rather than merely standing around or being "in peril," *Peligro*'s women characters do a lot of running, fighting, and shooting. And thus they are anything but passive.

Las Tigresas

The most striking examples of positive representation stem from Mexican Bond films featuring women as protagonists. For instance, the "Las Tigresas" series—*Muñecas peligrosas* and *Con licencia para matar*—center on highly competent women agents whose physical attractiveness is not exploited unduly. These films present a gender-swapped Bondian premise: instead of an intrepid man as secret agent, the protagonists are three women. Some possible sources of inspirations include the *Modesty Blaise* comic strip that began in 1963 (a film version was produced in 1966 and released in Mexico in late 1968), and the UK television series *The Avengers* (1961–1969). The black jumpsuits worn by the Tigresas are reminiscent of the costumes of Honor Blackman and Diana Rigg in *The Avengers*. A strong Bond-film influence was still present, as the title of the first "Tigresas" film—*Con licencia para matar* [With License to Kill]—makes plain.

While coincidentally all three of the Tigresa performers were foreign-born— Bárbara Angely (Austria), Emily Cranz (the United States), and Maura Monti (Italy)—they were dark-haired and are not depicted as noticeably "foreign," thus maintaining the Latin American hero/international villain schema.[18] The Tigresas are an assertive and competent trio of women who do not require assistance from men to battle evil, bail them out of trouble, or engage in any stereotypical acts of chivalry. While attractive, they are not simply used as eye candy, positioned as romantic interests, or relegated to the action periphery as sidekicks to the leading man. Instead, the Tigresas are specifically identified as free agents hired for their high level of expertise by the (patriarchal) New York–based JUS organization.

Few if any Mexican action films (versus melodramas, for instance) before or after the "Tigresas" series featured a group of such independent, assertive women. Prior to the 1960s, women rarely played protagonists in Mexican action films. The 1960s saw some exceptions prior to the "Tigresas" series, but this does not necessarily constitute a trend in Mexican popular culture in this period.[19]

Figure 1.3. **Las Tigresas confront the villain in *Muñecas peligrosas*.**
Source: Película Mundiales & T.V. Producciones, S.A., 1967. Screenshot by author.

In a twist on the familiar Bondian theme of betrayal—usually of the hero by a femme fatale—*Muñecas peligrosas* features a subplot in which Tigresa Emily's boyfriend is revealed to be the villain's henchperson. This is not presented in a manner that would suggest that Emily's gender has rendered her more susceptible to seduction and betrayal but is depicted as an occupational hazard of the secret agent's life: trust no one. *Con licencia para matar* also features a highly coincidental link between a Tigresa's romance and the case they are working on at the time. Regardless, the "Tigresas" series is impressive for its shattering of the Bondian-universe glass ceiling.

Conclusion

The Mexican Bond films were a response to the international success of the original movies. Unable to compete with Hollywood or other large cinema industries in terms of resources, Mexican versions of international blockbusters were necessarily made on lower budgets. The Mexican Bond films were, like most popular Mexican cinema of the era, chiefly aimed at a narrower, Spanish-speaking audience, which influenced the ideological content of these productions. At the same time, films such as the "Alex Dinamo" and "Tigresas" series could appeal to non–Latin American audiences—the language barrier aside—by appropriating the Bond formula.

Comparing the Mexican Bond films with the original series (and Bondian movies made in other countries at this time), one can observe how—while at first glance the Mexican Bond films may appear to simply be cheaper imitations of the originals—these pictures were subtly infused with cultural and sociopolitical content specific to their country of origin and their primary viewing audience. This would be readily understood by Latin American audiences, as the films received wider distribution, the fact that they contained many familiar elements of Bondian films would allow them to be consumed as global examples of the Bond phenomenon.

Notes

1. Non-Bond spy films exhibited in Mexico in this period included all eight of the stretch-out feature film versions of *The Man from U.N.C.L.E.* television series, serious spy dramas such as the "Harry Palmer" series with Michael Caine and *The Spy Who Came in From the Cold* (Ritt 1965), the "Matt Helm" and "Derek Flint" films, and Eurospy pictures like *OSS 117: Mission for a Killer* (Hunebelle 1965).

2. It appears that only *Peligro . . . ! Mujeres en acción* (René Cardona Jr. 1967) received extensive distribution outside of the traditional markets for Mexican cinema.

3. For example, *S.O.S. conspiración bikini* and *Peligro . . . ! Mujeres en acción* each contain one song. But, unlike many Mexican films featuring traditional or pop Mexican music, the first movie has a song by Charles Aznavour (although sung in Spanish), and the song in the second film is sung entirely in English.

4. "Jack" in *Peligro . . . ! Mujeres en acción* is an homage to "Oddjob" in *Goldfinger*, combining Oddjob's karate expertise and murder-hat into a razor-edged metal hand. Several Mexican-Bond film posters display a variation on the 007-pistol logo.

5. Films that reference the James Bond phenomenon in content (usually passing) or marketing but which had little direct Bond-like content include *Operación Tiburón* (de San Antón 1965), *Dr. Satán* (Morayta 1966), *Autópsia de un fantasma* (Rodríguez 1966), *No se mande, profe* (Crevenna 1967), *Agente 00 Sexy* (Cortés 1967), *Persíguelas y alcánzalas* (aka *Agente secretísmo*, de Anda Jr. 1967).

6. In *Machuchal agente 0 en Nueva York*, US citizen Machuchal is drafted into the US government agency CIA.

7. *The Man from U.N.C.L.E.* was shown on Mexican television (as *Agente secreto de C.I.P.O.L.*) as early as 1966.

8. The character of Alex Dinamo made the transition to comic books in October 1967, and at least sixty-three issues were produced until early 1969, by which time the "spy" genre had peaked and receded in Mexico.

9. This did not prevent Alemán and Rivero from occasionally playing indigenous characters, as in *El Yaqui* and *Indio*, respectively. It might also be noted that none of the Mexican Bond surrogates had moustaches, a cultural signifier for leading men in Mexican cinema for many years.

10. As described on the Pel-Mex (Películas Mexicanas, the company that handled international distribution of Mexican films) sales brochure; this tagline also appears in some newspaper advertisements for the film.

11. This is reminiscent of the death of Fiona Volpe in *Thunderball*, which was released in Mexico in April 1967. *Peligro . . . !* began shooting in June 1967.

12. "Neutrón" is another case, but the usual path was from comics to film ("Chanoc," "Alma Grande," "Kalimán"). The Mexican wrestler best known as "Abismo Negro" began his professional career in 1987 under the name "Alex Dinamo"; although it's unclear if his ring persona used any of the film character's attributes, the name itself clearly evokes the Mexican James Bond.

13. Three Mexican Bond films are comedies and make little attempt to have their protagonists emulate the Bond character, although the plots and settings are very Bondian. In *Machuchal, agente 0 en Nueva York*, Puerto Rican tourist Machuchal is mistaken for an assassin by a criminal organization, and the CIA convinces him to infiltrate the group. Capulina, in *Operación Carambola*, has taken (and flunked) a correspondence course in "how to become a secret agent," and is duped by a villain pretending to run a spy agency. Ricardo (Carlos East) in *Cazadores de espías* is an amateur who tries to solve the murder of his secret agent brother. These films illustrate how pervasive the Bond influence was in popular culture, but they are not strictly "James Bond spoofs."

14. *La Mujer Murciélago* also has certain elements of the *lucha libre* genre, combined with the Bond genre and the masked superhero genre (as the title suggests, the protagonist is to some extent modeled on Batman).

15. In *El tesoro de Moctezuma* it's implied that Santo has a brief relationship with one of a pair of twins (the other chooses Jorge), but this is not elaborated and he has no other romantic liaisons in the movie.

16. *S.O.S. conspiración bikini* revolves around a summit meeting of the S.O.S. organization disguised as a swimsuit manufacturer's convention, so there is some plot rationale for the bikinis. *Peligro . . . ! Mujeres en acción* has no such premise, and yet *every single female character* of any significance wears a bikini at least once.

17. In the "Alex Dinamo" comic book series (not written by René Cardona Jr.), the leader of S.O.S. was a man, Prof. Edgar Wolf.

18. Barbara Angely plays a German-speaking agent in *Peligro . . . ! Mujeres en acción*, and Maura Monti's character is apparently Italian in *Cazadores de espías*, but neither was typecast as a "foreigner," unlike Elizabeth Campbell and Amadee Chabot, for example.

19. The first four "Luchadoras" [Wrestling Women] films (1962–1966) teamed a woman wrestler from Mexico and one from the United States. Other female-centric action movies of the era included Mexican Revolution tale *Juana Gallo* (Zacarías, 1960) and the western *Las Hermanas X* (Curiel, 1962).

Bibliography

Amador, María Luisam and Jorge Ayala Blanco. 1986. *Cartelera Cinematográfica 1960–1969*. Mexico: Centro Universitario de Estudios Cinematográficos.

Bernal, Rafael. 2011. *El complot mongol.* Mexico City: Editorial Planeta Mexicana.

Black, Jeremy. 2001. *The Politics of James Bond: From Fleming's Novels to the Big Screen.* Westport: Praeger.

Chapman, James. 2007. *Licence to Thrill: A Cultural History of the James Bond Films.* 2nd ed. London: I. B. Tauris.

Funnell, Lisa. 2008. "From English Partner to American Action Hero: The Heroic Identity and Transnational Appeal of the Bond Girl." In *Heroes and Heroines: Embodiment, Symbolism, Narratives, and Identity,* edited by Christopher Hart, 62–80. Kingswinford: Midrash.

———. 2011. "Negotiating Shifts in Feminism: The 'Bad' Girls of James Bond." In *Women on Screen: Feminism and Femininity in Visual Culture,* edited by Melanie Waters, 199–212. New York: Palgrave Macmillan.

Funnell, Lisa, ed. 2015. *For His Eyes Only: The Women of James Bond.* London: Wallflower Press.

García Riera, Emilio. 1994. *Historia documental del cine mexicano.* 18 vols. Guadalajara: Universidad de Guadalajara.

Hoxha, Timothy M. 2011. "The Masculinity of James Bond: Sexism, Misogyny, Racism, and the Female Character." In *James Bond in World and Popular Culture: The Films are Not Enough,* edited by Robert G. Weiner, Lynn Whitfield, and Jack Becker, 193–205. Newcastle on Tyne: Cambridge Scholars Publishing.

McNeely, Tom L. 2011. "Somebody Does It Better: Competent Women in the Bond Films." In *James Bond in World and Popular Culture: The Films are Not Enough,* edited by Robert G. Weiner, Lynn Whitfield, and Jack Becker, 178–82. Newcastle upon Tyne: Cambridge Scholars Publishing.

Mills, Dan. 2015. "What Really Went on Up There James?" In *For His Eyes Only: The Women of James Bond,* edited by Lisa Funnell, 110–18. London: Wallflower Press.

Trejo, Héctor. 2018. "Espías a la mexicana a 24 por Segundo." https://www.mundiario.com/articulo/cultura/espias-mexicana-24-segundo/20181204103438139702.html.

Wilt, David. 1991. "Stereotyped Images of United States Citizens in Mexican Cinema, 1930–1990." PhD dissertation, University of Maryland.

———. 2007. "El Santo: The Case of a Mexican Multi-media Idol." 2007. in *Film and Comic Books,* edited by Ian Gordon, Mark Jancovich, and Matthew P. McAllister, 199–220. Oxford: University Press of Mississippi.

Chapter 2

James Bonds (OSS 117 and CID Shankar) in the Global South

Orientalism, "Mad Scientists," and Technology

Swarnavel Eswaran

This chapter engages with the "Bond of Tamil Screen" aka Thennagathu James Bond (South Indian James Bond) in the seminal film, *Vallavan Oruvan* (The Skilled One, 1966). It was produced by one of the major studios of South India, Modern Theatres, and was directed by its owner R. Sundaram, the son of the founder T. R. Sundaram. It starred Jaishankar, known by his mononym, who was frequently featured as a detective or CID (Crime Investigation Department) Officer on-screen. While *C.I.D. Shankar* (Sundaram, 1970), by the same production house, acknowledged the burgeoning popularity of (Jai) Shankar as the South Indian James Bond, this chapter will focus on *Vallavan Oruvan* as it features the initial reinvention of the James Bond figure for the local Tamil market. Shankar went on to play CID Shankar[1] or similarly styled agents[2] across numerous films of the 1960s and 1970s, and even reprised the role of CID Shankar in a guest-starring capacity in films like *Saranam Iyappa* (Dhasarathan 1980), *Saavi* (Raghunath 1985), and *Veerapandiyan* (Raghunath 1986) in the 1980s.

While many of the other Jaishankar films vary in terms of their style, blending the Bond aesthetic with other genres like the (rail)road movie (e.g., *Neelagiri Express* [Thirumalai and Mahalingam 1967]), *Vallavan Oruvan* remained true to the spirit of the James Bond genre in its investment in multiple locales for the various action sequences and depiction of beautiful women as seductresses, spies, and benevolent angels, apart from the enduring lover figure who is a fellow traveler. While its specificity as a Tamil/Indian mainstream film is marked by the many melodious songs, their imaginative picturizations, and the predominantly melodramatic mode of storytelling, *Vallavan Oruvan* is unique in not allowing the family to subsume the impulse toward the action of the Bond figure and, more importantly, not containing the objective of the action to be primarily linked to the safeguarding of the immediate family or its wealth, as in much Indian cinema. *Vallavan Oruvan* invokes the Bond figure as the savior of the larger society from the hands of a "mad" psychiatrist—punctuating it as a Global South film in its quest for subverting and retooling a Eurocentric Hero's energy beyond his machismo and womanizing abilities to foreground the predicament and the freedom of the people on the fringes.

Vallavan Oruvan could be considered a response to the French film director François Truffaut's scathing critique of the James Bond films and particularly the first one, *Dr. No.* (Young, 1962).

> For me, the film that marks the beginning of the period of decadence in the cinema is the first James Bond—*Dr. No* [1962]. Until then the role of the cinema had been by and large to tell a story in the hope that the audience would believe it. . . . For the first time throughout the world mass audiences were exposed to what amounts to a degradation of the art of cinema, a type of cinema which relates neither to life nor to any romantic tradition but only to other films and always by sending them up. What's more, [Alfred] Hitchcock's career began to suffer from the time of the arrival of the first Bond films, since they were a sort of plagiarized version of *North by Northwest* [1959], his finest thriller. He could not compete with the Bond films and after this he was increasingly obliged to make small-budget films. (Qtd in Allen 2022)

As Truffaut rightly points out, early Bond films like *Dr. No* (Young 1962), *From Russia with Love* (Young 1963), and *Goldfinger* (Hamilton 1964) reflect some of Hitchcock's aesthetics such as the back-projection technique and the awe-inspiring aerial shots. With an increasing production of $1 million, $2 million, and $3 million USD respectively, Bond filmmakers began developing their action choreography and engaging in more adventurous cinematography on picturesquely expansive and wild locales in the early films.

But what if your budget does not allow for such finesse in technology? What are the possibilities when technology becomes the center of discourse in a Bond film, beyond enabling the action to achieve the goal of spectacularly decimating the villain(s) during the climax? The James Bond of the Global South, particularly the South Indian James Bond in *Vallavan Oruvan,* provides opportunities to interrogate the role of technology for its local audience. What role does technology play in a detective film where it enables uncovering of the workings of a secret organization as well as the ideology that drives it? Can the use of technology shed light on the material as well as the dogmatic world of a delusional leader? Thus, this chapter could be read as a response to Truffaut's scathing criticism as it argues for the relevance of James Bond in the Global South and the way such a Bond genre film relates to the ground reality and resonates with our contemporary concerns.

Figure 2.1.   Poster of *Vallavan Oruvan*.
Source: Courtesy "Stills" Gnanam. Screenshot by author.

Banco à Bangkok pour OSS 117: The European Spy, Orientalism, and the Global South

Vallavan Oruvan, the film to launch the South Indian James Bond, is loosely adapted from the French film *Banco à Bangkok pour OSS 117* (Hunebelle 1964), released in the United States under the title *Shadow of Evil*. This French-Italian coproduction was based on *Lila de Calcutta* by Jean Bruce (1960), whose writings predate those of Ian Fleming in the wider European spy thriller genre. Like Ian Fleming's James Bond, Bruce created the popular character, secret agent Hubert Bonisseur de La Bath (Hubert Barton on the screen) aka OSS 117, who made his debut in 1949 in print, and in 1957 on-screen with *OSS 117 n'est pas mort/OSS 117 is Not Dead* (Sacha). Secret agent OSS 117 has been a popular character since then. The recent versions have seen Jean Dujardin playing the titular role in films like *OSS 117: Cairo, Nest of Spies* (Hazanavicius 2006), and its sequel *OSS 117: Lost in Rio* (Hazanavicius 2009). These were reflexive of the Bruce originals and in a lighter vein. Still, their massive box office success across borders indicates the popularity of the secret agent from France to this day.

The influence of European Spy Thrillers on South Asian filmmaking can be traced back to the founder of Modern Theatres, T. R. Sundaram. This prolific producer and director completed his undergraduate education in Engineering at Leeds, UK, and married Gladys Renee when he was still attending the college there. In fact, it was Gladys's father who got Sundaram, from a business community in Thiruchengodu in South India, interested in cinema and specifically European film (Eswaran Pillai 2015, 23). It is no wonder that R. Sundaram, the son who would continue his father's legacy as a director, chose a European spy thriller as the inspiration for his first South Indian Bond film. We know of the investment in the detective genre from the Sundarams—both the father and son—through the secret agent books, including those by Bruce and Ian Fleming, which were donated by Modern Theatres to the local libraries.

The point of entry is similar in the French and Tamil versions when the protagonist is introduced as the secret agent who has been assigned to investigate the murder of another agent. In *Banco à Bangkok pour OSS 117*, US agent Christopher Lemmon has been killed, and colonel Hubert de La Bath, aka Hubert Barton (Kerwin Mathews) investigates the incident, which is now part of a series of shocking murders. However, the French agent is dispatched from Washington, DC, thereby rendering him a Euro-American spy. The South Indian secret agent, CID Shankar, is also posited in a similar backstory (where the transnational is posited as national) regarding the unexpected death of a senior officer, CID Durairaj, from the Crime Investigation Department in Bombay where he works. He gets the orders to go down south to Chennai and find out the reasons for, and arrest the people behind, the gruesome murder of Durairaj. Both the French original and the Tamil adaptation share some of the key generic elements from the James Bond films, like actions being staged in picturesque locales and a number of (sensuous) women crisscrossing the path of the agent, often hiding their loyalty to the villain. There is also a love/romantic element as the sister of the villain falls in love and sides with the hero—another significant parallel in the French and the Tamil versions.

However, the villains are marked differently by the nature of their activities in the secret lair, a key generic element in Bond films, and through the nature and pursuit of strategic goals. More importantly, the original alludes to India through the villain, but in an Orientalizing mode, as detailed by Edward Said (Said 1978): The villain, seemingly anti-West in his ideology, is marked as a Westerner by proxy, who "believes it his human prerogative not only to manage the nonwhite world but also to own it, just because by definition 'it' is not quite as human" (108). Lemmon, who was murdered, had discovered that the Hogby Laboratories, who manufactures cholera vaccines in Bangkok for distribution in India, were trying to spread the plague in the supposed cholera vaccine and kill a multitude of Indians through an outbreak.[3]

In his attempt to bring such a sinister villain to justice, OSS 117 faces many obstacles. The antagonist Dr. Guna Sinn, played by a white French actor (Robert Hossein) with a turban, is an Indian doctor, much like the villain Dr. Sargunam (R. S. Manohar) in *Vallavan Oruvan*. However, Dr. Sinn is a psychologist, whereas Dr. Sargunam is marked as a psychiatrist and an FRCS (a Fellow in the Royal Society of Surgeons, London) by the nameplate in his office. Both the state detectives from France and India have to infiltrate the secret lair of the villains where the "mad scientists," Dr. Sinn and Dr. Sargunam, have hypnotized a mass of followers who abide by their words and carry out their orders without questioning them. While OSS 117 is able to intrude into the highly guarded hideout of Dr. Sinn with the help of his sister Lila (Pier Angeli), his Indian counterpart can do likewise with the help of Thara (L. Vijayalakshmi), Dr. Sargunam's sister. Even as the journey of OSS 117 toward Dr. Sinn's highly guarded den filled with obstacles is emulated in the case of CID Shanker, as he tries to uncover the mysterious activities surrounding Dr. Sargunam's lair, the climactic moment reveals the specificity of *Vallavan Oruvan* as a Global South film. While through the determined efforts of the spontaneous Hubert Barton, the OSS 117, we get a glimpse of the heart of darkness at the center of Dr. Sinn's ideology and activities, the perseverance and improvisational abilities of CID Shankar reveal the destructive potential and nihilism at the heart of Dr. Sargunam's secret society. The latter's objectives are far removed from those of the former.

The closed community of "People Elect" under the control of Dr. Sinn is working toward reducing the exponentially increasing population of the Earth by targeting one of the most populous countries in the World—India. In European narratives like *Banco à Bangkok pour OSS 117,* developing countries of the Global South, like India and Thailand, have to bear the brunt of being the hotbeds of manufacturing and experimenting with dangerous drugs, in connivance with the state/corporations, and finally murdering the local populace, intentionally. If Thailand is marked as the operational space for illegal laboratories and dangerous activities like incubating and nurturing plague-infected rats, India becomes a signifier of a space that offers free rein to the destructive imagination of a doctor who is depicted as being mentally unstable. Nonetheless, though referred to as an Indian doctor, the Malthusian narcissist (Shermer 2016), Dr. Sinn, is marked as a Thai native through his name, Sinn, which means treasure in the local language. Thus, the treasure becomes a disgrace in its land of origin, and only an outsider from Europe could bring order to the Global South in Bruce's novel and Hunebelle's rendering of it on-screen. Whereas, even if *Vallavan Oruvan*, without acknowledging it explicitly, borrows heavily for its narrative and key plot points from the original French film, it firmly denies its investment in Orientalizing the people of the Global South, particularly the people of India. It disavows the idea of extermination and ethnic cleansing through the archaic plague. Instead, Dr. Sargunam, though menacing and macabre in his nonconformist views and the challenging of what he perceives as an unjust and dystopic society, is savage in his ideas and activities regarding subverting the state machinery. However, in his anarchy, narcissism, and self-centeredness, he recalls the larger-than-life Bond villains and Dr. Sinn.

The maniacal plot of the villain in *Banco à Bangkok pour OSS 117* recalls Winston Churchill's regressive, repugnant, and Orientalist attack on Indians for "breeding like rabbits." Hogby Laboratories, through its manufacture of vaccines, the preeminent signifier of the West and its modern science, enables the "ethnic cleansing" of the Indian people not through war but invisible germs of the plague. By juxtaposing vaccines with plague, Bruce validates why he chose Thailand as the space for the action of his colorful and cavalier hero Hubert Barton—the OSS 117. The aporia of the coexistence of the past with the present enables the rendering of Global South as mythical through a European lens. In the mid-sixties when *Banco à Bangkok pour OSS 117* was released, plague was not an overriding concern, unlike in the 1940s, in India. Being a tropical country there are periodic outbreaks in small pockets. But the mythos surrounding the East and its frozen time and its differential temporality regarding the delay in technological/scientific advancement, another stereotype of Orientalism, enables the juxtaposition of the plague, and particularly of the fear surrounding the pandemic of the 1920s, with a modern laboratory manufacturing vaccines for the relatively contemporary cholera in the 1960s.

It is significant to note that in *Banco à Bangkok pour OSS 117* it is a European who is positioned to solve the issue involving the deaths of people in the Global South. Similarly, populations and vaccines become the chief signifiers of the reason and the cure, as per the Malthusian ideology–driven Dr. Sinn. The significance of OSS 117 lies in the way it resonates with the dominant issues of the present: population/migration and vaccine/pandemic could be argued to be the most significant issues of the contemporary and speedily globalizing world. Therefore, the erudite Truffaut's critique of the James Bond spy thrillers as "decadent" could be argued to be based on his predilection for European art cinema and the privileging of certain directors from Hollywood whose work he saw during his impressionable years (notably Hitchcock—see Truffaut 1969). His criticism justly alludes to the stereotypes and the shortcomings of a consumer-driven spy thriller genre but does not take into account the possibilities inherent in a cultural artifact like cinema to address our deeper anxieties like Western hegemony and Orientalism. Films can shed light on the instrumentalization of the Global South as a sweatshop, where products could be experimented, manufactured, and distributed. In a way, *Banco à Bangkok pour OSS 117* could be argued to forebode the current discourses surrounding the pandemic and the mysterious Orient and its laboratories as villains. Such possibilities of readings question the marking of an entire subgenre of Bond films as decadent and unconnected to life based on aesthetics which could be argued as subjective in its parameters.

In contrast to Truffaut's critical observations, the Bond genre films discussed here certainly relate to and resonate with life. For instance, the rhetoric of demonic villain Dr. Sargunam regarding the predicament and suffering of those convicts who have served their legal terms in prisons and remain excluded by society resonates with the realities of life not only in the Global South but across borders. His violent and illegal means to seek justice may be questionable and unethical (see discussion below), but the reasons for his anarchy are grounded in and relate to the lived experiences of many in the Global South. Though *Vallavan Oruvan* differs from *Banco à Bangkok pour OSS 117* in its preoccupation with the villain's agenda, leading to its differential climax in terms of the ideology of its egomaniacal villain, it is faithful in its form to the original French version.

Vallavan Oruvan: State, Subversion, and Technology

Vallavan Oruvan is a homage to *Banco à Bangkok pour OSS 117*, one could argue, frame by frame, except for the villain's objective and the provision of songs, a sine qua non for Tamil/Indian films, even in the case of a spy thriller. Today one wonders if such a remake with some significant changes could be made without copyright and the acknowledgment of the source. With the increasing presence of global corporates like Disney and Fox in India (IANS 2019), it has become more difficult to "plagiarize" a film than during the 1960s when *Vallavan Oruvan* was faithfully copied from its original to a large extent including some of the subtle details. Presently, we see Tamil films, like *Kadhalum Kadandhu Pogum* (Love Shall Also Pass, Kumarasamy 2016), acquiring the rights for the remake of a Korean gangster film (*My Dear Desperado*, Kim 2010) and acknowledging the source through their titles. Thus, the Global South is marked by the changes brought forth by globalization and the concomitant necessity to adhere to global copyright laws as a prerequisite for marketing the product, in this case, films, for a global audience.

Thus, *Vallavan Oruvan* occupies an interesting place in the history of Tamil/Indian cinema especially in relation to copyright laws in the 1960s when the Global South did *not* abide by Western regulations regarding intellectual property. There have been accusations that artists based in the West have also borrowed, copied, and/or stolen creative work from outside of their region. Nevertheless, copyright laws are contested across borders as privileging the haves at the cost of the have-nots. The Indian courts have acknowledged and supported the need for the accessibility of copyrighted books through photocopying for noncommercial, academic purposes/pursuits (Mathur 2016). While copyright laws are also contested in the West, particularly regarding the appropriation of copyrighted materials, for creatively reinventing and retooling by experimental artists (Balsom 2017), a mainstream film like *Vallavan Oruvan* complicates such a progressive intervention. However, *Vallavan Oruvan* marks its originality through the voice of its ambiguous yet dark villain. Dr. Sargunam's secret society has mostly ex-convicts for its members, and in his address to them during the climax of the film, Dr. Sargunam talks about how he created a space for them to work and earn money and enjoy life in an honorable way, unlike in the society where they were not included. On the face of it, such an objective certainly is progressive in social justice terms. But what undermines such a lofty ideal is Dr. Sargunam's investment in illegally procuring sulfur and manufacturing weapons and ammunitions through their labor and marketing the products to criminals, terrorists, and anti-national and antisocial groups.

Retroactively, the path leading up to Dr. Sargunam's lair with his captives, who seem to be under the spell of his hypnotism, is stereotypical of a Bond movie with a dreadful villain. More importantly, *Vallavan Oruvan* treads the same path as its predecessor, *Banco à Bangkok pour OSS 117*, right from the beginning. They also acknowledge their debt for having learned a lot more lessons from 007 than just that one: exotic locations, diabolical villains, and beautiful women await. As do a few other moments lifted pretty much whole-sale from *Dr. No*, such as when Hubert opens the door of his contact's office to reveal one of those beauties—the contact's secretary—eavesdropping with her ear to the door (Tanner 2010).

In the case of CID Shankar in *Vallavan Oruvan*, the contact person in Chennai (formerly known as Madras), is Mr. K. R. K. Menon, and the eaves-dropping secretary at his office is the beautiful Susheela (R. Sheela). Of course, in the French original, she is depicted as a blonde to differentiate her from the brunette who will follow suit. In the Tamil version, such demarca-tions are done through their belonging to other regional industries: Sheela was a top-tier star from Malayalam cinema, whereas the one to eavesdrop after her, the sensuous Vijayalalitha, was an emerging star from Telugu cinema, their paratexts enabling the local audiences to relish in the charm of the local Bond across borders. Thereafter, after flirting with Thara when Shankar meets her with her brother Dr. Sargunam at a party, it paves the way for a song sequence where we see and feel romantic love brewing between Shankar and Thara.

Figure 2.2.   Shankar and Thara in a romantic song.
Source: Courtesy "Stills" Gnanam. Screenshot by author.

Dr. Sargunam is initially depicted as a decent psychiatrist who cares for his sister and is well respected in society. Dr. Sargunam's affinity for his lover Susheela is also revealed. In the French original, however, Dr. Sinn is show-cased right from the beginning as a mélange of science and Oriental mysti-cism, rendering him as a curiously exotic and a regressive scientist:

> It's funny to listen to [Dr. Sinn] speak so disdainfully about "occidentals." Of course, despite the turban, Sinn is really as much of a grab-bag of pan-Asian ste-reotypes as Christopher Lee's Fu Manchu. He's prone to touting "the mysterious Orient" where he learned his powers of hypnosis and picked and chose whatever bits of Eastern mysticism would make him most villainous to xenophobic audi-ences. He's a doctor, he's a hypnotist, he's a mystic, he's a swami . . . you name it; he's got the credentials. (Tanner 2010)

Such a representation of stereotyping Asians, however, is not unusual when we look at the trajectory of the Bond films. For instance, Lisa Funnell and Klaus Dodds have written extensively about the representation and instru-mentalization of China and the "Yellow Peril" in Bond films as well as the transnationality of the Bond figure and his undermining of nation/culture (2017). In addition, Funnell has explored the problematic use of racial ste-reotypes for Asian women across the series including the "China Doll" and "Lotus Blossom" figures in *Dr. No* (Young 1962) and *You Only Live Twice* (Gilbert 1967) respectively. Thus, while *Vallavan Oruvan* adjusts the prob-lematic representation of India in the French source text, certain sentiments about East and Southeast Asia typical of the Bond genre continue forward in the Tamil/Indian remake.

Thus, *Vallavan Oruvan* remains in keeping with the spirit of the Bond genre spy thrillers. For instance, the villain plants his agents and moles who keep attacking CID Shankar. In one scene, he outwits them by entering through the balcony of the neighboring room in the hotel that he had rented in anticipa-tion, slipping in from behind, and surprising the henchpeople belonging to the villain's organization by successfully attacking them. Such violent encounters extend into the streets when gasoline is spread across the road and set on fire and the resultant inferno blocks the movement of Shankar, who reverses his car only to find a similar line of gasoline aflame at the rear end. True to his macho spirit, he daringly drives through the fire and ends up entering into a stream of water nearby, with the tires dangerously ablaze. The various fight scenes in *Vallavan Oruvan* frequently involve both the bodies and gadgets, with the local Bond encountering a range of diverse henchpeople, including a karate specialist and the people from across the borders in the north, par-ticularly Nepal—reflexively pointing to the stereotyping of Northeasterners in much Tamil cinema.

As with *Banco à Bangkok pour OSS 117, Vallavan Oruvan* gives its own nod to its investment in the Bond genre and the gadgets or technology right at the beginning when CID Shankar arrives at Chennai Airport and is welcomed by a mysterious photographer trying to literally frame him through his camera. This is a direct reference to an early scene in *Dr. No* only with a change in gender of the cameraperson. Shankar outwits his opponent by pretending to inadvertently brush aside them in a rush, forcing the camera to fall and exposing the film to light. When the photographer kneels to collect his camera from the ground, Shankar takes out his own mini camera, smaller than the size of a lighter, and clicks a snap. He further adds salt to the wound of his enemy's agent by asking if the photographer would like a copy of the photo; embarrassed by his error, the photographer refuses and rushes away. From the outset, *Vallavan Oruvan* marks its similarity with the preeminence and ubiquity of gadgets of the Bond genre films and their deft handling by iconic secret agents of the state like 007 and 117, not only through the tiny camera but also cars. *Vallavan Oruvan* showcases an array of vehicles, starting from the local and iconic Ambassador to the famous US car manufacturer, Chevrolet. It also modifies the Chevrolet as a closed and open van/truck as per the needs of its users. Between the capacious Ambassador car and the Chevrolet truck are the Fiats, Jeeps in their various versions, and the Standard sedans (Jain 2017). Today, *Valluvan Oruvan* is also a documentation of the rich history of the locally produced Ambassador, Fiat, and Standard Company's cars that have ceased manufacture and disappeared from the local car market. It recalls the fascination with cars in Bond novels as well as films, but also marks its difference through the sparseness of its resources, as with the many modifications and uses of the single Chevrolet truck in the film.

More importantly, the filmmaker makes interesting adaptive choices in *Vallavan Oruvan* that help to mark its specificity within the Bond genre through the inaugural sequence, wherein we see the backlot of the famous Modern Theaters in which a set has been constructed to display the billboard on the facade of the building that houses the "Aandhai Mark Theeppatti Thozhirchalai/The Owl Brand Matchbox Factory." In this initial scene, we see CID Durairaj driving in his car to the location. C. A. S. Mani, a veteran and an in-house cinematographer at Modern Theatres, shows his finesse in back projection during the night driving shots, while also displaying his knowledge of the noir aesthetics and his skills at chiaroscuro lighting once the car enters the studio backlot. Once Durairaj arrives, he carefully climbs up the wall to the roof of the building. In a nod to the infamous Istanbul-based billboard scene in the Bond film *From Russia with Love,* the exterior painting, here of an owl (rather than the face of a woman) reveals a hidden window in one of the eyes (rather than her mouth) from which Durairaj throws a rope down and tries to descend. Much like *FRWL*, the escape artist is shot (by two men in waiting) and falls dead. Unlike *FRWL*, where Bond and his Turkish ally Kerim Bey do the shooting, *Vallavan Oruvan* presents two northeastern-looking Indian men rushing toward the body on the ground to verify their target is dead. Thus, the Bond element has been retooled as a method of murder not by but for the state agent.

In a scene that references the debriefing of the beginning of Bond films through a similar scene in *Banco à Bangkok pour OSS 117,* we see CID Shankar is busy with his revolver and target practice inside his office building when his colleague informs him that the IG/Inspector General of Police (K. K. Soundhar) wants to talk to him. Once inside his office, the IG details the arms and ammunition on the table before deputing Shankar to investigate the untimely and shocking death of his senior colleague Durairaj. The IG lists the various crimes: "The recent railway and bank heists and the violent rebellion in villages." He also shows him the captured arms and ammunitions on his table: "The bombs used in the riots in Calcutta; the guns used in the train robbery at Nagpur; the revolvers used in the Bombay bank heist." What would be transnational use of arms in a Bond film becomes the transfer of arms and ammunition across borders within a nation in this localized Tamil/Indian Bond film. Additionally, this cataloging of destructive technology is also bookended in later scenes when we see the hidden factory in the lair of Dr. Sargunam; this is the location from which such arms and ammunition are manufactured, sold, and transported all over the nation to the rioters and rebels, including the terrorists. Both the agent of the state and its enemy are showcasing their strengths through their exceptional skills with technology and ability to accrue it.

Nonetheless, unlike the global unrest aimed at by the archvillains of a Bond film, the villain here is restricted to his aspirations of creating chaos within the nation. Here it is pertinent to look at the discourse surrounding technology and its discontents. The difference between the Global South Bond and his archenemy Dr. Sargunam is literally in the "stock reserve" at the latter's lair. Bond uses technology for his objectives, whereas the villain is under the grip of technology as he is addicted to the power it affords. Steven Zani argues that "when people have an incorrect relationship to technology, they relate to the world only in a way that turns everything into a stockpile, a 'standing-reserve' that serves no purpose but consumption and control" (2006, 178). In his astute engagement with Martin Heidegger's take on technology in the context of James Bond films, he quotes from the German philosopher:

> As soon as what is unconcealed no longer concerns man even as object, but exclusively as standing-reserve, and man in the midst of objectlessness is nothing but the orderer of the standing-reserve, then he comes to the very brink of a precipitous fall, that is, he comes to the point where he himself will have to be

Figure 2.3.   South Indian James Bond Jaishankar.
Source: Courtesy "Stills" Gnanam. Screenshot by author.

taken as standing-reserve. Meanwhile, man, precisely as the one so threatened, exalts himself to the posture of the lord of the earth. In this way the illusion comes to prevail that everything man encounters exists only insofar as it is his construct. (Heidegger 1977, 308)

Heidegger's words truly sum up the character of Dr. Sargunam, who when challenged by CID Shankar's intrusion into his own enshrouded and clandestine factory wants to immediately move the arms and ammunitions to an equally secretive and invisible locale. His "precipitous fall" as a psychiatrist, to an automaton who just wants to safeguard his accumulations in support of his delusional posture as "the lord of the earth" are aptly foreshadowed by Heidegger. Thus, his ideology regarding challenging the state for the injustice rendered to ex-convicts and his investment in supporting the rioters and rebels against the state is subsumed by his affinity with the standing reserve of technology at his disposal.

The use of microphones and audio speakers plays a critical role in differing notions of communications. On the one hand, Dr. Sargunam uses them to regularly communicate with the people of his closed commune with his hypnotizing voice becoming a gadget/commodity; his diktats metamorphize into a material that could be played over and again, as exemplified by the replay of his order to kill Shankar. By comparison, Shankar hides a microphone and is able to manipulate the content from the van. In the case of Shankar, as Steven Zani insightfully argues in the context of James Bond on-screen, the difference lies in the way he could use and throw away technology without being bound with any deep affinity to it (2006, 178–79). Thus Shankar, who is capable of near-constant innovation, keeps moving forward in his mission to bring Dr. Sargunam to justice and demolish his secret factory where illegal weapons are manufactured, in contrast to his technology-bound enemy. Guns, like cars, may be seductive, but they are also expendable for the Global South James Bond.

In addition to being adept with technology, Shankar uses his intuition to get the upper hand in challenging situations. For instance, he thwarts Thara's attempt to drug him and feigns unconsciousness to gain superiority during an interrogation. However, unlike Bond in *Goldfinger* who is strapped to a table and talks his way out of being killed, Shankar skillfully switches places with his interrogator Bhaskaran, who is now strapped to the chair instead of him. This gives Shankar the advantage, and he is able to interrogate the henchperson using an electrical charge to reveal information about the death of Durairaj and the location of his boss' secret factory.

It is Bhaskaran who outlines the imperatives of the Black Cat—the code name used by Dr. Sarguman within the organization—and his use of ex-convicts to manufacture and sell arms and ammunition at a profit to the antinational and antisocial elements. Much like the Bond megalomaniac Ernst Stavro Blofeld, leader of the SPECTRE organization in *Thunderball*, he is known only by his voice as his image and true identity are withheld from the group. This creates an opening for Shankar to manipulate recordings and emulate the Black Cat's voice, leading to his escape from the facility.[4] Eventually, technology, as exemplified by the exploding ammunitions inside his factory, engulfs the delusional Dr. Sargunam and kills him as he slips and falls while trying to cross a wooden pathway to safety and gets roasted in the inferno of his own ammunitions/standing reserve.

Nonetheless, *Vallavan Oruvan*'s specificity as a Global South film lies in its engagement with technology to focus on nature. The binary of the protagonist and the antagonist enable the clash between technology; this is exemplified by Shankar's use of technology for defense and the arrest of Dr. Sargunam, who uses it to fiercely defend his operation and attack any threats including the hero and his friends. The climax, set in Dr. Sargunam's secret and highly guarded factory, is spectacular due to the explosion of the ammunitions inside, a scene that recalls the extravagant climaxes of the early Bond films. Equally remarkable is the action choreography surrounding Dr. Sargunam's attempts to shoot Shankar and escape after switching on the alarm alerting his workers to the impending danger. Dr. Sargunam's fiery death where he falls into his own "standing-reserve" that are aflame and the black cat that comes and sits over his dead body is meticulously composed and staged. These scenes inside Dr. Sargunam's factory are painstakingly shot inside the Modern Theatres' Studios, where the spirals painted on the walls are direct references to the gun barrels that have become synonymous with Bond films.

In contrast are the exterior shots that frame the villain's lair when CID Shankar initially enters and finally exits to encounter the many guards outdoors. Unlike the finesse of the villain's habitat in a typical Bond film, Dr. Sargunam's hideout resembles an old house from outside. It is lined with thick pillars and is in a secluded area full of trees. The traditional terra-cotta roof tiles, preferred for their abilities to keep the interiors cooler, indicate it should have been a feudal lord's house once upon a time, which might have later been converted to an indigenous factory like a rice mill, as indicated by the massive exhaust fan at the top, not an uncommon phenomenon across villages in Tamilnadu. The dense greenery around recalls an earlier environment-friendly milieu, where such an organic clay-tile roofed and an elephant-pillared house should have been erected. However, unlike the finesse in a Bond film from the West, when CID Shankar cleverly evades the two guards as they keep religiously marching inside the compound to enter Dr. Sargunam's lair, his actions punctuate the peace and tranquility of the magisterial building and its green environs. His sprightliness is in opposition to the quietude of the backdrop.

The continuation of outdoor action remains jarring against the quietness of the aged building as the display of gunfire and dense smoke signifies the colossal destruction of human and natural life. This is exemplified when CID Shankar's confidante Kumar and his girlfriend Ammukutti join the fight and begin to gun down the workers of Dr. Sargunam. Although the greenery-filled backdrop marks the singularity of the James Bond/Secret Agent in the Global South—whether in Thailand or South India—the climactic sequence of *Vallavan Oruvan* is not only predicated on human and structural damage but also ecological destruction. This is a key generic element of the early Bond films in which the climactic settings located outside of the UK are subjected to harm through the indiscriminate use of technology on/within the environment.

Conclusion: Continuing the Legacy, While Carving a Distinct Path

While *Vallavan Oruvan* can be described as an extension of the Bond generic tradition, it can also be discussed as a local (re)iteration of a transnational hero through the figure of CID Shankar, who is a definitively South Indian detective. *Vallavan Oruvan* can be understood as both a broad homage to Bond films of the 1960s and a specific adaptation of *Banco à Bangkok pour OSS 117*, resulting in a distinctly local reinterpretation of the people, places, resources, and geopolitics frequently depicted in European spy thrillers. This is particularly evident in the way that the film challenges the stereotypical depiction of South Asians in Western films as well as their impulse toward depicting the unconditional development and testing of technology which renders local populations and ecosystems disposable. Unlike his British predecessor, the South Indian James Bond engages in a mission at home (rather than abroad) aimed at ensuring the safety of people and security of resources from threats located from within. Contrary to Truffaut's scathing criticism of Bond generic films, *Vallavan Oruvan* offers an opportunity for local audiences in the 1960s to (re)consider the expanding role of technology and its potential threats.

Notes

1. For instance, he was featured as C.I.D Agent Shankar in *Neelagiri Express* (Thirumalai and Mahalingam 1967) and *Nil Kavani Kaadhali* (Rajendran 1969)

2. For instance, played agent CID Raju in *Kettikaran* (Venu 1971) and CID Anand in *Thunive Thunai* (Muthuraman 1976).

3. The name of his laboratory, Hogby, exemplifies his being a conduit to the Western imagination of the fear surrounding the East and its vast population. When Officer Smith briefs Hubert Barton before deputing him to India, he recalls Lemmon having informed him of the widespread epidemic of the plague in India; Hubert responds by saying, "overpopulation . . . moderate hygiene," involuntarily mouthing the stereotypes regarding the people of the Global South.

4. Blofeld is often depicted holding and caressing a white cat. As a result, the code name Black Cat for Dr. Sarguman is another nod to Bond tradition.

Bibliography

Allen, Don. 2022. "'My Thoughts on the New Wave are Not Uplifting': Truffaut Interviewed in 1979." *Sight & Sound*, January 7, 2022. https://www.bfi.org.uk/sight-and-sound/interviews/francois-truffaut-1979.

Altman, Rick. 1999. *Film/Genre*. London: BFI Publishing.

Balsom, Erica. 2017. "Bootlegging Experimental Film." In *After Uniqueness: A History of Film and Video Art in Circulation*, edited by Erika Balsom and Shane Denson, 153–73. New York: Columbia University Press.

Benjamin, Walter. 2008. *The Work of Art in the Age of Its Technological Reproducibility, and Other Writings on Media*. Cambridge, MA: Belknap Press of Harvard University Press.

Brody, Richard. 2019. "The Truffaut Essays That Clear Up Misguided Notions of Auteurism." *New Yorker*, June 7 https://www.newyorker.com/culture/the-front-row/the-truffaut-essays-that-clear-up-misguided-notions-of-auteurism.

Bronfen, Elisabeth. 2015. "Screening and Disclosing Fantasy: Rear Projection in Hitchcock." Screen 56 (1): 1–24. https://doi.org/10.1093/screen/hjv004.

Bruce, Jean. 1960. *Lila de Calcutta*. Paris: Pr. de la Cité.

Eswaran Pillai, Swarnavel. 2015. *Madras Studios: Narrative, Genre, and Ideology*. New Delhi: Sage Publications.

Funnell, Lisa. 2015. "Objects of White Male Desire: (D)Evolving Representations of Asian Women in Bond Films." In *For His Eyes Only: The Women of James Bond*, edited by Lisa Funnell, 79–88. New York: Wallflower.

Funnell, Lisa, and Klaus Dodds. 2018. "For Your Eyes Only: James Bond's Secret China Mission." *South China Morning Post*, February 4. https://www.scmp.com/week-asia/geopolitics/article/2131818/your-eyes-only-james-bonds-secret-china-mission.

Guy, Randor. 2008. "Bond of Tamil Screen." *The Hindu*. November 7. https://www.thehindu.com/todays-paper/tp-features/tp-fridayreview/Bond-of-Tamil-screen/article15400631.ece.

Hansen, Miriam. 2012. *Cinema and Experience: Siegfried Kracauer, Walter Benjamin, and Theodor W. Adorno*. Berkeley: University of California Press.

Heidegger, Martin. 1977. "The Question Concerning Technology." In *Martin Heidegger: Basic Writings*, edited by David Farell Krell, 287–317. New York: Harper & Row. The German text appears in 1954. *Martin Heidegger, Vorträge und Aufsätze. Pfullingen: Günther Neske Verlag*, 13–44. Online version (University of Hawaii): http://www2.hawaii.edu/~freeman/courses/phil394/The%20Question%20Concerning%20Technology.pdf.

IANS. 2019. "Disney now owns Star India after $71bn Fox deal." *Business Standard* 20 March. https://www.business-standard.com/article/news-ians/disney-now-owns-star-india-after-71bn-fox-deal-119032000941_1.html.

Jain, Akanksha. 2017. "These 5 Vintage Cars Are Becoming Popular Among Indians. Here's the List." *Business Insider,* May 18. https://www.businessinsider.in/slide-shows/transportation/these-5-vintage-cars-are-becoming-popular-among-indians-heres-the-list/slidelist/58734858.cms.

Mathur, Aneesha. 2016. "Photocopying Allowed Under Law for Educational Use: Delhi HC." *Indian Express.* December 11. https://indianexpress.com/article/cities/delhi/delhi-university-photocopying-allowed-under-law-for-educational-use-delhi-hc-4419580/.

Richter, Gerhard. 2002. *Benjamin's Ghosts: Interventions in Contemporary Literary and Cultural Theory.* Stanford: Stanford University Press.

Safi, Michael. 2019. "Churchill's Policies Contributed to 1943 Bengal Famine—Study." *The Guardian.* March 29. https://www.theguardian.com/world/2019/mar/29/winston-churchill-policies-contributed-to-1943-bengal-famine-study.

Said, Edward W. 1978. *Orientalism.* New York: Pantheon Books.

Sharf, Zack. 2020. "Sam Mendes Says Making James Bond Films Is 'Not a Healthy Way to Work.'" *Indiewire.com.* March 9. https://www.indiewire.com/2020/03/sam-mendes-james-bond-not-healthy-work-1202216364/.

Shermer, Michael. 2016. "Why Malthus Is Still Wrong: Why Malthus Makes for Bad Science Policy." *Scientific American,* May 1. https://www.scientificamerican.com/article/why-malthus-is-still-wrong/.

Tanner, Matthew Bradford. 2010. "Movie Review: *Banco a Bangkok pour OSS 117* aka *OSS 117—Panic in Bangkok* aka Shadow of Evil (1964)." *Doubleosection.b logspot.com.* May 13. http://doubleosection.blogspot.com/2010/05/movie-review-banco-bangkok-pour-oss-117.html.

Truffaut, François, and Helen G. Scott. 1969. *Hitchcock.* London: Panther.

Zani, Steven. 2006. "James Bond and Q: Heidegger's Technology, or 'You're Not a Sportsman, Mr. Bond.'" In *James Bond and Philosophy: Questions Are Forever,* edited by Jacob M. Held and James B. South, 157–72. Chicago: Open Court. http://site.ebrary.com/id/10960221.

Chapter 3

Nostalgic Humor and Cultural Memory in the Remakes of Hong Kong Jane Bond Films

Jessica Siu-yin Yeung

Asian Cinema's Answer to the James Bond Craze

The production of Hong Kong James Bond spoofs or *Bondpian* is often attributed to the Bond craze that started after the screening of *Dr. No* (Young 1962) in Hong Kong on May 9, 1963 (Lee 2017, 350). According to the film critic Sam Ho, "In the 1960s, after the box office success of the Hollywood James Bond films *Dr. No* (1962), *From Russia with Love* (Young 1963) and *Goldfinger* (Hamilton 1964), spy films became a global phenomenon. Imitations sprang up all over the so-called free world, the parts of the world huddled under the anti-communist banner (2009, 221; Ho's original)." Critics have examined cosmopolitanism (Tan 2015, 195), representations of women killers (Desser 2017, 117–23), gender performativity and gender traits (Yau 1997), and categorization of these 1960s Hong Kong *Bondpin* or "Bond films" as crime thrillers (Van den Troost 2014, 64–66) and as "spy films without spies" (Ho 2009, 223; Ho's original).

This chapter focuses on the cultural legacy of James Bond spoofs in their comedy remakes in the 1990s. Juxtaposing two trilogies featuring the archetypal Cantonese Jane Bond character, Black Rose in Chor Yuen's *Black Rose* Trilogy (1965–1967) and Jeff Lau's *La Rose Noire* Trilogy (1992–1997), it argues that nostalgia and humor are key to understanding the cultural memory of Hongkongers in popular culture. This is especially true as the British colonial rule was approaching its end on July 1, 1997.

Black Rose in Chor Yuen's *The Black Rose* (1965), *Spy with My Face* (1966), and *To Rose with Love* (1967) is central to Jeff Lau's comedy remakes, as in *92 Legendary La Rose Noire* (1992), *Rose Rose I Love You* (Pang dir., Lau as producer, 1993), and *Black Rose II* (Lau and Yuen 1997). Chor's trilogy has an enduring influence on Hong Kong popular culture, including cinema, media, and Cantopop (Lai 1997, 97). Lau's trilogy intertextualizes with Chor's trilogy and met with critical success, as its first film is ranked 92nd in the "100 Hong Kong Must-See Movies" list compiled by the Hong Kong Film Archive selection panel (Hong Kong Film Archive 2011).

The Hong Kong Jane Bond genre is a product of long-established cultural traditions. Despite referencing the Bond franchise, Sam Ho conceived the term "Jane Bond" with the tradition of *nuxia* (female-knight) in the Chinese cinema of the 1920s and Hong Kong pulp fiction of the 1940s–1950s in mind (1996, 34). The "Jane Bond" genre should not be perceived as a mere "trendy imitation" (my translation) of James Bond (Van den Troost 2014, 65), or a colonial and feminized response to the Bond craze. It should be contextualized in Hong Kong popular culture, especially the 1950s and 1960s, which is seen as "the beginning of the history of Hong Kong and, simultaneously, as the golden age of the colonial time" (Chan 2000, 265). A major influence is the pulp fiction written by the southbound or Mainland Chinese intellectuals who fled from Shanghai to Hong Kong in the 1950s. Two writers are pivotal. The first writer published under the pseudonym "(Zheng) Xiaoping" and serialized *Oriole, the Heroine* series (1948–1960), where the three martial women friends and former burglars, Wang Ang (Oriole), Wu Nga (Raven), and Heung Kit (A-Heung) assist police to solve difficult cases (Ng 2008, 206). The second writer is Ni Kuang. He creates *The Black Musketeer 'F'* series (1966–1978) by synthesizing the leading characters of the British comic strip *Modesty Blaise* (1963–2002) and the Chinese folk heroine Hua Mulan into a black-clad, feminine, and righteous heroine Muk Lan-fa, her younger cousin, Muk Sau-chen, and Muk's male inspector sidekick Ko Cheung (Wei 2016, 146–55). Resembling Wang Ang and her cohorts, Muk Lan-fa and her assistants do a better job in investigating, fighting, and tracking down the criminals than the cops. These two fictional series create two Jane Bond characters, Wang Ang and Muk Lan-fa, prior to the Bond craze (*Oriole*: 1954–1962; Wei 2016, 139–40) and during the Bond craze (*Musketeer*: 1966–1967) respectively on-screen. They justify the local and literary origins of the Jane Bond archetype before the Hong Kong Bond craze began in 1963. In the 1980s and 1990s, the Jane Bond genre inspired the D & B Films' (1984–1992) "girls with guns" subgenre, which, like its predecessor, was an exploitation genre produced "on small budgets, featured low production values and unknown female stars, and earned less revenue at the box-office than male-driven gunplay films" (Funnell 2012, 172). In the 1990s, *The Black Musketeer 'F'* series also informed Johnnie To's cult Bond spoof, *The Heroic Trio* (1993), which features three women fighters fighting a baby-stealing eunuch.

Most of these *Bondpin* or "Bond films" revolve around a woman Bond or a pair of Bond sisters, who have come to be known as "Jane Bond" (Ho 1996) as women resorting to violence to promote social justice. "Jane Bond" is a character type coined by Sam Ho that defines the peak of the Bond craze (1960–1977) in Hong Kong cinema between 1965 and 1967 in his essay "Licensed to Kick Men: The Jane Bond Films" (1996, 34–46). Ho elaborates on his coinage in the essay "Spy Films Minus Spies: Hong Kong Cinema's Answer to the James Bond Craze" (2009) by attributing the absence of spies in Jane Bond films to the colonial government's avoidance of politics through film censorship during the Cold War (221, 223). These films were made in multi-dialects and different languages, including Cantonese, Mandarin, Amoy-dialect, and East Asian or Southeast Asian languages.

Beyond Hong Kong, there are many Bond spoof variants in Asian cinema during the 1960s and 1970s, including South Korea, Japan, Taiwan, Malaysia, Singapore, and Philippines (Garcia 2011, 15; Shih 2020). Hong Kong right-wing film companies, especially Shaw Brothers, capitalized on the Bond craze by hiring South Korean and Japanese film workers during the peak (1965–1967) and the later stage (1967–1977) of the trend. Hong Kong Bond spoofs with South Korean contributions include *The International Secret Agents* (Choi 1966), *Special Agent X-7* (Cheng 1967), and *Temptress of a Thousand Faces* (Cheng 1969). The Hong Kong-Taiwan coproduction film, *Golden Rose* (Ahn and Yeung 1971) also involves South Korean film workers. Japanese contributions to Hong Kong Bond spoofs include *Inter-Pol* (Nakahira 1967), *Asia-Pol* (Matsuo 1967), *Operation Lipstick* (Inoue 1967), *The Lady Professional* (Matsuo and Kuei 1971), and *The Venus' Tear Diamond* (Inoue 1971), with the last three films featuring the Taiwanese actresses Cheng Pei-pei and Lily Ho and the Taiwanese filmmaker Kuei Chih-Hung, who all worked for the Shaw Brothers. These East Asian collaborations (not necessarily coproductions) belong to the Hong Kong Mandarin cinema, which had a bigger market and production budget than dialect cinema like the Taiwanese-language cinema, though it also managed to make Bond spoofs like *The Best Secret Agent* series (Chang 1964–1966, five films; Wang 2022). Japan, moreover, initiated the genre of comedic Bond spoofs with *International Secret Police: Key of Keys* (Taniguchi 1965; Garcia 2011, 15). The genre was revived in 1990s–2010s Hong Kong cinema by films such as *From Beijing With Love* (Chow and Lee 1994) and *Agent Mr. Chan*

(Cheung 2018), which respectively parody *The Living Daylights* (Glen 1987) and *For Your Eyes Only* (Glen 1981)'s film posters.

The Malay–Hong Kong coproduction Bond spoofs directed by the Shaw Brothers filmmaker Lo Wei, *Nora Zain: Female Agent 001* (1967), *Shadow of Death* (1968), and *Danger Valley* (1968) (Bernard 2008, 169; Yeo 2021, n.p.) show a similar pattern with the Hong Kong–East Asian collaborations, although Malaysia has its local productions such as *Jefri Zain: Operation Lightning* (Sulong 1966; Yeo 2021, n.p.). The Singaporean Bond comedy, *Mat Bond* (Sentul and Amin 1967; Garcia 2011, 15) was filmed in Malay and released in Malaysia. Like the Shaw Brothers coproduction Bond spoofs, it was produced by Cathay-Keris Film Productions, a studio co-owned by Dato Loke Wan Tho (Jia, n.p.), who founded the Hong Kong right-wing film company Motion Picture & General Investment Co. Ltd. (MP & GI) in 1956. Filipino cinema responded to the trend with *For Y'ur Height Only* (Nicart 1981; Garcia 2011, 15) and about a dozen comedic Bond spoofs starring the Filipino comedian Dolphy, beginning with *Dolpong Scarface* (San Juan 1964) and *Dr. Yes* (San Juan 1965; Warped Factor 2021, n.p.). Demonstrating localisms, regionalisms, and humorous turns, Asia cinema has remade the Bond originals into their own since the 1960s.

Hong Kong Jane Bond Films

At least sixty-six Hong Kong Jane Bond films in were released in the peak of the trend of this exploitative genre between 1965 and 1967 (Hong Kong Film Archive 2007). The hybridity of this genre changed from combining the elements from the national defense and *wuxia* genres reminiscent of Hong Kong cinematic tradition in the 1930s–1950s, to adding modern and urban elements such as sci-fi, musical, gambling movie, and rom-com. Examples of these entertainment-oriented films are *The Black Musketeer 'F'* Trilogy (Law 1966–1967), *The Lady Information Agent* (Yeung 1967), *Double Exposure* (Tu 1966), and *Golden Butterfly, the Lady Thief* (Mok 1965), respectively.

In comparison with the popularity of foreign (mainly Hollywood) and Mandarin (especially Shaw Brothers) films in the 1960s, the Cantonese films did poorly in terms of box office receipts, and access to finance, studios, and technology pertinent to moviemaking (Fu 1997, 40, 42–43).[1] A major reason for this is that one of the primary sources of income for the Cantonese film industry was the Southeast Asian market, which was overtaken by the Shaw Brothers' movie theater chains (Kwok 2007). The political instability in Southeast Asia, Singapore's expulsion from Malaysia, and its adoption of the Bilingual Policy (Mandarin and English) further marginalized the Hong Kong

Cantonese film industry (Kwok 2007). The Cantonese film workers strived to keep up with the youthful expectations and westernized tastes of the postwar baby boomer audience (Law 1996, 9). But their efforts were constrained by the limited budget, the tight production schedule, and the colonial government's film censorship, therefore reflecting their comparative disadvantage in the local film market. These operating conditions contrast to the James Bond franchise with increasing generous budgets and the spectacular ambition of Ken Adam (Bond films' production designer, 1962–1979). These constraints also contribute to the "niche appeal" (Tan 2015, 206) of the Hong Kong Jane Bond films, which is perhaps the most obvious when Cantonese-speaking Jane Bond films deploy technical devices and futuristic weapons.

The workings of these "futuristic" devices and weapons often rely on verbal narrative or diegetic soundtracks (Ho 1996, 36). Their appearances are ordinary, which ironically meet the needs of the Bonds carrying them to disguise their identities. These low-budget yet innovative gadgets include the infrared glasses and headband, the anesthetic water gun, and the lock-pick ring in *The Woman in Black and the Black Dragon* (Law 1966), and the gun lighter and the remote-controlled model airplane that fires tear gas at the cops in *To Rose with Love* (Chor 1967). In the comedy remakes, this niche appeal becomes cult humor when the postwar baby boomer Hong Kong filmmakers such as Jeff Lau, Jacky Pang, and Corey Yuen poke fun at the playfulness, contradictory technology, and fantasy of these gadgets.

Figure 3.1. The model airplane in *To Rose with Love*.
Source: Hung faa hap dou, Rose Motion Picture Company, 1967. Screenshot by author.

Cantonese Jane Bond Films

Featuring the mid-1960s' rising star, Lily Ho, as Mandarin Jane, *Angel with the Iron Fists* (Lo 1967) and its sequel *The Angel Strikes Again* (Lo 1968) inaugurated the Shaw Brothers' Mandarin domination (1967–1977) of the Hong Kong Jane Bond craze, which until 1967 was preoccupied by Cantonese films (1960–1967). Before the Shaw Brothers' internationalization of the genre, the Cantonese Jane Bond film is a genre "with its deep root in the local culture" (Fu 1997, 46). Cantonese Jane Bond films target "a pre-dominantly female audience" of factory workers with "financial security and social freedom" and leisure to go to the cinema (Ho 1996, 41). Film depiction of Cantonese Janes must orient commercially by responding to the fantasies of these female spectators, who project their financial, social, and cultural empowerment on their screen heroines. Two of these memorable heroes were represented by the Cantonese stars Connie Chan and Nam Hung, who played the Jane Bond sisters in the *Black Rose* trilogy. Youth culture was a major trend in Cantonese cinema during the mid-1960s (Law 1996, 9), there-fore Cantonese-based stardom of the Jane Bond actresses, Connie Chan and Josephine Siao, and their sidekicks Lui Kei and Patrick Tse, were consecrated and emphasized in the comedy remakes of the 1990s.

The dialect divide between Cantonese Jane Bond films and Mandarin Jane Bond films matters, as "Mandarin Jane is less innocent, more worldly, less meek, more edgy and a whole lot more sexual" (Ho 2009, 224). The Cantonese Jane, as in *"Lady Bond* [(Mok 1966)] only kicks people, while [the Mandarin Jane in] *Lady Professional* really kills" (Ho 2009, 224; Ho's original). This rule is largely true, except for the Cantonese Jane Bond film, *The Female Chivalry* (Lo 1967), where a Bond sister, Wan Wai-ping (Connie Chan) kills two villains to avenge her father's death. Sam Ho elaborates on this point in his second essay, "Jane is not licensed to kick the bejesus out of men and the detective does not have a pass to break into others' houses. . . . To justify their means, the films establish ends of social equality and criminal justice" (Ho 2009, 223–34; Ho's original). While the most recent Bond film *No Time To Die* (Fukunaga 2021) has won applause by transforming the womanizing Bond into a family-oriented secret agent, this virtue has always been part of the Cantonese Jane's characterization from the outset: "Unlike Agent 007, who sets out to save the world for democracy, Jane's calling is to save the family" (Ho 1996, 45). Such family-orientation not only dovetails the avoidance of politics during the colonial period, it also speaks to the grassroots audience's Confucian moral universe and wins their approval.

Targeting a local audience and "appealing mostly to the semi- and illiter-ate masses" (Fu 1997, 42) more than five decades ago, these Cantonese Jane

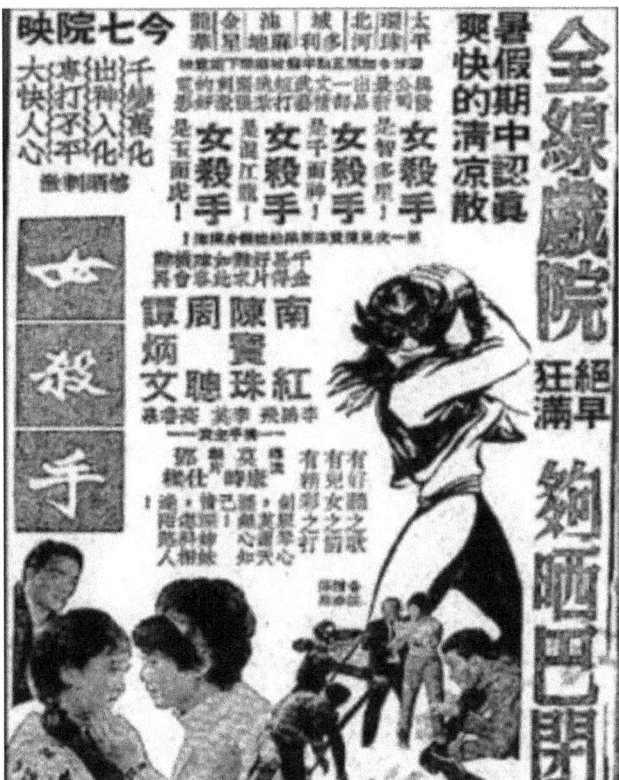

Figure 3.2. An advertisement for *Lady Bond* (Neoi saat sau, Mok, 1966) in newspapers.
Source: Chang Chun-chiang.

Bond films were still progressive and relevant in today's international standards with a Chinese and humane female lead. On a local level, Jane Bond still resonates in the 1990s and now, as she personifies the "moral values and social expression" of the 1960s on-screen (Chan 2000, 260) that the audience of the contemporary Hong Kong cinema cherishes, as evidenced in their engagement and the marketing of the remakes. These Jane Bond films, therefore, have edified a generation of young entertainment-seekers growing up with the didacticism of Cantonese cinema during the 1950s and 1960s and have become part of the audience's collective memories.

Jeff Lau's *La Rose Noire* Trilogy:
Memory Archive of a Hong Kong Pasticher

Being made during the transitional period of Hong Kong cinema during the 1960s (Fu 1997, 46), the Cantonese Jane Bond films deal with the subject of

Hongkongers' cultural identity subtly. This is not unlike the nostalgia cinema in the 1980s and 1990s, when Hong Kong cinema and Hongkongers were again facing another transitional period during the impending transfer of the city's sovereignty to China (Chan 2000, 263). Jeff Lau's *La Rose Noire* Trilogy belongs to this trend to cash in on Hongkongers' nostalgia through representing the iconic Jane Bond from Cantonese cinema. *Tomorrow Never Dies* (Spottiswoode 1997) similarly profits from the UK-China geopolitics by having a subtext of Hong Kong's transfer of sovereignty to China, though Hong Kong popular cinema always has a distant relationship with Hollywood cinema in the same period, unless there are intertextual references or remakes in the former. In other words, the 1990s Hong Kong Jane Bond comedy remakes are spoofs of spoofs, which have few "Bond" elements from the originals.

Jeff Lau's *La Rose Noire* trilogy is heavily encoded with classical forms in terms of Cantonese cinema's memorable elements such as soundtracks, genres, actresses and actors, characters, costumes, plot, props, and settings in canonical films. According to Thomas J. Flamson and Gregory A. Bryant, humor's role as a means of "signaling compatibility within local groups by relying on the detection of 'encrypted' information" is rarely noticed (2013, 50). Such cryptography of humor is an excess of form, as it relies on double coding to enable signs such as visuals and soundtracks to be read in more than one ways. Knowledge of the originals, however, is essential to perceiving the semiotic richness of the subtle pastiche (Hoesterey 2001, 81). This knowledge can be conceived as an "archive of classical forms" (Hoesterey 2001, 33). Such knowledge of the originals allows the in-group to grasp the humor, as "spectators familiar with '60s Cantonese movies can laugh knowingly" (Lai 1997, 96). The spectators with both the knowledge of the originals and nostalgic longing (Boym 2001, 38–39) for 1950s and 1960s Hong Kong culture are thus the targeted audience of the trilogy. In the following section, an examination of the trilogy's visual and musical codes would reveal it as an archive of cultural memory curated through pastiche by merging "horizons past and present" (Hoesterey 2001, xi).

A major sign in the trilogy is Cantonese scores, especially the soundtracks of the *wuxia* fantasy series, *Buddha's Palm* (Ling 1964–1968; seven films). *92 Legendary La Rose Noire* opens with the Cantonese tune "The Hungry Horse Is Shaking the Bells," thereby setting up the stylistics of the film as nostalgic comedy. The tune appears three times in the film: The first during the opening sequence; the second when the two apprentices of Black Rose, Piu-hung (Bobo Fung) and Yim-fun (Wong Wan-si) are introduced; the third when Butterfly Wong (Maggie Siu) wakes up in the Rose Mansion. When Butterfly gets to know Piu-hung and Yim-fun, she realizes that Piu-hung, as the rightful heir of Black Rose's legacy, has a Master

Bell. The Bell compels Yim-fun to practice martial arts stunts when it rings. The bell is rung three times. Whenever the bell is rung, the Chinese folk music used by the *Wong Fei-hung* film series between the 1940s and 1970s, "The General Mandate" (McGuire 2018, 49) would come up on the soundtrack. "Dagger Society Suite Overture" also contributes to the suspenseful mood. It is played when Lui Kei (Tony Ka-fai Leung) arrives at the Rose Mansion to rescue Butterfly while Piu-hung and Yim-fun hide away and use the traps that appeared in Cantonese Jane Bond films to hold him captive. This tune is best remembered by the postwar Hongkongers in the *Buddha's Palm* series, and by the 1980s–1990s generation in Stephen Chow's movies, especially *Kung Fu Hustle* (2004). The last appropriated tune is "Daring General," a Chinese orchestral ensemble score composed during the Cultural Revolution (1966–1976). Resembling "Dagger Society Suite Overture," "Daring General" is uplifting, which makes it apt when Piu-hung practices the Rose Swordplay to kill Mo Leung (Cheung Kwok-leung). Despite the seeming creativity of these appropriations, Chor Yuen and other Hong Kong Jane Bond filmmakers had ripped off the original soundtracks (the most-used ones are the James Bond theme, the percussive theme "007" and "Girl Trouble" from *From Russia with Love*, and "Auric's Factory" from *Goldfinger*) since the 1960s.

Another sign is Cantonese film genres, which include melodrama (*leon-leipin*), *wuxia* fantasy, Cantonese opera film, sentimental and tragic love story, absurdist comedy, and musical (Lau 2003, 124). The "sentimental and tragic love story" is referenced through the highly recognizable tune "Butterfly Lovers' Violin Concerto" from *The Love Eterne* (Li 1963), a film representative of the 1950s and 1960s *Huangmei* opera film trend. It is played in *92 Legendary La Rose Noire* when Lui Kei attempts suicide upon hearing Butterfly, his love interest, has a husband overseas. In *Black Rose II*, "Butterfly Lovers' Violin Concerto" is deployed when Lui Kei spoon-feeds Black Rose Chinese herbal medicine in bed when their past romance rekindles. The melancholic and grandiose tune joins *The Love Eterne*'s tragic love story with those in *92 Legendary La Rose Noire* and *Black Rose II*. This exemplifies pastiche effacing the temporal differences (Hoesterey, 69) between the two golden ages of Hong Kong cinema in the 1960s and 1990s. Inserting "Butterfly Lovers' Violin Concerto" into a postmodern comedy, Jeff Lau makes use of the incongruous music to create a hilarious effect, which ironically harmonizes the stylistics and narratives of his remake. Ingeborg Hoesterey quotes Vincenzo Giustiniani in discussing hilarious pastiche: "the most incompatible subjects make the best friends" (2001, 67). This applies to the *Rose Noire* Trilogy, where the "lush visuality and extravagant stylization . . . create the semiotic framework for a cultural critique" (Hoesterey 2001, 70) of the postwar generation's downplay of the socio-moral values at the heart of the Cantonese cinema of the 1950s–1960s in the late capitalist age, Hongkongers' identity displacement when 1997 approached, and the lack of cultural memory of these old Cantonese films among the younger generation of Hongkongers growing up in the 1980s and 1990s. Lau's "imaginative theft of the past" (Hoesterey 2001, 68) has made Cantonese cinema's iconic elements accessible to many members of the audience "who might otherwise never have cared for" looking up their origins (Hoesterey 2001, 68).

The second film in Jeff Lau's Trilogy, *Rose Rose I Love You*, corresponds to Chor Yuen's second film in his Trilogy, *Spy with My Face*. Lau's film pays tribute to Chor's original through similar characterization, costumes, footages, plot, and settings. *Spy with My Face* is about the private investigator Cheung Man-fu (Patrick Tse) getting captured by the gang of Golden Satan (Cheung Wood-yau), who assigns Jade-faced Tiger (Patrick Tse)[2] to replace Cheung at work in the insurance company and to steal the valuable belongings of the clients. This theme of double is replicated in *Rose Rose I Love You*, where the secondary school teacher Pearl (Carina Lau) turns out to be the villainous flying burglar White Rose. White Rose stole the sapphire Marat's Star years ago. Yet the more famous Black Rose (Veronica Yip) is blamed for the theft, so she appears as Pearl's neighbor, Beauty, to investigate the case. White Rose replaces Golden Satan in Chor's original as the Head of the gang and the skull emblem of the Golden Satan's gang is appropriated for hers.

In addition to the formal similarities between *Rose Rose I Love You* and *Spy with My Face*, the former commemorates the 1950s and 1960s as the golden age of musical and song-and-dance films in Hong Kong Mandarin and Cantonese cinema. When the undercover police officer who secretly admires Beauty, Leung Sing-por (Kenny Bee), arrives at the warehouse where she and her students and Headmaster/White Rose's gang members are, she lies that they are rehearsing for the graduation ceremony. The song they are dancing to is the theme song "Lady Bond" from the first film of the *Lady Bond* series (Mok 1966–1967; 4 films). The series has a slightly different theme song in the opening to imitate those in the Bond originals. The *Lady Bond* series incorporates musical numbers or song-and-dance elements in each film, especially in the second one, *Return of Lady Bond* (1966). This film adapts "Do-Re-Mi" from *The Sound of Music* (Wise 1965) into "Martial Arts Practice Song" and plays it when Kong Yin/Lady Bond teaches the slum children and the teenager (Lydia Shum) martial art skills to defend themselves from gang violence. The incorporation of these musical elements in the Hong Kong Mandarin and Cantonese cinema of the mid-1960s was illustrative of its time, during when major studios such as MP & GI and Shaw Brothers enjoyed higher production budgets. *Rose* pays tribute to this glorious era with Yao Surong's "Won't Go Home Tonight," Paula Tsui's "It's Like Fog Flowers," Harlem Yu's "The Passionate Desert," and Yao Lee's "Rose Rose I Love You."

The above intertextual references are *Rose Rose I Love You*'s nostalgic aspects while its funniest ones are the in-jokes. Laughing at them requires knowledge about Mak Gei and Sek Kin, the two actors in Cantonese cinema typecast to play Teddy boy and villain roles respectively. Teddy boy (*A-fei*) is a character type common in the 1960s Cantonese cinema. "A unique Hong Kong term with a negative connotation," *A-fei* was "used to describe trendy young men with a propensity for crime" (Ho 2018, 23 note 12). Toward the end of *Rose*, the escaped prisoner Mak Gei (Simon Yam Tat-wah) holds the inspector hostage while having a standoff with the undercover officers Leung Sing-por and Lui Kei (Tony Ka-fai Leung). Leung and Lui try to delay the time given by Mak to hand him the key for the safe with the sapphire by playing a clip of *Spy with My Face*. But the footage has been dubbed, so that the Black Rose (Connie Chan) in it addresses Mak (the character) directly. Mak (the actor) was cast in some of the Cantonese Jane Bond films but not this one. Despite the incongruity with the original, the plot still makes sense as the villain's name in *Rose* is Mak. But the footage has been mixed up with that of other Cantonese films, as Sek, who did not play in the original *Spy with my Face*, appears in it. The standoff becomes intense as Mak interrogates Leung and Lui about why Sek is in it and the two look at each other and wonder why. This exemplifies encrypted humor in Hong Kong popular culture that depends on double-coding, which joke to the in-group while commemorating a bygone age.

Figure 3.3. The in-joke of Mak Gei in *Rose Rose I Love You*.
Source: *Mui gwai mui gwai ngo oi nei*, Pang dir., Regal Films Co Ltd, 1993. Screenshot by author.

Conclusion

This chapter contends nostalgia and humor are key to making sense of Hongkongers' cultural memory through examining Jeff Lau's comedy remakes of Chor Yuen's *Black Rose* trilogy. Referring to Ingeborg Hoesterey's view on pastiche and cultural memory, it unravels the double coding of humorous elements in Lau's *La Rose Noire* Trilogy by identifying the canonical elements in Cantonese cinema of the 1950s–1960s and Hong Kong popular culture. Through juxtaposing the formal elements of the trilogy with their sources, this chapter sees Lau's remakes as an encoded memory archive of the Cantonese cinematic canon that speaks to the locals about the handover in a manner both similar and distinct from how *Tomorrow Never Dies* addresses it to an international audience. The double encoding of local identity in these spoof-of-spoof films prompts a reflective historicism of the cultural and social history of Hong Kong. The 1950s and 1960s as the golden past in the colonial era are remembered not for their economic and social reality of hardship and exile, but for their fruitful cultural production, "individual freedom and autonomy" (Chan 2000, 268). As minor histories and revisionist historiographies, these nostalgic films fill in the void of Hong Kong colonial history by recalling collective memories, social belonging, and cultural identity in a transitional time.

Comedic Bond spoofs are a phenomenon around the world paralleled with the unveiling of the films in the Bond franchise since the 1960s. As we have *Dr. No*, we also have *Dr. Yes* as its double. While Asian cinema of developing countries might not have the production budget on par with Hollywood to film explosive sequences, they might be able to afford to bomb the audience with laughs while domesticating Bondmania for the locals by inserting some in-jokes. In the West, the spoofing trend includes films such as *Casino Royale* (Huston et al. 1967) and novels such as Mabel Maney's Jane Bond series. While in Hong Kong, the *Aces Go Places* series (1982–1997; six films), Stephen Chow's *From Beijing with Love* (Chow and Lee 1994) and *Forbidden City Cop* (Kok and Chow 1996), and Jingle Ma's *Tokyo Raiders* (2000) and *Seoul Raiders* (2005) continues to reinvigorate the trend and they become classics on their own terms.

Acknowledgements

I am grateful to Lisa Funnell, Klaus Dodds, my anonymous reviewers, Sam Ho, Priscilla Chan, Carmen Tsoi, William Wilber, and the staff at the Hong Kong Film Archive for their help in enabling the writing of this essay.

Notes

1. Cantonese films always had lower budget (investment) than Mandarin films but that did not affect their box-office performance in the 1940s–1950s. One reason for the lower investment was Mandarin cinema's Shanghai connection, resulting in more generous budgets, a situation that became more pronounced in the postwar era. It was when Shanghai filmmakers and businessmen moved their operations to Hong Kong and produced a number of films with escalated budgets that set the tone for the differences between the two dialect cinemas. Audiences of Mandarin cinema tended to be more educated and therefore indirectly resulted in better production quality. In some instances, ticket price for Cantonese films might have been lower than for Mandarin films. According to the historian Chung Po-yin, the ticket price for Cantonese films in the postwar period were mostly HKD 1.70–2.40 while that for Mandarin films were just more than HKD 2.00 (2011, 158, 187 note 35). The ticket price for Chinese films (both Cantonese and Mandarin) was lower than that of Hollywood films, which mostly cost HKD 2.00–3.00 (2011, 158, 187 note 35). The decline of Cantonese films in the 1960s was caused by several factors: the manipulation of Southeast Asian exhibition by Shaw Brothers was a major one. Another factor was losing touch with a changing audience: while youth films with Connie Chan and other rising stars did well with young working-class women, they did not connect well with the more-educated audience, especially young men. They also resulted in losing of older audiences, who were not into the "miniskirts and go-go boots" trend. Mandarin films triumphed over Cantonese films partly because of their better connection with Chinese roots. This means that, in addition to investment, market and cultural forces played important roles in the differences between Cantonese cinema and Mandarin cinema. As economy and education improved, audiences became more demanding of production quality, but Cantonese cinema was unable to muster better investment in response to match the budgets of Mandarin films partly because of the market and cultural factors above. This added to its poorer performance, thus a vicious circle that eventually led to its demise. I thank Sam Ho for this point.

2. Probably an appropriation and sinologized name of the protagonist, Napoleon Solo (Robert Vaughn) in the American spy fiction series *The Man from U.N.C.L.E.* (1964–1968).

Bibliography

Bernard, Timothy P. 2008. "The Shaw Brothers' Malay Films." In *China Forever: The Shaw Brothers and Diasporic Cinema*, edited by Poshek Fu. 154–73. Urbana and Chicago: University of Illinois Press.

Chan, Natalia Sui Hung. 2000. "Rewriting History: Hong Kong Nostalgia Cinema and Its Social Practice." In *The Cinema of Hong Kong: History, Arts, Identity*, edited by Poshek Fu and David Desser, 27–46. Cambridge, UK: Cambridge University Press.

Chung, Po-yin. 2011. "Xing ma zijin denglu (The Arrival of Investment from Singapore and Malaysia)." In *Xianggang yingshi ye bainian (Zengding ban) (A*

Hundred Years of Hong Kong Film and Audiovisual Industries, Revised Edition), edited by Esther C. M. Yau, 124–87. Hong Kong: Joint Publishing.

Desser, David. 2017. "Beyond *Hypothermia*: Cool Women Killers in Hong Kong Cinema." In *Hong Kong Neo-Noir*, edited by Esther C. M. Yau and Tony Williams, 118–39. Edinburgh: Edinburgh University Press.

Flamson, Thomas J., and Gregory A. Bryant. 2013. "Signals of Humor: Encryption and Laughter in Social Interaction." In *Developments in Linguistic Humour Theory*, edited by Marta Dynel, 49–73. Amsterdam: John Benjamins.

Fu, Poshek. 1997. "The Turbulent Sixties: Modernity, Youth Culture, and Cantonese Film in Hong Kong." In *Fifty Years of Electric Shadows*, edited by Law Kar, 34–46. Hong Kong: Urban Council.

Funnell. Lisa. 2012. "Fighting for a Hong Kong/Chinese Female Identity: Michelle Yeoh, Body Performance, and Globalized Action Cinema." In *Asian Popular Culture in Transition*, edited by John A Lent and Lorna Fitzsimmons, 171–85. London: Routledge.

Garcia, Roger. 2011. "Asia: The Comedy." In *Asia Laughs! A Survey of Asian Comedy Films*, edited by Garcia, 13–16. Udine, Italy: Centro Espressioni Cinematografiche.

Ho, Sam. 1996. "Licensed to Kick Men: The Jane Bond Films." Translated by Ma Shan. In *The Restless Breed: Cantonese Stars of the Sixties*, edited by Law Kar, 34–46. Hong Kong: The Urban Council.

———. 2009. "Spy Films Minus Spies: Hong Kong Cinema's Answer to the James Bond Craze." Translated by Wai Ling. In *The Cold War and Hong Kong Cinema*, edited by Wong Ain-ling and Lee Pui-tak, 221–30. Hong Kong: Hong Kong Film Archive.

———. 2018. "A Man of His Time: Lung Kong and His Cantonese Films." *Nang* 5: 10–23.

Hoesterey, Ingeborg. 2001. *Pastiche: Cultural Memory in Art, Film, Literature*. Bloomington: Indiana University Press.

Hong Kong Film Archive. 2007. *Hong Kong Filmography Volume VI (1965–1969)*, edited by Kwok Ching-ling. Foreword by Wong Ain-ling. Hong Kong: Hong Kong Film Archive.

———. 2011. "100 Must-See Movies." https://www.filmarchive.gov.hk/documents /18995340/19057011/100_Must_See_Booklet.pdf.

Jia, Joshua Chia Yeong. 2022. "Cathay-Keris Studio." Singapore Infopedia. https:// eresources.nlb.gov.sg/infopedia/articles/SIP_1159_2007-07-01.html.

Kwok, Ching-ling. 2007. Preface. In *Hong Kong Filmography Volume VI (1965– 1969) (In Chinese)*. Hong Kong: Hong Kong Film Archive. https://www.lcsd .gov.hk/CE/CulturalService/HKFA/zh_TW/web/hkfa/rp-hk-filmography-series-7 -2.html.

Lai, Linda Chiu-han. 1997. "Nostalgia and Nonsense: Two Instances of Commemorative Practices in Hong Kong Cinema in the Early 1990s." In *Fifty Years of Electric Shadows*, edited by Lar Kar, 90–99. Hong Kong: Urban Council.

Lau, Jeff. 2003. "The Local Flavour of Hong Kong None Like It on Earth: Jeff Lau's Mischievous Creativity." Interview by Bono Lee. In *Hong Kong Panorama 2002– 2003*, 120–26. Hong Kong: Hong Kong Arts Development Council.

Law, Kar. 1996. Foreword. *The Restless Breed: Cantonese Stars of the Sixties*, edited by Law, 8–9. Hong Kong: The Urban Council.

Lee, Sangjoon. 2017. "Destination Hong Kong: The Geopolitics of South Korean Espionage Films in the 1960s." *The Journal of Korean Studies* 22 (2): 343–64.

McGuire, Colin P. 2018. "Unisonance in Kung Fu Film Music, or the Wong Feihung Theme Song as a Cantonese Transnational Anthem." *Ethnomusicology Forum* 27 (1): 48–67.

Ng, Ho. 2008. "Anye dushi: Linglei shehui xiaoshuo-shilun wushi niandai Xianggang zhentan xiaoshuo (Twilight City: 'Alternative Social Fiction'—A Study of Hong Kong Detective Fiction from the 1950s)." In *Gucheng ji: Lun Xianggang dianying ji su wenxue (A Record of the Isolated City: Studies on Hong Kong Film and Popular Literature)*, edited by Esther M.K. Cheung, 201–40. Hong Kong: Subculture.

Shih, Evelyn. 2020. "No Longer Bond's Girl: Historical Displacement of the Top Female Spy in 1960s *Taiyupian*." *Journal of Chinese Cinemas* 14 (2): 115–26.

Svetlana, Boym. 2001. *The Future of Nostalgia*. New York: Basic Books.

Tan, See-Kam. 2015. "Shaw Brothers' *Bangpian*: Global Bondmania, Cosmopolitan Dreaming and Cultural Nationalism." *Screen* 56 (2): 195–213.

Van den Troost, Kristof. 2014. "Born in an Age of Turbulence: Emergence of the Modern Hong Kong Crime Film." In *Always in the Dark: A Study of Hong Kong Gangster Films*, edited by Po Fung, 62–77. Hong Kong: Hong Kong Film Archive.

Wang, Chun-chi. 2022. "*The Best Secret Agent* (1964): The First Female Spy Hero of *Taiyu pian*." In *32 New Takes on Taiwan Cinema*, edited by Emilie Yueh-yu Yeh, Darrell William Davis, and Wenchi Lin, 36–51. Ann Arbor, United States: University of Michigan Press.

Warped Factor. 2021. "The Bizarre (& Unauthorised) James Bond Films of The Philippines." Warpedfactor.com, October 6. http://www.warpedfactor.com/2021/03/the-bizaare-unauthorised-james-bond.html.

Wei, Vivian Yan. 2016. "Transforming the Image of Female Chivary—Popular Detective Fiction from the 1940s to 1960s, from Shanghai to Hong Kong, in 'Huang Ying, the Female Cat Burglar' Series and 'The Dark Heroine Mulan Hua' Series." *Journal of Modern Literature in Chinese* 13 (1–2): 131–55.

Yau, Esther Ching-mei. 1997. "Ecology and Late Colonial Hong Kong Cinema: Imaginations in Time." In *Fifty Years of Electric Shadows*, edited by Lar Kar, 100–13. Hong Kong: Urban Council.

Yeo, Min Hui. 2021. "Malay 'Bond-ing' in Hong Kong: The MFP-SB(HK) Connection in the Malay Bond Films." Paper presented at the Asian Cinema and the Cultural Cold War Virtual Conference, Nanyang Technological University and Singapore Management University, May 22.

Chapter 4

Contrasting Sensibilities

Golgo 13, *Japanese Masculinity, and Differing Expectations of the Bond Archetype*

Aaron D. Horton

In Japan, the rising international popularity of the James Bond films, including *You Only Live Twice* (Gilbert 1967), filmed in Tokyo, Kobe, and numerous other locations throughout the country, coincided with the emerging *gekiga* ("dramatic pictures") movement in the Japanese comic industry. *Gekiga* originated in 1956, when artist/writer Saito Takao,[1] among others, sought to produce adult-oriented comics that were visually and thematically distinct from the more child-friendly, mainstream *manga* ("whimsical pictures"), exemplified by the works of Tezuka Osamu, often referred to as the "Walt Disney of Japan" and creator of popular series such as *Astro Boy* (manga 1952–1968; anime series in 1963, 1980, and 2003). The *kawaii* ("cute") style of much modern manga and anime, with childlike characters (even those who are adults), large eyes, and an overall "cartoony" feel, reflects Tezuka's lingering influence, decades after his death in 1989. Saito and like-minded artists sought, however, to distinguish their own works, both thematically and visually, with images that more closely resembled Western comics, and stories featuring violence, sex, and other mature elements, ostensibly intended for adult readers. Saito became the most famous and successful *gekiga* artist through *Golgo 13*, a series about a globe-trotting assassin-for-hire inspired, at least initially, by the artist's earlier comic adaptations of four of Ian Fleming's James Bond novels.

At first glance, *Golgo 13* resembles the slew of Bond imitations that appeared in the 1960s, particularly in Europe, in hopes of capitalizing on the success of films such as *Goldfinger* (Hamilton 1964). While there are many Bond-like elements in *Golgo 13* stories, including exotic locales, fisticuffs, gunplay, and glamourous women, Saito's character reflects distinctly Japanese sensibilities, and is intended primarily for an adult male Japanese audience. As such, the aspirational aspects of *Golgo 13* often differ from Bond's, perhaps one of several reasons for the former's failure to find much success in the West. As of 2022, *Golgo 13* is the longest-running Japanese comic series of all time, spawning film, television, and video game adaptations, a testament to the character's enduring popularity in Japan, and perhaps indicative, given the Bond film franchise's ongoing success, of the wide-ranging appeal of narratives featuring political intrigue, action, exotic locations, and beautiful women. Despite sharing such elements in common with the Bond novels and films, the series has had little success among Western anime and manga fans; indeed, the vast majority of *Golgo 13* comic stories remain untranslated into English, a reflection of limited interest and demand.[2] Drawing primarily from Saito's Bond adaptations and early *Golgo 13* stories, this chapter will examine Saito's distinctly Japanese interpretation of the Bond archetype, seeking to explain its enduring appeal in Japan, as well as its relative lack of success among Western audiences.

Saito's Bond

From December 1964 to August 1967, Saito published serialized versions of the Fleming novels in *Boy's Life* (Shogakugan, 1963–1969), a monthly publication intended, as the name implies, for a young male (*shōnen*) audience. Of the four Japanese versions (*Live and Let Die* (1964), *Thunderball* (1965), *On Her Majesty's Secret Service* (1966), and *The Man with the Golden Gun* (1967)), only *Thunderball* had been adapted to film prior to Saito's treatments, so the stories were, theoretically at least, drawn from the Fleming novels. However, in a 2015 interview included with a new edition of his *Shinuno wa Yatsura Da* ("Live and Let Die")[3] comic, Saito admitted he had not read the relevant novels before producing his own versions, though he had seen the *Thunderball* film, which he thought would make an interesting comic, before beginning work on the adaptations (Saito 2015d, 306–7). While they do feature some elements from Fleming's stories, Saito's adaptations engage in a great deal of creative license, reflecting, among other things, concessions to Japanese sensibilities and to the intended young male audience. As Gary R. Bortolotti and Linda Hutcheon have argued, the value of adaptations should not depend entirely on the adaptation's "fidelity" to the original source; a more productive approach is to view the original source as an "ancestor" to the adaptation (Bortolotti and Hutcheon 2007, 446).

Accordingly, my analysis of Saito's Bond adaptations seeks to explain how a distinctly Japanese depiction of the character was tailored for a presumably young male Japanese readership.[4]

For example, there are no sex scenes, a regular feature of Fleming's original stories (sometimes explicit) and the Bond films (usually implicit), in the four stories. In fact, Saito's Bond never even kisses anyone, though there are a few extremely tame romantic moments with female characters. Kissing itself is typically considered a far more risqué activity in Japanese culture, something reserved usually for sexual encounters (Easton 1994; Masuda 2012). Its absence, much less any implied sexual activity, is likely a concession to the sensibilities of a younger audience. In contrast, *Golgo 13* stories often contain both nudity and explicit sex scenes, reflecting the adult-oriented nature of *gekiga*. Visually, Saito's Bond is modeled after Sean Connery, unsurprising given the author's admission that the *Thunderball* film helped inspire his adaptations. Accordingly, Saito's Bond is gregarious, smiling and joking frequently, a far different figure than the taciturn and emotionless Golgo 13. Unlike Golgo 13, Bond is depicted as deeply emotional; for example, in *Ōgon no Jū o Motsu Otoko* ("The Man with the Golden Gun"), a crime boss named Kurt Hyman (rather than the Soviets in the Fleming novel) brainwashes him to kill M by using the agent's childhood trauma of seeing a truck driver accidently run over his friend Rick (Saito 2015b, 66–70). Even after Bond's attempt on M's life fails, the former suffers nightmares and immense guilt for his actions, despite M's repeated assertions that he does not hold his agent responsible for the incident (Saito 2015b, 120–22). While there were moments of such emotion and vulnerability in Fleming's novels, only the Daniel Craig series of Bond films (2006–2021) consistently depicted such a deeply emotional Bond on-screen.

The first story, *Shinuno wa Yatsura Da* ("Live and Let Die") sets the tone for Saito's adaptations by diverging significantly from the source material. As in the novel, Harlem crime boss Mr. Big is the primary villain, but Fleming's fortune-telling Solitaire is replaced by Kitty, a blonde CIA agent who works with Felix Leiter. This may have been a concession to the potential difficulty of rendering "Solitaire" in *katakana*, a phonetic script used primarily for foreign words, though it would still not explain the completely different characterization of the leading woman as a CIA agent. In Saito's adaptations, most of the female characters, including Moneypenny (written in *katakana* as "Money Penny," presumably representing her first and last names), are blonde, a common trope in manga and anime to signify that someone is American or European (Sevakis 2016). In Fleming's novel, Mr. Big threatens to break a captive Bond's fingers; in Saito's version, Mr. Big threatens Bond with a flamethrower embedded in his desk, a scene visually similar to "Number One" (Blofeld)'s use of a hidden execution switch on an underling in the *Thunderball* film. The train scene, loosely inspired by Fleming's novel, features Bond and Kitty travelling to Florida and Leiter being murdered[5] by the henchmen of a little person named "G," who poses as a child. Bond fights G atop the train, shooting the latter, who falls to his death. Eventually, Bond travels to Jamaica, where a local Caucasian boy named Tonto serves as his guide, replacing Quarrel, a Black Jamaican, from the novel. When Kitty is kidnapped and offered as a voodoo sacrifice, the ritual occurs in front of an enormous stone gargoyle, with the voodoo adherents wearing what appear to be traditional Japanese *oni* ("demon") masks. The bizarre depiction of the voodoo scene suggests, as one might expect of a Japanese person in the 1960s, that Saito had little to no familiarity with actual voodoo imagery. As in the novel, Mr. Big's ship explodes (due to a bomb planted earlier by Bond) while dragging Bond, Kitty, and a male CIA agent, in a three-person bundle, through shark-infested waters, though the ship is a stereotypical wooden pirate sailing vessel, rather than a modern yacht.

Unlike Fleming's novel, Mr. Big is revealed to have survived his apparent death in Saito's *Live and Let Die*, and becomes the series' recurring villain, similar to Blofeld's role in the novels and films. In the second adaptation, *Sandāboru Sakusen* ("Thunderball"), Mr. Big, now with a robotic hand, is revealed to be in cahoots with Emilio Largo in the latter's plot to steal nuclear bombs for the purpose of extortion. In the finale, Big escapes yet again, and then serves as the primary villain in Saito's third story, *Jo'ō Heika no Zero Zero Sebun* ("On Her Majesty's Secret Service"). Although Saito has not directly addressed his reasons for this particular change, it is possible that Mr. Big, as a Black character, seemed a more exotic antagonist for Japanese readers. Dating back as far as the 700s, white skin has been idealized in Japan as a mark of beauty, associated partly with social class, as elites would have spent less time outdoors, exposed to the sun. Conversely, as Hiroshi Wagatsuma argues, dark skin was historically viewed as "ugly" long before any sustained Japanese contact with South Asians or Africans (Wagatsuma 1967, 407). Historically, the color black has been associated with negative concepts, such as evil, uncleanliness, or death, in contrast to the purity, cleanliness, and beauty associated with pale skin (Wagatsuma 1967, 431).

Bald, tall, muscular, with an eye patch and robotic hand, Mr. Big represents a menacing threat to the slender Bond throughout the first three Saito Bond stories, a threat perhaps intensified by his dark skin, given its historically negative connotations in Japanese culture. When Mr. Big finally dies, due to being trapped in a room with an errant poison grenade thrown by an underling, Bond laments his rival's death, noting that Big was a great opponent who deserved better than such an accidental, ignoble demise (Saito 2015a, 288). Pausing to honor a fallen enemy, especially one responsible for tormenting and killing several of Bond's allies over the course of three stories, would seem out of place both in Fleming's work and the Bond films. However, this moment is a distinctly Japanese characterization of Bond, one that evokes the classic (though often exaggerated or misunderstood) samurai Bushido[6] ethic of respect toward one's opponent, even when bearing great animosity toward them, a trend Karl Friday argues was driven primarily by the practical need to use defeated enemy soldiers and civilians for the purposes of supplementing one's own forces and maintaining agricultural production, rather than an adherence to lofty ideals (Friday 1994, 346).

The Bond films clearly influenced Saito's action scenes, though the Japanese adaptations often bear little resemblance to their source material. For example, in Saito's *The Man with the Golden Gun*, there is an extended chase scene involving M, Moneypenny, and Bond, featuring M engaging in a shoot-out with assassins (Saito 2015b, 99–115). The final scene of Saito's *Thunderball* features Emilio Largo attempting to escape an undersea base via submarine, only for Bond to close the bay door exit to crush it (Saito 2015c, 232–34). Perhaps the most incongruous action scene in all of Saito's adaptations is a bizarre sequence in *On Her Majesty's Secret Service*, in which Mr. Big, housed in a hideout in the Alps, forces Bond, dressed in gladiator attire, to fight tigers in a Roman-style arena, from which he eventually escapes via a ski-chase reminiscent of those in Fleming's novel and its film version (Saito 2015a, 230–55). In these and other instances, Saito was probably attempting to extend the stories to meet length requirements, but also to incorporate more exotic, over-the-top sequences that might resonate with younger readers.

Aside from Moneypenny, the leading female characters are all Saito creations. As in most of Fleming's novels and the early films, leading female characters usually serve as passive figures in need of rescue; for example, Kitty's capture for the voodoo ritual in *Live and Let Die*. As noted above, romance plays very little role in Saito's adaptations, likely due to content concerns for a young audience. The closest Saito's Bond comes to a romantic connection is in *On Her Majesty's Secret Service*, in which he encounters the dark-haired Sofia Largo, the deceased Emilio Largo's younger sister, who serves a similar role in the story to Tracy di Vicenzo, Bond's love interest in the Fleming story, though without the eventual marriage or her demise (Saito 2015a, 70). Visually, Sofia resembles Domino from the *Thunderball* film, another indication of its influence on Saito's adaptations. Despite Sofia Largo becoming the closest romantic connection for Saito's Bond, the depiction is quite tame, and does not even lead to a single kiss between the characters. As mentioned above, kissing itself is widely viewed as a sexual, intimate, and "adult" activity in Japan, an act inappropriate to perform in public (Easton 1994; Masuda 2012), so it is rarely depicted in manga or anime intended for younger or broader audiences as of this writing, much less in the 1960s. In pioneering the *gekiga* movement, Saito and other artists sought to free themselves from such restraints, as reflected in the far more explicit sexual content of *Golgo 13*.

Furthermore, despite the rising number of manga and anime heroines in the 1980s and beyond, a Victorian-like notion of "separate spheres" for men and women has proved far more durable in Japanese society, especially when compared to the dramatic gains achieved by women in practically every facet of political, social, and cultural life in the West. From the Meiji era (1868–1912) of rapid modernization and cultural westernization to the post–World War II era and beyond, Ofra Goldstein-Gidoni argues, various social and cultural norms, including women wearing traditional kimono (which often cost the equivalent of $10,000 or more) for festivals, coming-of-age ceremonies, and other formal occasions, serve to reinforce traditional notions of femininity in which women embody a "good wife, wise mother" ideal (Goldstein-Gidoni 1999, 365). While the percentage of women ages 24–54 in the workforce between 1948 and 2002 increased from 35 percent to roughly 75 percent in the United States, the percentage in Japan remained just under 50 percent, despite a brief increase in the immediate postwar period due to labor shortages. This, as argued by Kristen Shultz Lee and her coauthors, is indicative of ongoing social and political norms that discourage women from continuing to work after marriage, which the authors note is an outlying anomaly among similar "postindustrial" states, whose percentages of women working outside the home more closely resemble those of the United States (Lee et al. 2010, 188–89). Accordingly, it is unsurprising that women in Saito's 1960s Bond stories are most often characterized as "damsels in distress," demonstrating little of the agency seen in characters such as Teresa di Vicenzo in the *On Her Majesty's Secret Service* novel and film.

In a 2015 interview, included in segments in the new editions of his Bond adaptations, Saito was asked if his Bond stories inspired the creation of Golgo 13. Acknowledging that the Bond character represented a "lighter" attitude and approach to the problems and obstacles he encounters, a characterization evidently based almost entirely on the films, Saito confirmed that he created Golgo 13 due to his desire to create "more serious" Bond-style stories. In that sense, he believes that his Bond work "gave birth" to Golgo 13 (Saito 2015a, 294). The interview did not mention the fact that, in 1967, the Fleming estate's Gildrose Productions withdrew Shogakugan's license to publish Bond adaptations (Bradford 2016), forcing Saito to create a new character in order to continue writing similar stories. Losing the Bond license led to Saito's creation of a darker, adult-oriented character who, although bearing some resemblance to the artist's version of Bond, was not only a departure from many aspects of the Bond archetype (including the countless Eurospy imitations), but also a figure more likely to appeal to a largely adult male Japanese audience. Saito's Bond was restrained by its presumably youthful audience, limiting the violence and almost entirely eliminating sexuality, but *Golgo 13*, published weekly in Shogakukan's *Big Comic* magazine, intended for adult readers, would allow the artist to fully embrace the mature themes of the *gekiga* movement.

Golgo 13 and Idealized Japanese Masculinity

The first Golgo 13 story, "Biggu seifu sakusen" ("Operation Big Safe"), appeared in serialized form in *Big Comic* in November 1968. From the first few pages, the adult-oriented nature of *gekiga* comics, in contrast to manga norms, is evident. The first few panels depict Golgo 13 gazing out a brothel window, with a naked woman lying in bed behind him. Startled when she approaches him from behind, Golgo 13 punches her squarely in the face, a shocking action for a story's protagonist. His suspicions of a setup are confirmed when armed men rush into the room, leading to an action sequence in which he escapes out the window. Over the course of the series, one of Golgo 13's rules of conduct is to never allow anyone to stand behind him, lest they attempt to ambush or otherwise harm him; his reaction to the woman's approach in the first story, seemingly justified by the subsequent attack by armed men, establishes the individualistic, cynical, and distrustful nature of the character before he speaks a single line of dialogue.

The first story also establishes that Golgo is Asian, though Saito never fully reveals his origins. During a high-level government meeting in Britain, in which the participants are discussing hiring freelance assassin Golgo 13 to kill a former Gestapo agent, the shadowy figures speculate about whether Golgo is Japanese. While this is never confirmed over the course of the series, other characters frequently refer to him as "Asian," sometimes using pejoratives, inviting male Japanese readers to identify with the character. The fourth story, "Ori no naka no nemuri" ("Sleepers in the Cage," March 1969), features the first use of Golgo 13's presumptive "real" name, Duke Togo, with the surname written in *kanji*,[7] another hint of his potential Japanese origins. Bart Beaty and Stephen Weiner argue that Golgo's murky origins essentially render him a "cipher" with whom readers can easily identify (Beaty and Weiner 2013, 147). I would add that other characters' frequent acknowledgment of him as Asian, or even specifically Japanese, is especially important to his resonance with Japanese male readers.

The first story also features his potential employers speculating about the meaning of "Golgo 13," for which they have no clear answer. The name derives from a juxtaposition of "Golgotha," the Biblical site of the crucifixion, and Judas's status as the disgraced thirteenth apostle, having been replaced after his betrayal of Christ to Roman and Jewish authorities. Accordingly, the series' logo features a standing skeleton wearing a crown of thorns, another crucifixion reference. Golgo 13 is a contract killer, owing loyalty to no one but himself and his client, so the allusions to Judas's betrayal and its ultimate consequence, Jesus's crucifixion, are apt. The use of Christian imagery is common in Japanese media, often as an exotic or mysterious element (Kincaid 2017). For example, Anno Hideaki's acclaimed apocalyptic anime series, *Neon Genesis Evangelion* (1995–1996), relied heavily on Christian and Jewish imagery, albeit in forms that would strike adherents of those faiths as rather bizarre. Accordingly, while Judas is reviled within the Christian tradition as a betrayer, Golgo 13, while often cold and ruthless, is clearly a protagonist with whom readers are meant to identify.

Individualism and the Unbreakable Code

In sharp contrast to Bond, an MI6 agent who serves "queen and country," Golgo 13 is an assassin whose primary motivation is money. Despite accumulating a great deal of wealth, he seems disinterested in Bond's conspicuous consumerism, reflecting pervasive negative attitudes toward ostentatious wealth and excessive spending in Japan (Hill 2018). While Bond enjoys expensive cars, food, and drink, featured heavily in the films and to which Fleming devotes much detail, including frequent mention of name-brand cars, champagne, and other items in the novels (Berberich 2012, 17), Golgo 13 lives relatively inconspicuously, using his financial resources largely to acquire equipment necessary for the completion of his current contract rather than to acquire material goods or fund a lavish lifestyle. Bond's conspicuous consumerism and refined enjoyment of luxury goods, which both Christine Berberich and James Chapman describe as "snobbery" (Berberich 2012, 17; Chapman 2007, 64), is a key element of the character's appeal. This element of Bond's character, argues Berberich, may have resonated especially in the immediate postwar era in Britain, when memories of wartime rationing and scarcity were still fresh (Berberich 2012, 18). While consumerism plays very little role in Saito's stories, Golgo 13's extreme individualism, owing no loyalty or obligations to anyone except his current client (which frequently includes the CIA, KGB, MI6, and other agencies), would resonate especially with Japanese male readers accustomed to subordinating their own wishes to the collective interests of their workplace, where conformity is expected and individualism discouraged, oft-embodied in the "salaryman" office worker cultural trope (Cheng 2019). The fantasy of functioning and thriving as a completely independent actor, who still manages to retain fundamentally Japanese reservations about excessive spending, likely contributes greatly to the character's appeal.

While it certainly has its opponents and hypocritical interpretations, individualism is frequently encouraged and celebrated in Western culture, while in Japan, conformity and subordination to collective needs are fundamentally engrained in society, from strict codes of conduct in school to workplace culture. In modern Japanese history, individualism has often been derided as a source of social or cultural ills, and an undesirable product of rebellious youth culture, which, in the late 1960s, inspired nationwide leftist protests on college campuses against established conservative values and practices within universities as well as in society more broadly. As Sharon Kinsella argues, comics became a popular venue for the values of youth culture, including individualism and sexual liberation, elements that feature frequently in Golgo 13's characterization and behavior (Kinsella 1998, 291). In *Amae no kōzō* ("Anatomy of Dependence," 1971), psychoanalyst Doi Takeo likened individualism in Japan to a "childishness" that sought to unravel both traditional social bonds, such as those between youth and their elders, as well as social distinctions, such as those between men and women. Doi's assertions, building upon traditional Confucian concepts of hierarchy and obedience, underscore the tremendous appeal of comics such as *Golgo 13*, which offers the "fantasy" of extreme individualism in a character beholden to no form of authority, other than his own code of conduct. Frederick Schodt describes Golgo 13 as a "super-samurai" who embodies ultimate individualism, the type of "Nietzschean superman" archetype that is particularly appealing to Japanese men who must "sublimate their own personal desires to those of the majority in the organization[s] [they belong] to" (Schodt 2012, 78–79).

While Golgo 13 is largely amoral, he adheres to a strict code of conduct that echoes popular stereotypes of the samurai Bushido ethic, which emphasized loyalty to one's lord, even to the point of committing suicide in the event of failure or betrayal. In popular imagination, such values were universal among samurai, lending the Sengoku ("Warring States") era (1467–1615) a certain romantic appeal in subsequent Japanese culture, though in reality, Bushido was no more uniformly interpreted or universally implemented than the medieval European concept of chivalry (Friday 1994, 514–16). Regardless, adhering honorably to a code of conduct has long been celebrated as ideal in Japanese culture, embodied in classic works such as *Chūshingura* ("Treasury of Loyal Retainers"), an early eighteenth-century drama based on the 1701 killing of government official Kira Yoshinaka by a group of forty-seven ronin (masterless samurai). These wayward samurai believed Kira provoked their daimyo, Asano Naganori, into violating courtly protocol, which resulted in the Tokugawa shōgun ordering Asano to commit suicide. Upon completing their act of revenge, the forty-seven men commit seppuku (ritual suicide), having violated the shōgun's order not to retaliate against Kira (Friday 1994, 523–25; Turnbull 2011). The story, which has spawned countless stage, film, and television adaptations, idealizes the importance of following the Bushido code, even when it results in one's own death.

Just as Bushido emphasizes loyalty to one's lord, Golgo is unwavering in his commitment to carrying out his contracts, an element Leo Lewis, reflecting on his 2015 interview with Saito, says is "subconsciously attractive" to Japanese readers (Lewis 2015). In that interview, Saito acknowledged his love of samurai movies and culture, and asserted that Golgo's code of conduct[8] was a key part of the character's enduring appeal. Despite his amoral, individualist nature, Golgo never breaks a contract, even when offered more money by other parties. He also displays incredible patience, sometimes waiting at great length to set up an assassination, as in "*Merankorī natsu*" ("Melancholy Summer," August 1969), where he spends many days in Malta secretly observing his target's abandoned wife, expecting, correctly, the man would eventually return to see her. In the Lewis interview, Saito equated Golgo's legendary patience and endurance to that of the average salaryman, noting that such characteristics signified that the character was "purely Japanese" (Lewis 2015). In "Melancholy Summer," even when pressured by MI6 to leave Malta to search elsewhere for his target, a former MI6 agent who had sold information to the Soviet Union, Golgo stubbornly refuses, insisting that his patience will pay off. In the end, Golgo's patience triumphs over Western impatience when his target returns to Malta, validating what Saito described as a "purely Japanese" trait.

Among his other rules, including refusing to shake hands or to allow others to stand behind him, both indicative of Golgo's suspicious, distrustful nature, the character will also kill anyone who witnesses him carry out an assassination. In *Byakuya wa ai no umeki* ("The Midnight Sun Wails for Love," April 1969), Golgo bonds with a woman he encounters on a turbulent flight to Norway. After spending a night together, she follows Golgo and sees him kill his target. When Golgo discovers her, a single panel shows a regretful expression on his face, before he fatally shoots her. The juxtaposition of his brief moment of regret with the killing of a woman with whom he'd displayed an unusual level of tenderness illustrates Golgo's unwavering commitment to his own rules, even when he might personally have preferred a different outcome. Thematically, the scene resembled the *Chūshingura* protagonists' revenge killing that resulted in their own suicides. Their own desires, including family attachments, were secondary to their need to fulfill their obligations to their disgraced and deceased lord, just as Golgo might personally have wanted to spare his lover, but was forced, by unwavering devotion to his own code, to kill her. Men who display cruelty and unjustified violence (i.e., not in self-defense, for example) toward women are consistently and unequivocally portrayed as reprehensible villains in Saito's stories (as well as more generally in many other manga and anime series[9]), but Golgo's action in this particular story is understood to be justified by his commitment to his rules, and he does so with seeming regret, rather than from any malice or hostility.

"Conquest" of the West?

Just as most Bond adventures occur somewhere other than Britain, the vast majority of Golgo 13 stories, both in the comics and their adaptations, take place in locations likely to seem exotic to a Japanese audience. The Golgo stories serve not only as entertainment, but also as part travelogue, allowing readers or viewers to experience foreign locations they may never visit in reality, just as Bond serves as a white male avatar through which readers and viewers can project themselves into exotic locales (especially in the novels and early films), besting foreign enemies and bedding foreign women. Gregory Daddis argues that Western adventure stories, specifically those in pulp magazines, but whose themes certainly appear in the Bond novels and films, often placed male protagonists (and male readers) in a position to "objectify" exotic women, who contrasted strongly with the "overbearing" women back home (Daddis 2021, 98–99). In this sense, Golgo achieves the same function for male Japanese readers and viewers, serving as a Japanese/ Asian avatar traveling the world, outwitting foreign (mostly Western) individuals and governments while often achieving sexual conquests of mostly Western women, an appealing embodiment of Japanese masculinity. The prevalence of Western, particularly white, women among Golgo's sexual encounters is evident in the *The Golgo 13 Encyclopedia* (2000), which provides the following breakdown of all the women the character slept with by race: seventy-two White, fourteen Asian, six Black, six "Other," three Native American, one Inuit, and five "Unknown." Reversing widespread post–World War II Japanese sexual anxieties regarding mostly white American soldiers and Japanese women, Golgo, an ostensibly Japanese man, frequently engages in the "conquest" of white American and European women, a seeming confirmation of his libidinal masculinity.

In their depiction of locations around the world, Saito's production team developed a reputation for historical and factual accuracy, with several members of his staff responsible for conducting extensive research to ensure the accuracy of each story's setting (Thompson 2012). This attention to detail included not only political and historical details, but also highly accurate depictions of cityscapes, landscapes, firearms, vehicles, and other photorealistic imagery in the comic. In the pre-internet era, this was a time-consuming process, with Saito's staff scouring newspapers and other sources to acquire reference photographs and other information to ensure the comics' accuracy (Kuroda 2021). The team accumulated an extensive collection of model firearms, stored in the studio's "gun room," so that artists could easily access realistic replicas to ensure the accuracy of guns in the comic (Lewis 2015). Saito's commitment to realism set Golgo stories in the context of exhaustively researched real-world political, social, and cultural developments, offering readers a window to the wider world, through which they not only could experience exotic locales and situations, but also learn about the real histories and cultures of unfamiliar people and places.

After Japan's defeat in World War II, Japanese men in particular experienced pervasive feelings of powerlessness and inferiority, especially in the wake of American military occupation and global ascendancy, a phenomenon discussed at length in Igarashi Yoshikuni's *Bodies of Memory: Narratives of War in Postwar Japanese Culture, 1945–1970* (2000). The widespread sense of emasculation and defeat, argues Igarashi, contributed directly to the incredible popularity of pro wrestler Rikidōzan,[10] whose matches in the 1950s drew massive crowds and television ratings, relying most often on the dynamic of the star battling (and usually defeating) Western, mostly American, villains, rendering his matches a means of producing a "new narrative for the nation," one in which the valiant, smaller Asian man overcomes his larger Western opponent (Igarashi 2000, 129). Igarashi's explanation of Rikidōzan's appeal could easily apply to Golgo 13 as well. Golgo travels the world, carrying out assassinations of mostly Western targets, remaining calm and collected while outwitting and overcoming Western and other foreign opponents, many of whom are depicted as overly emotional and thus more susceptible to error, with frequent sexual conquests throughout. The mostly Western women Golgo encounters and usually sleeps with are drawn to him despite, or perhaps because of, his taciturn nature.

While Western audiences sometimes find Golgo's characterization baffling and unappealing, his commitment both to his unbreakable, Bushido-like code of conduct, as well as his employment of *harage*, a Japanese concept of verbal economy by which one speaks only as absolutely necessary (Lewis 2015), partly to gain information from others, are, to a Japanese audience, positive qualities that provide Golgo an advantage over his foreign foes, who often make pivotal mistakes due to their emotionality. For example, in the 1983 anime film *Golgo 13: The Professional*, in which American oil tycoon Leonard Dawson resorts to increasingly desperate and depraved measures to kill Golgo, who assassinated the former's son (who, it turns out, hired Golgo as a means of committing assassin-assisted suicide). Among other actions, Dawson, prone to emotional outbursts throughout the film, allows a mutant-like killer, "Snake," to rape his daughter-in-law in exchange for the killer's services, in hopes that the bizarre figure can manage to kill Golgo. In contrast, Golgo, pursued throughout the film, remains calm, eliminating each threat until finally confronting Dawson, who attempts to commit suicide by

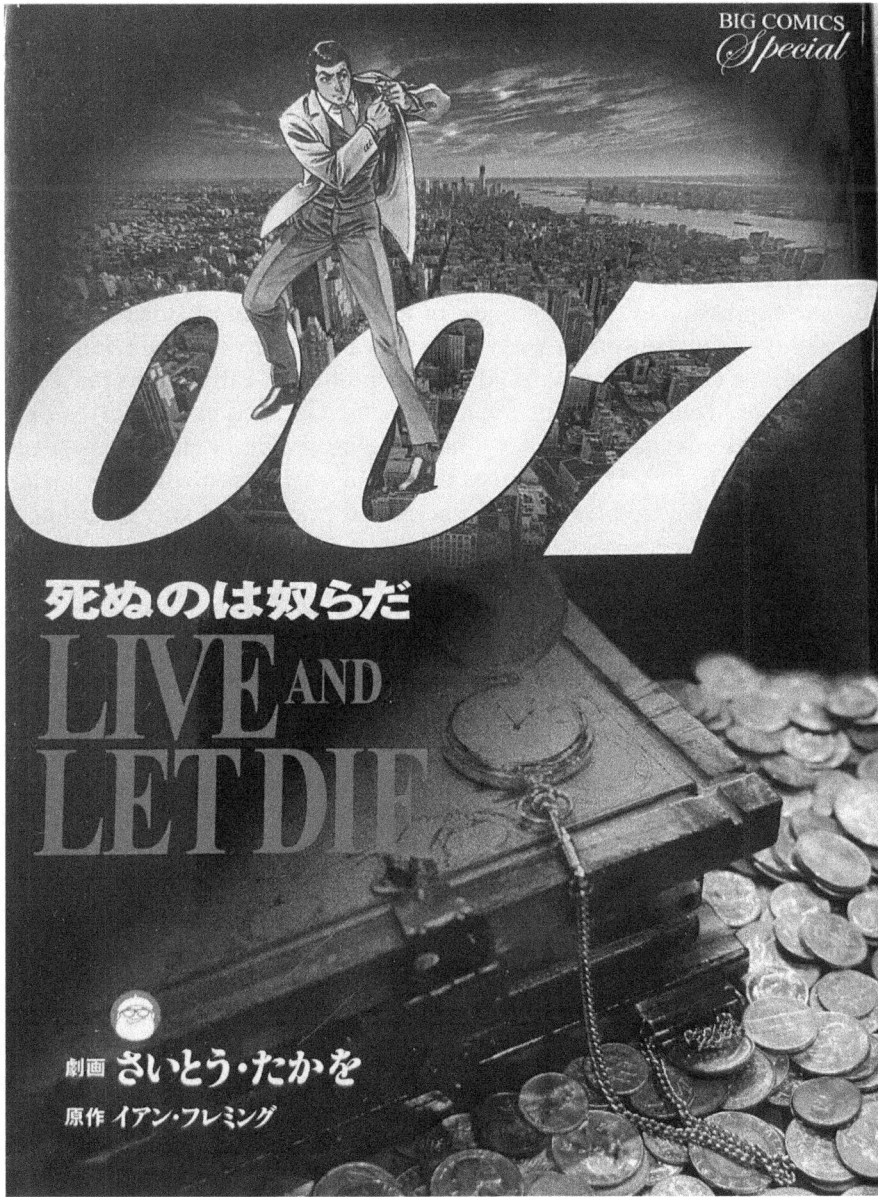

Figure 4.1. Saito Takao, *Shinuno wa Yatsura Da* ("Live and Let Die").
Source: 2015 reprint. Photo by author.

jumping from his office atop a skyscraper. As a nod to his true sentiments, Golgo calmly shoots Dawson in the head as he falls, presumably for the satisfaction of killing his tormenter, mere seconds before he would have died from the fall. Much as Bond served, for Fleming at least, as a means of reasserting Britain's importance in the midst of its declining empire and increasingly subordinate role to the United States in 1950s geopolitics (Berberich 2012, 24–25; Chapman 2007, 62), Golgo overcoming obstacles, often in the form of emotional, verbose Western antagonists, validates the Japanese ideal of concealing one's emotions while adhering to a strict code of conduct.

In contrast to Bond, Golgo rarely shows any outward interest in the women he encounters, maintaining his usual cold, taciturn disposition. The women he sleeps with almost all initiate the encounter, with Golgo displaying a dispassionate expression even in the midst of intercourse. Part of Bond's appeal is his ability to seduce women, even those who are initially reluctant. For example, both the *Goldfinger* novel and film, he problematically "converts" Pussy Galore, a lesbian (plainly stated in the novel and implied in the film) through his relentless advances, which, to modern eyes, might be defined as sexual harassment. Gregory Daddis argues that Bond's "conquest" of Pussy Galore embodied an idealized reversal of a perceived post–World War II decline of "manliness" in Western society (Daddis 2021, 59). Golgo, on the other hand, occasionally turns down opportunities for sex, as in the story "*Eki basha no GT*" ("GT the Sniper," August 1969), when a female Chinese agent offers him two willing Chinese women to help him "kill time" while waiting for their operation to begin. The female agent is visibly impressed by his refusal, leading to her own sexual encounter with him later in the story. In a similar situation, Bond's contact in Egypt offers him a pair of willing women in *The Spy Who Loved Me* film, but he does not refuse. Despite his emotional coldness toward them (and everyone else), Golgo's relations with women appear almost gentlemanly when compared to Bond's aggressive sexual pursuits. A recurring theme in Japanese popular culture is the figure of the lonely male who struggles to relate to those around him, especially romantically. From the novels of Murakami Haruki to countless representations in anime, manga, film, and television, depictions of men who struggle to form romantic connections are pervasive in Japanese media. In this context, Golgo's standoffish posture toward women provides male readers a fantasy by which a man who speaks little and does not actively pursue women (thus never risking rejection) is nonetheless irresistibly attractive to them.

In Japanese media, men who aggressively (but nonviolently, as violence would render them villains) pursue women à la Bond often serve as comical figures, frequently rejected by women in over-the-top, slapstick fashion; for example, Moroboshi Ataru in the *Urusei Yatsura* manga (Takahashi Rumiko, 1980–1987) and anime (1981–1986), and Saeba Ryo, a private detective who possesses Golgo's skills for marksmanship, albeit with a gregarious and at times silly personality, in Hojo Tsukasa's popular *City Hunter* series (manga, 1985–1991; anime, 1987–1991). In contrast, Golgo's seeming disinterest proves attractive to many of the women he encounters, and he often displays subtle hints of compassion and sympathy for them. In *"Merankorī natsu"* ("Melancholy Summer," August 1969), when he notices that his target's lonely, long-suffering wife is waiting for her estranged husband at the docks, Golgo attaches a silencer to his rifle so that she won't notice him kill her husband, approaching via boat. This spared her seeing her husband die, and prevented her noticing the nearby Golgo commit the act, which would've required the assassin to kill her as well. In the final scene of *The Professional*, Laura Dawson, the widow of the man who hired Golgo as a means of assisted suicide, confronts the latter on a busy street, threatening to shoot him. He simply turns his back, allowing her to shoot him (which he survives, walking away into the surrounding crowd), without retaliating, as a gesture of sympathy or pity for the suffering she had endured due to her husband's death and the whims of her vengeance-obsessed father-in-law.

Western Receptions

Despite its status as the most prolific comic series in Japanese history, along with its many adaptations, Golgo 13 has met with limited success in the Western world, where manga and anime have grown both in popularity and accessibility since the 1990s. Of the 205 (and counting) comic volumes published in Japan, containing over five hundred individual stories, only a handful have been translated and published in English, most recently Viz Media's thirteen-volume collection, totaling twenty-six selected stories (2006–2008). The second live-action film (*Golgo 13: Assignment Kowloon*, 1977), both anime films (*Golgo 13: The Professional* in 1983 and *Golgo 13: Queen Bee* in 1998), and the fifty-episode anime series (2008–2009) have all been released in the West, though the latter quickly went out of print and is currently unavailable on any major streaming service in the United States.[11] Two of the six *Golgo 13* video games were released in North America and Europe on the Nintendo Entertainment System (NES): *Golgo 13: Top Secret Episode* in 1988, and *Golgo 13: The Mafat Conspiracy* in 1990, both accompanied by English-translated comics to introduce potential players to the character. With the exception of the 1983 anime film, Western editions of Golgo media have failed to resonate, as indicated by their generally poor sales, which, among other things, led Viz to discontinue their English translations after only thirteen volumes (Thompson 2012).

A survey of Western reviews and reactions to various Golgo 13 stories provides some insight into the character's lack of appeal to Western manga and anime fans. Many reactions address the series' sex and violence. Because it is the most widely available Golgo 13 story, the vast majority of reviews focus on *Golgo 13: The Professional* (1983), which Jason Thompson referred

Figure 4.2.   Saito Takao, *Golgo 13*, volume 96: *Nō Rireeshon* ("No Relation").
Source: Tankōbon volume (Shogakukan, 1990). Photo by author.

to as "deeply depressing" and a "nihilistic hellscape" and ultimately a film "about evil people doing terrible things to one another" (Shuster 2019). In a 2014 review for *Teleport City*, "Keith" acknowledged that the 1983 film was "a shamelessly over-the-top work of grindhouse theater exploitation," but that he very much enjoyed it ("Keith" 2014). Female reviewer "Kisha" (*Admit One Film Addict*) admitted that parts of the 1983 film were "sexist and exploitative," but described herself as a "total fangirl for Golgo," awarding the film a score of 8/10 ("Kisha" 2018).

Beyond reactions, both positive and negative, to the sex and violence, many Westerners who disliked Golgo 13 point to his taciturn characterization. For example, in her *New York Times* review of what she called the "crude and idiotic" 1983 anime film, Janet Maslin noted that she found the protagonist especially "dull" (Maslin 1992). In a May 5, 2021, *Vintage Anime Club* podcast review of the film, the hosts frequently complained about Golgo 13's seeming "lack of character," with one summarizing by saying "imagine if James Bond was a Terminator, except without any charisma" (Vintage Anime Club 2021). Such reactions are common, even among those who enjoy Golgo 13, illustrating the differing expectations of Japanese and Western audiences. As noted above, Golgo's stoic persona projects Bushido discipline and strength to a largely male Japanese fanbase, who understand that those qualities are often key to the character's success in a variety of situations, while some Westerners view such qualities as dull rather than admirable.

There may also be a simpler explanation, particularly for the manga's failure to achieve success in the West: Saito's "old-fashioned" art style. Golgo fan Jason Thompson posits that the comics' visual style is unappealing to American and European manga fans because it features odd quirks such as long noses, exaggerated sweat beads, and "goofy expressions," albeit with ultrarealistic backgrounds and technical details. Thompson points out that Saito's style contrasts greatly with Western expectations of *moe* (a term, along with *kawaii*, "cute," used to refer to a character's cuteness and visual appeal to readers or viewers) in their manga and anime (Thompson 2012). Beaty and Weiner suggest that, while the grittier, hyperrealistic "Western style" of the Golgo 13 manga made it *more* appealing to Japanese readers, the art had the opposite effect on Western audiences, who prefer more "typical" manga and anime artwork, which tends more toward fantastical, highly stylized imagery (Beaty and Weiner 2013, 149–50). As these examples indicate, the distinctly un-*moe* style of Golgo 13 is likely a factor in the series' general lack of appeal to Western audiences, though probably in combination with the other issues discussed above.

Conclusion

Although inspired by Saito's work on Bond adaptations, Golgo 13 embodies and appeals to distinctly Japanese sensibilities. His absolute independence, owing loyalty to no one but himself and his own code, offered an appealing fantasy to Japanese men whose daily lives were defined by expectations of submission and conformity. The character's rigid code and stoic nature evoke romanticized images of the samurai ideal, however inaccurate it often was in reality. Golgo stories typically feature many elements in common with Bond, such as action, exotic locales, stylish clothing and cars, and "conquests" of foreign enemies and women, elements that have, as with Bond, contributed to the series' enduring popularity, but the character has largely failed to appeal to Western audiences. While these elements frequently feature in Western entertainment, they differ significantly from the manga and anime series most popular in the West. Golgo's serious tone, ultrarealistic art style, and emphasis on real-world political intrigue contrast sharply with Western expectations of manga and anime, embodied in series such as *Naruto*, *One Piece*, and *Full Metal Alchemist*. The character himself, as noted by several Western observers above, possesses none of the good-natured gregariousness, frequently bordering on the comedic, often associated with male manga and anime protagonists, or the film version of Bond, for that matter. Accordingly, the very traits that have made Golgo 13 an appealing and enduring character in Japan have limited his appeal in the West. Despite the increased availability and popularity of manga and anime in the United States and Europe since the 1990s, there remain some series and characters that are perhaps *too* Japanese to elicit much interest from Western readers and audiences.

Notes

1. As in other East Asian countries, Japanese names are written with surname first.

2. In contrast, each chapter of Oda Eiichiro's popular *One Piece* manga typically appears in English translation within a week of publication in Japan.

3. After the first mention of each, I will use the English title to avoid confusion.

4. There have been numerous other Japanese adaptations of Western media, many of which differ significantly from the source material in order to follow Japanese visual and thematic conventions. One of the most famous such adaptations was Toei's *Spider-Man* series (1978–1979), in which motorcycle racer Takuya Yamashiro gains his powers from a wizard from Planet Spider, and goes on, as Spider-Man, to fight giant monsters and other enemies with the help of an enormous mech called Leopardon in scenes reminiscent of *Godzilla* or *Power Rangers* (Davidson 2019). A more recent example is an anime adaptation of Agatha Christie's novels, *Agatha Christie's Great Detectives Poirot and Marple* (2004–2005), that mostly follows the outlines of the original stories, save the addition of a new character (Mabel West, Miss Marple's niece) and her pet duck, Oliver.

5. In Fleming's novel, Leiter is maimed, but not killed, by sharks when captured by Mr. Big.

6. The Bushido ideal of the disciplined, respectful, loyal-unto-death samurai was popularized in the largely peaceful Edo period (1603–1867) in countless plays and other literature, partly as nostalgic, romanticized reinterpretations of Sengoku-era

culture and conflicts. The most influential voice in shaping Western views of Bushido was Nitobe Inazō's *Bushido: The Soul of Japan* (1899), published in English in the United States, which presented Westerners an idealized view of traditional samurai culture and values.

7. Chinese characters used for many native Japanese words, and all Japanese surnames.

8. His rules, including never breaking contracts, never shaking hands, never allowing anyone to approach him from behind, and killing anyone who witnesses one of his assassinations, among others, comprise this code.

9. With the exception, perhaps, of some pornographic *hentai* (literally, "pervert") materials.

10. Ironically, this icon of Japanese masculinity was actually a Korean named Kim Sin-rak who immigrated to become a sumo wrestler. Concerned about contemporary negative views of Koreans, Rikidōzan strove constantly to conceal his true national origins.

11. A quick search on Amazon's website in 2022 reveals that the cheapest option for purchasing the collected series on Blu-ray is over $350, due to its scarcity and absence from streaming services.

Bibliography

Beaty, Bart H., and Stephen Weiner, eds. 2013. *Critical Survey of Graphic Novels: Manga.* Ipswich, MA: Salem Press.

Berberich, Christine. 2012. "Putting England Back on Top? Ian Fleming, James Bond, and the Question of England." *The Yearbook of English Studies*, vol. 42, Literature of the 1950s and 1960s, 13–29.

Bortolotti Gary R., and Linda Hutcheon. 2007. "On the Origin of Adaptations: Rethinking Fidelity Discourse and 'Success': Biologically." *New Literary History* 38 (3): 443–58.

Bradford, Matthew. 2016. "Classic Japanese James Bond Comics Reprinted and Reviewed." *Double O Section*, https://doubleosection.blogspot.com/2016/02/classic-japanese-james-bond-comics.html.

Chapman, James. 2007. *Licence to Thrill: A Cultural History of the James Bond Films.* 2nd ed. London: I. B. Tauris.

Cheng, Jamie. 2019. "Japan's Salaryman Culture: Consequences of Corporate Governance." *Medium*, August 14. https://medium.com/@jami3jam/the-japanese-salaryman-452692b485e5.

Chiu-Tabet, Christopher. 2021. "Takao Saito, Creator of 'Golgo 13,' Dead at 84." *Multiversity Comics*, September 29. http://www.multiversitycomics.com/news/takao-saito-dead/.

Daddis, Gregory A. 2021. *Pulp Vietnam: War and Gender in Cold War Men's Adventure Magazines.* Cambridge: Cambridge University Press.

Davidson, Chris. 2019. "Leopardon: The Secret History of Spider-Man's Giant Robot." *CBR*, April 5. https://www.cbr.com/leopardon-spider-man-robot-explained/.

Del Callar, Carlos Miguel. 2021. "Golgo 13 and the Globalization of James Bond." *Aero*, December 3. https://areomagazine.com/2021/12/03/golgo-13-and-the -globalization-of-james-bond/.

Easton, Thomas. 1994. "Amorous Pairs Peck Away at Japan's Taboo on Kisses." *The Baltimore Sun*, September 26. https://www.baltimoresun.com/news/bs-xpm-1994 -09-27-1994270147-story.html.

Goldstein-Gidoni, Ofra. 1999. "Kimono and the Construction of Gendered and Cultural Identities." *Ethnology* 38 (4): 351–70.

Hill, Andy. 2018. "A Lesson in Saving from Japan." *Tiller*, March 16. https://www .tillerhq.com/a-lesson-in-saving-from-japan/.

Holmberg, Ryan. 2011. "Saitō Takao and the 'Gekiga Factory.'" *The Comics Journal*, May 18. https://www.tcj.com/saito-takao-and-the-gekiga-factory/.

Igarashi, Yoshikuni. 2000. *Bodies of Memory: Narratives of War in Postwar Japanese Culture, 1945–1970*. Princeton, NJ: Princeton University Press.

Keith. 2014. "A Gaggle of Golgo 13." *Teleport City*, April 20. https://web.archive.org /web/20160923231213/https:/teleport-city.com/2014/04/20/golgo-13/.

Kincaid, Chris. 2017. "Influenced By . . . Judaism and Christianity: Saviours, Angels, Robots, Nuns and Vampires!" *Japan Powered*, July 2. https://www.japanpowered .com/japan-culture/influenced-by-judaism-and-christianity.

Kinsella, Sharon. 2000. *Adult Manga: Culture and Power in Contemporary Japanese Society.* Honolulu: University of Hawai'i Press.

———. 1998. "Japanese Subculture in the 1990s: Otaku and the Amateur Manga Movement." *The Journal of Japanese Studies* 24 (2): 289–316.

Kisha. 2018. "ゴルゴ13 / The Professional: Golgo 13 (1983)." *Admit One Film Addict*, October 20. https://admitonefilmaddict.wordpress.com/2018/10/20/%E3 %82%B4%E3%83%AB%E3%82%B413-the-professional-golgo-13-1983/.

Kuroda, Kenro. 2021. "'Golgo 13' Tops Guinness World Record for Most Manga Volumes." *Asahi Shimbun*, July 29. https://www.asahi.com/ajw/articles/14396652 #:~:text=Guinness%20World%20Records%20announced%20that,earned%20the %20ranking%20in%202016.

Lee, Kristen Schultz, Paula A. Tufiş, Duane F. Alwin and Jay Teachman. 2010. "Separate Spheres or Increasing Equality? Changing Gender Beliefs in Postwar Japan." *Journal of Marriage and Family* 72 (1): 184–201.

Lewis, Leo. 2015. "Interview: 'Golgo 13' creator Takao Saito." *Financial Times*, October 16. https://www.ft.com/content/734f95c0-7260-11e5-a129-3fcc4f641d98.

Maslin, Janet. 1992. "Review/Film; Animated Violence From Comic Books." *The New York Times*, October 23. https://www.nytimes.com/1992/10/23/movies/review -film-animated-violence-from-comic-books.html.

Masuda, Karen. 2012. "The State of Kissing in Japan." *Japan Today*, September 8. https://japantoday.com/category/features/lifestyle/the-state-of-kissing-in-japan.

Melan. 2016. "Golgo 13, Japanese Superspy." *Beyond Formalhaut*, December 16. https://beyondfomalhaut.blogspot.com/2016/12/beyonde-golgo-13-japanese -superspy.html.

Miyake, Kan, ed. 2000. *The Golgo 13 Encyclopedia*. Tokyo: Shogakukan.

Saito, Takao. 1993a. *Gorugo 13* (1): *Biggu seifu sakusen*. Tokyo: Leed Publishing.

————. 1993b. *Gorugo 13* (3): *Eki basha no GT*. Tokyo: Leed Publishing.

————. 1995. *Gorugo 13* (2): *Ori no naka no nemuri*. Tokyo: Leed Publishing.

————. 2015a. *Jo'ō Heika no Zero Zero Sebun* [On Her Majesty's Secret Service]. Tokyo: Shogakukan.

————. 2015b. *Ōgon no Jū o Motsu Otoko* [The Man with the Golden Gun]. Tokyo: Shogakukan.

————. 2015c. *Sandābōru Sakusen* [Thunderball]. Tokyo: Shogakukan.

————. 2015d. *Shinuno wa Yatsura Da* [Live and Let Die]. Tokyo: Shogakukan.

Schodt, Frederik L. 2012. *Manga! Manga! The World of Japanese Comics*. New York: Kodansha USA.

Sevakis, Justin. 2016. "Why Are Americans in Anime Always Blonde?" *Anime News Network*, February 5. https://www.animenewsnetwork.com/answerman/2016-02 -05/.98341.

Shuster, Jeffrey. 2019. "The Curator of Schlock #265: *The Professional: Golgo 13*." *The Drunken Odyssey—A Podcast About the Writing Life*, March 15. https: //thedrunkenodyssey.com/2019/03/15/the-curator-of-schlock-265-the-professional -golgo-13/.

Thompson, Jason. 2012. "Golgo 13." *Jason Thompson's House of 1000 Manga*, March 1. https://archive.ph/7bBSl#selection-2373.0-2373.36.

Turnbull, Stephen. 2011. *The Revenge of the 47 Ronin: Edo 1703*. Oxford: Osprey.

Vintage Anime Club. 2021. "Because That's What Pros Do (Golgo 13: The Professional)." Episode 120. May 5. https://podtail.com/en/podcast/vintage-anime -club-podcast/episode-120-because-that-s-what-pros-do-golgo-13-t/.

Chapter 5

Assassins, Cigars, and Revolution

James Bond's Cuba

Antti Korpisaari

Against all odds, the Cuban revolution[1] has managed to survive both its decades-long political confrontation with the United States and the collapse of the Soviet Union in 1991, remaining the only former Eastern Bloc country not to have formally abandoned communism. During the Cold War and beyond, these historical peculiarities of Cuba have made it a frequent topic of spy fiction (e.g., Greene 1958; Scott 2020), including of James Bond stories. In what follows, I analyze the depiction of Cuba in both Ian Fleming's twelve Bond novels and nine short stories, and the twenty-five Eon-produced Bond films released to date. From *Live and Let Die*, Fleming's second Bond novel published in 1954, to *No Time to Die*, the latest Bond film released in 2021, the series offers a rich, almost seventy-year-long corpus to work with. After Fleming's beloved Jamaica and perhaps the Bahamas, Cuba receives the second- or third-most attention of any Latin American and Caribbean country in the Bond corpus.[2]

As the largest island in the Caribbean, Cuba has always had significant regional importance. When Fleming wrote his first Bond novels, Dictator Fulgencio Batista was still firmly in power, and the island was under heavy American political and economic influence, including by the Mafia. After Fidel Castro and his revolutionary forces toppled Batista, however, Cuba soon joined the Eastern Bloc. The country whose capital Havana had been a favorite gambling spot and holiday destination for well-off Americans became an ideological and political opponent, and travel to and from the island was severely restricted. Fictional depictions of Cuba changed accordingly and arguably gained more relative weight too, as fewer non-Cuban people had a chance to experience the country firsthand. As I will show in this article, Fleming and the Bond films have certainly done their part in casting Cuba in the role of an "other" and an enemy of the Western capitalist world in the minds of hundreds of millions of people the world over. Significantly, too, the Brosnan-era Bond films continued to reproduce such a problematic and even dehumanizing depiction of Cuba well after the Cold War had ended.

Cuba in Ian Fleming's Bond Novels and Short Stories

While Ian Fleming was captivated by the (British) Caribbean, he never traveled to Cuba, and neither did his character James Bond. The closest Bond gets to doing so is in Fleming's last novel, *The Man with the Golden Gun* (1965). Having unsuccessfully chased his target Francisco Scaramanga for six weeks in the Caribbean, Central America, and Venezuela, Bond is at Kingston Airport waiting for a flight to Havana—Scaramanga's "home ground . . . *with which Bond was barely familiar*" (Fleming [2006] 1965, 42; my emphasis).[3] Bond ends up canceling his reservation, however, when he learns that Scaramanga is soon to arrive in Jamaica. Still, Cuba as a geographical place and geopolitical space factored largely in Fleming's thinking, as social and/or political issues related to the country are mentioned in six of his Bond novels and two of his Bond short stories. I see two main reasons for this relative richness of Cuba-related content in Fleming's prose. First, Fleming wintered—and wrote his Bond stories—in Jamaica (Parker 2014), whose nearest neighboring countries are Cuba and Haiti.[4] Second, the period in which Fleming produced his Bond texts, 1952–1964, encompasses the victory of the Cuban revolution and other key developments in Cuba. Fleming, whose background was in journalism and intelligence, likely followed these major historic events of the late 1950s and early 1960s with keen interest, and they also seeped into his fiction writing, framed and interpreted through a distinctly white male colonial lens.

For the first time, Fleming brings up Cuba in his second Bond novel, *Live and Let Die* (1954). We learn that Bond's first assignment in Jamaica just after World War II had links to Cuba as "the Communist headquarters in Cuba was trying to infiltrate the Jamaican labour unions" (Fleming [2003] 1954, 168; see also Black 2001, 14). In the book's present, the villain Mr. Big's yacht *Secatur* regularly sails from St. Petersburg, Florida to Jamaica via Cuba. The heroine Solitaire comments to Bond that Mr. Big's business in Cuba is "probably mixed up with Communism." She believes that "Cuba comes under Harlem [that is, Mr. Big's main theater of operations] and runs red agents all through the Caribbean" (Fleming [2003] 1954, 111). When Bond stops Mr. Big's operation to smuggle pirate gold and gemstones from Jamaica to the United States to finance the Soviet espionage system there, Bond, therefore, strikes a blow against Cuban communists too. The Cuban

Popular Socialist Party (see Sweig 2012, 37–38) might conceivably have tried to spread its ideology to Jamaica in the 1940s and 1950s, but it is just as likely that Fleming's references to such prerevolution attempts are figments of his imagination, motivated by the general East-versus-West framework of his pre-SPECTRE-era Bond stories. Whether Fleming was historically accurate or not, however, is not the most important point here. What is imperative, rather, is that in the ideologically polarized times following the end of World War II and the onset of the Cold War, most of Fleming's contemporary readers first in Britain and later in the Western world more generally were prone to accept his depiction of Cuba as a place capable of considerable extraterritorial impact (see Goodman 2016).

In *Dr. No* (1958), Fleming again alludes to (prerevolution) Cuba spreading communism in the Caribbean when Bond's chief M comments to him that the quiet routines of the Caribbean station include dealing with "an occasional communist trying to get into the island [i.e., Jamaica] from Cuba" (Fleming [2006] 1958, 32). More important to the plot of the novel is that the villain's island, Crab Key, is located between Jamaica and Cuba, and that Dr. No hired people for his guano operation from both islands (Fleming [2006] 1958, 220). Furthermore, he has "established a watch on the intelligence services in Jamaica and Cuba" (Fleming [2006] 1958, 224) and mentions Havana (together with Kingston and Miami) as a possible future target for the American rockets, fired from Turks Island, that he is jamming (Fleming [2006] 1958, 236; see also Black 2001, 33). As Cuba and Jamaica are often treated together in this way, *Dr. No*'s depiction of Cuba could arguably be read as the least judgmental in Fleming's oeuvre. Another possible reading, however, is that both Cubans and Jamaicans are as culpable for having helped Dr. No build up and run his criminal operation. Nevertheless, following Dr. No's violent demise, the Jamaican police superintendent agrees with Bond in that "most of these Negro gangsters [i.e., Dr. No's surviving henchmen] will probably be in Cuba by now. Have to get in touch with my opposite number in Havana and catch up with them before they take to the hills or go underground" (Fleming [2006] 1958, 297). This indicates that "normal" channels of communication and at least some level of cooperation exist between Jamaica and Cuba, but also insinuates that it is relatively easy for criminals to escape capture in Cuba.

In his Bond stories, Fleming repeatedly mentions the strong control that American organized crime exerted over the Cuban casino and hotel sector in the Batista era (see Simons 1996, 262–63). *Live and Let Die*'s Mr. Big could perhaps be read as an early representative of this phenomenon. For the first time the theme comes up explicitly in *Goldfinger* (1959), as one of the gangster bosses whose services Auric Goldfinger requires for the taking of Fort Knox is "Mr. Jed Midnight of the Shadow Syndicate operating out of Miami and Havana" (Fleming [2006] 1959, 262). In the short story *For Your Eyes Only* (1960), Colonel Havelock regards Cuba as being "riddled with crooks and gangsters" (Fleming [2006] 1960, 42). A bit later in the story, M tells Bond that the FBI has "been interested in Havana ever since the big American gangster money started following the casinos there" (Fleming [2006] 1960, 57). Finally, *The Man with the Golden Gun* contains a reference to hoods of "the type that had owned the Havana hotels and casinos in the old Batista days" (Fleming [2006] 1965, 83). All these cases allude to the shady, highly corrupt side of Batista's Cuba, where American (and other) criminal organizations were able to operate rather freely.

The short story collection *For Your Eyes Only* (1960) features the first mentions of (Fidel) Castro and his insurgency as well as some of the most nuanced Cuba-related content in the Fleming Bond corpus. The negative, and in many cases racist, framing of Cuba and the Cubans in the collection's second short story, *For Your Eyes Only*, is quite telling. The story is set in September–October 1958, with the Castro insurgency's victory over the Batista regime in Cuba only months away (Fleming [2006] 1960, 41, 52, 57). This has led to a situation in which many Cubans, wanting "to get their money out of Cuba and into something else quick" (Fleming [2006] 1960, 42), are buying up properties in Jamaica. For Fleming, himself a Brit of high-class background and the owner of the Goldeneye property in Jamaica, this was a horrific scenario. Alternatively, however, the situation could be read as one (welcome) facet of the rapidly advancing decolonization of Jamaica, or even as the "recolonization" of parts of the island by people of Spanish inheritance, as Jamaica was a Spanish colony for some 150 years prior to its takeover by the British in 1655.

For Your Eyes Only begins with the murder of the elderly Havelock couple in Jamaica because they refuse to sell their ancestral plantation to the "head of Batista's Counter Intelligence," ex-Gestapo-man von Hammerstein (Fleming [2006] 1960, 56). The Cuban Major Gonzales and his two gunmen commit the actual killing. Gonzales's accent is "the sham American of a Jamaican taxi-driver" (Fleming [2006] 1960, 45), and Mrs. Havelock thinks of him as "a common, greasy little man" (Fleming [2006] 1960, 48) and a "mangy Cuban crook" (Fleming [2006] 1960, 50). Later in the story, Bond, who sets out to avenge the Havelocks' deaths after von Hammerstein is sacked by Batista and, for the time being, settles on a ranch in Vermont (see Amis 1966, 26–29; Black 2001, 41–42), regards the three Cubans as "very small and dark" (Fleming [2006] 1960, 82). Gonzales's two gunmen are "low peasant types" (Fleming [2006] 1960, 82) who have a shooting match to decide which one should get to spend a night with one of two Cuban women also present on the ranch. Bond thinks that these "swarthy brunettes" look like "cheap

Cuban whores" and laugh and chatter "like pretty monkeys" (Fleming [2006] 1960, 82–83).

For Your Eyes Only and the *Quantum of Solace* short story that immediately follows it, however, also feature startlingly positive treatment of the Castro insurgency. In the former story, Station C of the British Secret Service, looking into the Havelocks' deaths on M's request, "didn't get anywhere with the Batista people" but has "a good man with the other side" (Fleming [2006] 1960, 56). M continues: "Castro's Intelligence people seem to have the Government pretty well penetrated. I got the whole story a couple of weeks ago" (Fleming [2006] 1960, 56).[5] The Batista government is framed much less favorably as, among many other things, it "won't raise a finger" to help get the Havelocks' murderers on trial (Fleming [2006] 1960, 58). In *Quantum of Solace*, Castro's revolutionary fighting provides the reason for Bond being in Nassau, thus framing the narrative otherwise totally unrelated to Cuba (see Black 2001, 43). As the U.S. Coast Guard had seized two shipments of arms meant for the Cuban rebels, "the Castro supporters had turned to Jamaica and the Bahamas as possible bases" (Fleming [2006] 1960, 99). The British "government had a big export programme with [Batista's] Cuba . . . , and a minor condition of the deal was that Britain should not give aid or comfort to the Cuban rebels" (Fleming [2006] 1960, 99–100). Therefore, Bond had been sent to intervene and had used thermite bombs to destroy "the two big cabin cruisers that were being fitted out for the job" of running arms to Cuba (Fleming [2006] 1960, 100). What is of great interest here is that Bond had not wanted the job as, "if anything, his sympathies were with the rebels" (Fleming [2006] 1960, 99). This represents a rare case of Bond "taking sides" in a national conflict (that at the time was) quite unrelated to British geopolitical interests. For however briefly, then, Fleming apparently saw in the (victory of the) Castro insurgency the promise of a better Cuba. After some sixty years of largely negative geopolitical sentiments toward communist Cuba, this may seem strange, but prior to taking power in Cuba, Castro and his guerrillas received sustained positive coverage in US (and other international) media (Anderson 1997). Furthermore, in 1958, the US administration first put an embargo on arms shipments to Cuba and then, on December 10, withdrew recognition of Batista's government (Black 2001, 44; Parker 2014, 250). That is, Fleming was far from alone in feeling that Castro could be a better ruler than Batista ever was.

After the *For Your Eyes Only* short story's von Hammerstein, *Thunderball* (1961) contains Fleming's second reference to fugitive Nazi war criminals residing in (prerevolution) Cuba: Ernst Stavro Blofeld lists "former SS Gruppenführer Sonntag, living under the name of Santos in Havana" as one of the SPECTRE criminal organization's successful blackmail victims (Fleming [2006] 1961, 66). In his prose, Fleming develops this ex-Nazi theme most fully in *Moonraker* (1955), set in England. In regards to Latin America, it is a well-established fact that many ex-Nazis, including Adolf Eichmann and Josef Mengele, sought refuge there after World War II. Because of its proximity to and close ties with the United States, however, prerevolution Cuba was probably not one of their most preferred destinations. Rather, as Black (2001, 43) puts it, "this linkage by a Conservative writer [i.e., Fleming] of ex-Nazis with right-wing Latin American regimes was designed to damn the latter."

Up to this point, most of the content we have covered has referenced pre-Castro Cuba. Fleming's last two Bond novels, however, reflect his clear disillusionment with the communist path revolutionary Cuba took in 1959–1960. Although the first of these works, *You Only Live Twice* (1964), is set almost totally in Japan, Fleming brings up Cuba on two occasions. The first is when M has lunch with the neurologist Sir James Molony at the exclusive gentlemen's club Blades. As cigars are offered to M's guest, Sir James, raising a quizzical eyebrow, comments: "I see the Havanas are still coming in" (Fleming [2006] 1964, 16). The first thing to note here is that Cuba is epitomized as a product, the cigar, in a dehumanizing way. The second is that in a series of novels and short stories replete with descriptions of the characteristics of different kinds of cigarette brands (see Amis 1966, 30–31; Hartvelt 2022, 7–8), this is the only instance of any tobacco products specified as being Havanas/Cuban. This is surely no coincidence. Rather, Sir James's remark alludes to the nearly total embargo the United States imposed on trade with Cuba in the early 1960s (Sweig 2012, 88–89) and/or to the relocation of several well-known Cuban cigar and liquor brands elsewhere in the first years of the revolution. Arguably, this passage could be read more as criticism of US policy than of Cuba itself. In light of the following example from *You Only Live Twice*, however, I feel that it indeed is aimed at Cuba and Castro for having taken up communism, forcing the Western world and many private companies to resort to drastic countermeasures.

The second time Cuba is referenced in *You Only Live Twice* is when, prior to his fatal fight with Bond, Blofeld seeks to justify SPECTRE's stealing of two atomic weapons in the earlier *Thunderball* story (Fleming [2006] 1964, 248; my emphasis):

> These were dangerous toys which, in the poor boy's hands, or let us say, to discard the allegory, in the hands of *a Castro*, could lead to the wanton extinction of mankind. . . . If I had been successful . . . , might not the threat of a recurrence of my attempt have led to serious disarmament talks, to an abandonment of these dangerous toys that might so easily get into the wrong hands?

Blofeld's arguments clearly carry echoes of the Cuban missile crisis of 1962, which brought the world closer to the brink of nuclear war than it has perhaps ever been (Black 2001, 49–50; 2017, 21; Chapman 2007, 70–71; Sweig 2012, 84–87).[6] Furthermore, Fleming employs Castro as short hand for a particular understanding of Cuba in a problematic manner.

Of Fleming's Bond stories, *The Man with the Golden Gun*, published posthumously in 1965, contains by far the most Cuba-related content. Bond is sent to kill Francisco Scaramanga, "the greatest pro gunman in the world" (Fleming [2006] 1965, 177). After working in organized crime in the United States and then briefly as a kind of real estate agent in the Caribbean area, Scaramanga settled in Havana in 1959, obtaining "an influential post as foreign 'enforcer' for . . . the Cuban Secret Police" (Fleming [2006] 1965, 30–31). In this capacity, Scaramanga has undertaken numerous assassinations, including of several British agents, in Latin America. He carries a Cuban diplomatic passport and "appears to have no difficulty in obtaining foreign currency from *the slim resources of Cuba* when he needs it" (Fleming [2006] 1965, 31–32; my emphasis). Therefore, Scaramanga is further vilified through his association with and being part of a system of oversight and oppression in revolutionary Cuba. It is noteworthy, however, that he is not Cuban per se but of Catalan origins (Fleming [2006] 1965, 30). That is, like the ex-Nazi von Hammerstein in *For Your Eyes Only*, he is a foreigner who has found a lucrative niche befitting of his unique "skills" in Cuba (see Halloran 2005, 173–74).

In *The Man with the Golden Gun*, Scaramanga, the KGB's resident director for the Caribbean Mr. Hendriks, and five American gangster bosses have formed the "Group." Fleming, therefore, highlights Cuban-Russian relations, adding American criminal organizations into the conspiracy to vilify Cuba further. Besides developing the Thunderbird Hotel in western Jamaica, the Group is engaged in various illegal activities that serve the Soviets' (and, by extension, the Cubans') interests of creating social and political unrest in Jamaica and the Caribbean. In the novel, the burning of the West Indies Sugar Company's Jamaican sugarcane crops receives special attention. Its estates were "run by expatriate British and white Jamaicans" (Parker 2014, 31), so Bond is once again fighting to protect British economic interests in the Caribbean. We learn that in its previous meeting in Havana, the Group, against Hendriks's (that is, the Soviet Union's) minority vote, had decided, "in exchange for certain favours, to come to the aid of Fidel Castro and assist in maintaining and indeed increasing the world price of sugar to offset the damage caused by Hurricane Flora" (Fleming [2006] 1965, 106). As Bond's former secretary Mary Goodnight tells him, Castro is trying to keep the price of sugar up to get more in exchange for it from the Soviets. Jamaica is Cuba's main rival in sugar production, so one way to accomplish this is to burn and otherwise sabotage Jamaican sugarcane crops (Fleming [2006] 1965, 52–54). Fleming's portrayal of Cuba's dependency on sugar is accurate: Despite

Castro's initial dreams of industrializing the country, it actually had little choice but to continue producing and exporting as much sugar as possible. Instead of the United States, however, this sugar now mostly went to the Eastern Bloc countries. The part about sabotaging competing production in Jamaica, however, is in all likelihood only figment of Fleming's imagination, inserted in the story to discredit revolutionary Cuba.

At the tail end of a private meeting between Scaramanga and Mr. Hendriks, the former expresses the following views regarding Fidel Castro and his thinking (Fleming [2006] 1965, 147–48; see also Black 2001, 77–78):

> My Mister C is not expecting great results in the States. Even the Mafia can't buck the anti-Cuban feeling there. . . . As for Mister C, he seems to be going along all right. Flora was a body-blow but, largely thanks to the Americans leaning on Cuba the way they do, he's kept the country together. If the Americans once let up on their propaganda and needling and so forth, perhaps even make a friendly gesture or two, all the steam'll go out of the little man.

Scaramanga's ideas are more sensible than the tongue-in-cheek "advice" Fleming reportedly gave to future President John F. Kennedy over dinner in March 1960 on how to topple Castro[7] and which, quite incredibly, the CIA still took rather seriously (see Moran 2011; Parker 2014, 260–61; Willman 2005).

Cuba in the Bond Films

Fleming's discussion of Cuba was strongly influenced by events of the 1950s and early 1960s, as well as how they would affect Britain and (de)colonial Jamaica. In other words, it was never about Cuba per se but instead what it meant for Bond and the UK and its colony of Jamaica. Furthermore, as Fleming did not set any of his stories in Cuba, it is no wonder that very little of his commentary on Cuba made it to the movie versions of his stories, released from 1962 onward.[8] Still, starting with 1995's *GoldenEye*, three Bond movies, their stories totally unrelated to Fleming's oeuvre, have had 007 operate in Cuba, and four others reference the country in their dialogue.

The first Bond films to mention Cuba—*Goldfinger* (1964), *The Man with the Golden Gun* (1974), and *For Your Eyes Only* (1981)—are (mostly rather unfaithful) adaptations of Fleming's stories. In *Goldfinger*, after the eponymous villain's Operation Grand Slam fails, Bond boards a private jet that is to take him to the White House to meet the US president. Goldfinger has hijacked this plane, however, and holding Bond at gunpoint, tells him: "In two hours, I shall be in Cuba." Goldfinger's plot was backed up by China, so in light of the Sino-Soviet split of 1960 (Black 2001, 95, 182) this is a bit surprising. Goldfinger's attempt to escape to Cuba is perhaps a carryover from the Fleming novel in which, when Goldfinger and his top gangster allies initially evade capture, Felix Leiter tells Bond: "for my money, that Jed Midnight [a gangster boss operating in Miami and Havana] has somehow got them out to Cuba" (Fleming [2006] 1959, 328). Nevertheless, the movie depicts Cuba as a rogue place where Western law enforcement could not touch Goldfinger.

If *Goldfinger* depicts Cuba as the would-be refuge for an evil genius, in *The Man with the Golden Gun* and *For Your Eyes Only*, the focus is on the country's links to transnational criminal networks. Besides some of the assassin Francisco Scaramanga's early life events and personal attributes, the former film bears little resemblance to Fleming's last Bond novel (see Chapman 2007, 144–48). Whereas in the book Scaramanga is a foreigner working for the Cubans, in the film his father is "possibly Cuban," but he was trained by the KGB and "went independent in the late '50s," that is, around the time Castro assumed power in Cuba. Scaramanga's possible Cuban roots are never brought to the fore with the sole exception of his use of the Spanish term mano a mano (face-to-face) shortly prior to his fateful duel with Bond.

For Your Eyes Only features another assassin whose Cuban nationality is in no doubt. At the beginning of the film, this "Cuban hit man, Hector Gonzales," guns down the marine archaeologist Sir Timothy Havelock and his wife. Gonzales acts under orders from the Greek villain Aris Kristatos, hired to acquire the sunken British electronic surveillance ship *St. Georges*'s automatic targeting attack communicator (ATAC) transmitter for the Soviets. Shortly thereafter, the Havelocks' daughter Melina kills Gonzales at a villa near Madrid. The assassin gets little screen time and speaks only once (in English to Bond). Besides his profession and nationality, we only learn that he seems to enjoy both killing and the company of beautiful women (see also Black 2001, 141–42). Gonzales's surname and Cuban nationality are the only elements the film retains from the *For Your Eyes Only* short story's ample Caribbean content. However, Cuba also comes up on two occasions toward the end of the film, most notably when Kristatos tells his not-at-all-pleased protégée, figure skater Bibi Dahl, that "we are going to live in Cuba for a few months." Whereas Fleming's short story highlights the ruthless and violent nature of the Batista administration and its supporters, the film takes place over twenty years later in a more "mature" Cold War atmosphere. Accordingly, it depicts Cuba as working in close tandem with the Soviet Union—as it certainly did at the time. Cuba provides Kristatos both an efficient killer and the promise of a safe haven in which to lay low after the ATAC affair is over.

As for Bond's first actual visit to Cuba, Black (2001, 43; 2017, 127) argues that this would take place in the pre-title sequence of *Octopussy* (1983). It is set in an unnamed Spanish-speaking country, where Bond destroys a military airplane hangar. The sequence indeed highlights a cigar-smoking military officer greatly resembling Fidel Castro (see Figure 5.1). In light of the hostile depiction of Cuba in the preceding *For Your Eyes Only* and the intensification of the Cold War in the early 1980s (see Black 2001, 143–44; 2017, 125–26), Black's interpretation certainly has its merits. However, it has its problems, too: Making his escape, Bond flies over a rather loosely guarded land border crossing point. Furthermore, the Castroesque character, played by Brian Coburn, is listed in the end credits as a "South American V.I.P." Although Cuba has a (very heavily guarded) land border of a kind with the US Naval Station Guantanamo Bay, the island is not part of South America. Therefore, I am hesitant to qualify *Octopussy* as the first movie in which Bond actually operates in Cuba. Still, a great many people who saw *Octopussy* around the time of its release probably associated its pre-title sequence with Cuba, a geopolitical hot spot close to US shores: Bond does not need to go to Cuba for the film to reference notable Cuban imagery.

In *Licence to Kill*'s (1989) pre-title sequence, the villain, Latin American drug lord Franz Sanchez, attempts to avoid arrest by the Americans by flying toward Cuban airspace, just as Goldfinger did twenty-five years earlier. A bit later in the story, he escapes and travels by mini-submarine and fast boat to Cuba on his way home to the fictional Republic of Isthmus. Whereas the writers of this original screenplay chose to invent the Republic of Isthmus as a substitute for actual Panama (see Korpisaari and Hakola 2021), they did not feel the need to resort to similar measures in their negative depiction of Cuba. As Black (2001, 152) nicely puts it, this situation "focuses two central features of American demonology: drugs and Cuba." In 1989, the year of *Licence to Kill*'s release, several Cuban military and government officials were indeed convicted (in Cuba) of having aided the Colombian Medellín

Figure 5.1.   A Castroesque military officer shows more interest in Bond's helper Bianca than in show jumping in *Octopussy*.

Source: EON Productions et al., 1983. Screenshot by author.

cartel to ship several tons of cocaine through the island into the United States. Furthermore, "according to [Cuban] defectors' accounts, the Castro regime was actively manipulating the drug trade . . . to earn hard currency for the revolution and *to demoralize and destabilize U.S. society*" (Lee 1997, 51; my emphasis). It is hard to evaluate the validity of such charges, but they do uncannily resemble some of the Soviets' plans in Fleming's *The Man with the Golden Gun*. Nevertheless, writing a bit later, Rodríguez Beruff and Cordero (2005, 308) state that "U.S. officials' comments on Cuban antidrug efforts have generally been positive."

1995's *GoldenEye* is an important film in many ways. Bond returned after a six-year hiatus, played by a new actor, Pierce Brosnan. Even more importantly, the Cold War had ended, the Soviet Union had dissolved, and, as a result, geopolitical boundaries had experienced dramatic shifts. Still, in many ways, *GoldenEye*'s plot taps into past technology and alliances, including the former Soviet Union–Cuba partnership. It is in this context that Bond's first unequivocal visit to Cuba takes place.

GoldenEye's villain, Alec Trevelyan, needs a satellite dish built by the Soviets in Cuba to launch a powerful electromagnetic pulse over London. Cuba, then, remains a dangerous geopolitical hot spot even in the post–Cold War era. Bond and the heroine Natalya Simonova use a plane provided by the CIA's Jack Wade to follow Trevelyan into an apparently uninhabited corner of Cuba. They encounter no interference from Cuban authorities and, according to Bond, "there's no one within 25 miles." Russians still operate the satellite dish's underground control facility, and no characters readily recognizable as Cuban/Latin American appear on-screen during the whole twenty-six-plus-minute Cuba sequence. Only English and Russian are spoken and a single *"PERSONAL AUTORIZADO SOLAMENTE"* sign is the only indication that the action takes place in a Spanish-speaking country. Furthermore, no actual filming was done in Cuba, but the on-location shooting for the film's "Cuba" took place in Puerto Rico (Field and Chowdhury 2018, 485). Therefore, Cuba and the Cubans are symbolically annihilated in *GoldenEye*. The Cuban people are not even important enough to appear on-screen, while Russian criminals and soldiers, a British secret agent with his Russian helper, and, at the very end of the film, the U.S. Marines seem to have the run of the place. As Wade boasts to Bond, "You can't light a cigar in Cuba without us [the Americans] seeing it" (see Black 2001, 165). No mention is made of the severe socioeconomic hardships caused by the collapse of the Soviet Union, especially the end of its $4–5 billion annual subsidy to Cuba, or the (limited) economic reforms implemented in Cuba to overcome these (see Sweig 2012, 126–38). In *GoldenEye*, therefore, Cuba, the only ex-Soviet bloc country still clinging to its old regime and mode of governance, is just an anomalous relic, comparable to the "cemetery" of old communist statues shown earlier in the film and, in Judi Dench's new M's words, to Bond himself.

Brosnan's last Bond film, *Die Another Day* (2002), links Cuba with North Korea, a rising geopolitical menace arguably even "more evil" (and certainly more enigmatic) than the Soviet Union/Russia ever was. Bond flies commercially to and from Cuba and can move around it at will, with no Cuban "tail." The first 3.5 minutes of the Cuba sequence are set in Havana although, again, no actual footage shot in Cuba is included in the film.[9] The establishing shot, filmed in Cádiz, Spain (Field and Chowdhury 2018, 556), shows some of "Havana's" waterfront populated by carefree people and the famous prerevolution American cars, kept running for decades through creative engineering (see Hill 2011). In the next shot, Bond walks past a wall onto which posters of the revolutionary hero Camilo Cienfuegos have been plastered. Inside the Raoul cigar factory, female employers roll tobacco leaves into cigars using their hands and thighs, while a man reads a newspaper to them. *Die Another Day*'s Havana is certainly no mere relic, but a living, breathing entity, although quite rustic, stereotypical, and nostalgic in character (see figure 5.2).

Asking for Delectado cigars and proving his knowledge of their characteristics, Bond enlists the help of the factory manager Raoul, a British sleeper agent. He provides Bond with information, a revolver, and a beautifully kept old American car. In his conversation with Bond, Raoul alludes, among other things, to corruption ("favors called in, some dollars spread about") and the longing many Cubans have for the "decadent," prerevolution times. Through his "friends in high places," Raoul learns that the North Korean terrorist Zao whom Bond is pursuing is on the island of Los Organos, where

> there is a strange clinic run by Dr. Alvarez. He leads the field in gene therapy, increasing the life expectancy of our beloved leaders. And, of course, the richest

Figure 5.2. Bustling city life in "Havana" featured in *Die Another Day*.
Source: EON Productions et al., 2002. Screenshot by author.

Westerners. We may have lost our freedom in the revolution, but we have a health system second to none.

Raoul uses the words "beloved leaders" ironically and refers to the Cubans' significant loss of individual freedoms under communism, but also praises his country's achievements in medical care. The Castro regime's significant investments into education and public health indeed quickly turned Cuba into one of the Latin American leaders in these areas (Simons 1996, 25–32). This excellence in medical sciences also created an avenue for earning foreign currency and/or political goodwill, with Cuba exporting "doctors, drugs and other medical facilities . . . to Africa, Asia and the Americas" (Simons 1996, 31; see also Sweig 2012, 51, 143–46) and welcoming "medical tourists" into the country (Hill 2011, 10). Dr. Alvarez, who receives very limited screen time, is an "evil genius," harvesting DNA from "orphans, runaways, people that won't be missed" and charging huge sums for DNA transplants. The extensive gene-therapy work he has done on Zao and—especially—*Die Another Day*'s North Korean villain Tan-Sun Moon/Gustav Graves, is pure science fiction, of course (see Field and Chowdhury 2018, 546; Metz 2004, 66–67). Such highly unethical and racist treatments would surely be prohibited in Western democracies, but the Cuban state fully sanctions and supports Dr. Alvarez's work: the Policía Nacional Revolucionaria and the Cuban military provide security for the Alvarez Clinic, and the entrance to its "inner sanctum" is through a wall covered in images of revolutionary heroes and Cuban flags and the entrance to its "inner sanctum" is through a wall covered in images of revolutionary heroes and Cuban flags (see figure 5.3). Despite these heavily negative connotations, however, Dr. Alvarez's scientific excellence arguably also alludes to a modern, cutting-edge side of Cuba, very different from the film's depiction of Havana.

Both Bond's mode of travel to and from Havana and the scenes set in the El Gran Palacio seaside hotel where Dr. Alvarez's patients[10] await boat transportation onto Los Organos Island hint at how, after the fall of the Soviet Union, international tourism was quickly developed into an important avenue for Cuba to earn much-needed foreign currency. Since the late 1990s, Canada has been the leading source of international tourists, followed by the UK, Germany, France, and Italy (Salinas, Mundet, and Salinas 2018). In *Die Another Day*, we also see Bond smoking (a cigar) for the first time since the 1980s, which caused controversy because of supposedly endorsing tobacco-product use (e.g., Rogers 2002). However, this (and other) cigar-smoking in the film actually helps make its depiction of Cuba more accurate, as most foreigners visiting the island either want to taste real Cuban cigars themselves or buy these to take home as presents.

Figure 5.3. Hidden entryway covered in nationalistic and revolutionary imagery in *Die Another Day*.
Source: EON Productions et al., 2002. Screenshot by author.

In January 2002, President George W. Bush introduced the phrase "Axis of Evil" to group Iran, Iraq, and North Korea, countries that, in his view, supported terrorism and sought weapons of mass destruction. Some months later, Under Secretary of State John Bolton added Cuba, Libya, and Syria to the list (Chapman 2007, 234; Van Der Borght and Strawson 2002, 66). This political rhetoric, grouping Cuba together with North Korea as some of the world's most dangerous countries (Field and Chowdhury 2018, 545), certainly made *Die Another Day* very topical upon its release. However, it also opens cigar-factory-manager Raoul's comment that "one man's terrorist is another man's freedom fighter" for several new readings, including criticism of the then-US government's warmongering.[11]

To date, Bond's last visit to Cuba occurs in *No Time to Die* (2021). He is retired and living "under the radar" in Jamaica, surely as a kind of an homage to his creator Fleming, who wintered on the island from 1947 until his death. Bond breaks his retirement, however, when Felix Leiter asks him to "pick up" the missing scientist Valdo Obrutšev from Santiago de Cuba.[12] Bond arrives there by boat as dusk is beginning to settle, and most of the thirteen-plus-minute Cuba sequence takes place at night. This clearly differentiates *No Time to Die*'s depiction of Cuba from that of the above-treated movies, in which almost all action takes place in daytime. Furthermore, *No Time to Die*'s color palette emphasizes blues and other cool tones, marking a clear departure from the yellow filter and palette more typical of filmic representations of the Global South. In part, all this may also owe to the revisionist nature of the last two Craig-era films, which make Bond face his past in several ways (see Funnell and Dodds 2017).

As opposed to *Die Another Day*, *No Time to Die* contains no spoken commentary on Cuban politics and/or society. For any references to these, one needs to be able to decode sporadic visual clues: two murals celebrating revolutionary heroes, an old American car, and the Soviet Ladas driven by Cuban police officers. Cuba only provides a (semi-)exotic Caribbean location for the Spectre "*bunga bunga*" (sex) party. Otherwise, the country receives surprisingly little negative (or positive) framing. At the Spectre party, however, there are a number of exotic dancers and (probable) escorts, alluding to the resurgence of prostitution in Cuba alongside the growth of tourism (see Salinas, Mundet, and Salinas 2018, 224). The fact that dozens of Spectre agents are able to convene in Cuba might also be interpreted as negative framing. Still, recalling earlier Spectre board meetings in Paris in *Thunderball* (1965) and Rome in *Spectre* (2015), Santiago de Cuba is in illustrious company. Moreover, if one was very bold, one could perhaps see in Leiter's death and the sinking of the Americans' vessel in the Caribbean after Bond has flown in with Obrutšev an allegory of the failure of US Cuban policy, which, despite over sixty years in effect, has failed to force a regime change in Cuba. Be that as it may, *No Time to Die* has to be lauded for featuring the first Cuban (American) supporting character, Bond's efficient CIA helper Paloma, actually played by a Cuban-born person (Ana de Armas). Although Paloma is introduced in a rather comic light, making her seem unprofessional and nervous, she actually proves to be a competent operative and highly skilled in various modes of combat. Very refreshingly, therefore, her character strongly departs from traditional Latin American gender expectations (see Korpisaari and Hakola 2021, 8–9).

Overall, *No Time to Die*'s depiction of Cuba differs quite substantially from that we see elsewhere in the Bond corpus. One possible way to read this is that with the passing of first Fidel Castro's and then also his brother Raúl's leadership, Cuba's revolutionary agency is no longer as threatening as before. It is at least as likely, however, that due to the drawn-out, rather "chaotic" production process of the film (as well as the possible late addition of the Cuba sequence) the filmmakers just did not have time to contextualize and vilify Cuba in a more "traditional" manner.

Conclusion

With small exceptions, the above-treated James Bond texts, published between 1954 and 2021, depict Cuba in a very hostile, even dehumanizing way. Fleming was keen to criticize the Batista administration, having no good things to say about it. In the *For Your Eyes Only* short story collection, he depicted the Castro insurgency in a rather favorable light, but his political conservatism clearly shows in how fast this optimism faded after the Castro-led Cuba allied with the Soviet Union. In this regard, it may be noteworthy that Fleming never alluded to the Bay of Pigs invasion (1961) that aimed to overthrow Castro and, through its catastrophic failure, gave revolutionary Cuba a great propaganda boost. Conversely, in his last two Bond novels, Fleming referred to the Cuban missile crisis, which, arguably, resulted in a "victory" for the United States and its allies. More importantly, however, in his Bond prose, Fleming was never actually interested in Cuba per se, but in its influence on Jamaica and British/Western geopolitical interests more generally.

The first Bond film was released some years after the victory of the revolution, and all references in the series are to communist Cuba. In the 1960s and 1970s, the country received little attention from the franchise, and the relative thawing of the Cold War in the 1970s may have contributed somewhat to the decision to eliminate nearly all links to Cuba from the movie version of *The Man with the Golden Gun*. As the Cold War reintensified in the early 1980s, the narrative use of Cuba in the Bond films clearly increased. Thereafter, although the world had changed, the Brosnan-era Bonds carried on depicting Cuba in a hostile way, first, in *GoldenEye*, as a dangerous relic of the Cold War past and later, in *Die Another Day*, as North Korea's "partner in crime." Refreshingly, *No Time to Die* treats Cuba somewhat more humanely. Still, although Bond has operated in Cuba several times and spent close to an hour of total screen time there, no footage actually shot in Cuba is included in any Bond film. Ultimately, the Bond franchise has shown little interest in the actual country and the fortunes of its inhabitants. Rather, it has repeatedly used Cuba as a convenient geopolitical tool, sufficiently well known to most members of any given audience to eliminate the need to provide any real context. In so doing, the Bond stories have both drawn from and helped reinforce the depiction of Cuba as a geopolitical troublemaker, both spawning and harboring international criminals and willing to endorse any endeavor to strike a blow against Western hegemony.

Notes

1. The Cubans think of their revolution as an ongoing process rather than only the single act of toppling Dictator Fulgencio Batista at the turn of 1958–1959. I use the term similarly throughout this article.

2. For the treatment of continental Latin America in the James Bond films, see Korpisaari and Hakola (2021).

3. Although the main point of this quote is to highlight Bond's unfamiliarity with Cuba, it is also important to note the negative connotations Cuba receives here and elsewhere in Fleming's works as the (paternal or, as here, adoptive) "home ground" of many evildoers.

4. Haiti receives much less attention from Fleming, and when it does—almost exclusively in *Live and Let Die*—this is in the context of vodou/folk beliefs, not, say, politics.

5. The deceased Havelocks' daughter Judy, also seeking to—and ultimately managing to—kill von Hammerstein, had to come by this information in a very different way, "flirting" with the Cuban underworld and finally getting the whole story from a "sort of high-up policeman" in exchange for sex (Fleming [2006] 1960, 81).

6. Fleming actually makes a (fictional) connection between nuclear weapons and Cuba in *Thunderball*: SPECTRE tells Giuseppe Petacchi, who hijacks a British military airplane carrying two atomic weapons, that "a Cuban revolutionary group who wanted to call attention to its existence and aims by a dramatic piece of self-advertisement" (Fleming [2006] 1961, 111) commissioned the undertaking.

7. "Advice" such as dropping "leaflets saying that the fallout from American nuclear tests provoked a strange reaction in men with facial hair, reducing them to sexual impotence. All the famous 'bearded ones' of the uprising would immediately shave off their beards, and the revolution would be over" (Parker 2014, 261).

8. According to Funnell and Dodds (2017, 47), however, the first version of *Dr. No*'s (1962) screenplay would have had Bond encounter Cuban agents working in Jamaica.

9. According to Field and Chowdhury (2018, 556), key members of the *Die Another Day* production team actually visited Havana "but were prohibited under US law from shooting there."

10. One prospective international patient of Dr. Alvarez first calls a Cuban waiter "Fidel" and then threatens to turn him into "Fidel Castrato" (see Metz 2004, 78). These are the only mentions of the longtime Cuban leader's name in the Bond films.

11. In total, the Cuba sequence of *Die Another Day* lasts for eighteen-plus minutes. Following his visit to Los Organos, Bond briefly returns to Raoul's office, where it turns out that the Cuban is, quite implausibly, also an expert in the chemical composition of diamonds.

12. Before Leiter and Bond actually meet in *No Time to Die*, the former has visited the latter's home, leaving behind the stub of a Cuban Delectado cigar—an intertextual reference to *Die Another Day*.

Bibliography

Amis, Kingsley. 1966. *The James Bond Dossier*. London: Pan Books.

Anderson, Jon Lee. 1997. *Che Guevara: A Revolutionary Life*. London: Bantam Press.

Black, Jeremy. 2001. *The Politics of James Bond: From Fleming's Novels to the Big Screen*. Westport, CT: Praeger.

———. 2017. *The World of James Bond: The Lives and Times of 007*. Lanham, MD: Rowman & Littlefield.

Chapman, James. 2007. *Licence to Thrill: A Cultural History of the James Bond Films*. 2nd ed. London: I. B. Tauris.

Field, Matthew, and Ajay Chowdhury. 2018. *Some Kind of Hero: The Remarkable Story of the James Bond Films.* Updated edition. Stroud: The History Press.

Fleming, Ian. (1954) 2003. *Live and Let Die.* New York: Penguin Books.

———. (1958) 2006. *Doctor No.* London: Penguin Books.

———. (1959) 2006. *Goldfinger.* London: Penguin Books.

———. (1960) 2006. *For Your Eyes Only.* London: Penguin Books.

———. (1961) 2006. *Thunderball.* London: Penguin Books.

———. (1964) 2006. *You Only Live Twice.* London: Penguin Books.

———. (1965) 2006. *The Man with the Golden Gun.* London: Penguin Books.

Funnell, Lisa, and Klaus Dodds. 2017. *Geographies, Genders and Geopolitics of James Bond.* London: Palgrave Macmillan.

Goodman, Sam. 2016. *British Spy Fiction and the End of Empire.* New York: Routledge.

Greene, Graham. 1958. *Our Man in Havana: An Entertainment.* London: Heinemann.

Halloran, Vivian. 2005. "Tropical Bond." In *Ian Fleming & James Bond: The Cultural Politics of 007,* edited by Edward P. Comentale, Stephen Watt, and Skip Willman, 158–77. Bloomington: Indiana University Press.

Hartvelt, N.F. 2022. "'The Texan With Whom He Shared So Many Adventures': Reassessing the Role of Felix Leiter in Fleming's Bond Novels." *The International Journal of James Bond Studies* 5 (1): 1–24. http://doi.org/10.24877/jbs.79.

Hill, Sarah. 2011. "Recycling History and the Never-Ending Life of Cuban Things." *Anthropology Now* 3 (1): 1–12. https://doi.org/10.1080/19428200.2011.11869116.

Korpisaari, Antti, and Outi J. Hakola. 2021. "The Portrayal of Continental Latin America in the James Bond Films." *The International Journal of James Bond Studies* 4 (1): 1–19. http://doi.org/10.24877/jbs.66.

Lee, Rensselaer W. III. 1997. "Cuba's Drug Transit Traffic." *Society* 34 (3): 49–55.

Metz, Walter. 2004. *Engaging Film Criticism: Film History and Contemporary American Cinema.* New York: Peter Lang.

Moran, Christopher. 2011. "Ian Fleming and CIA Director Allen Dulles: The Very Best of Friends." In *James Bond in World and Popular Culture: The Films Are Not Enough,* Second edition, edited by Robert G. Weiner, B. Lynn Whitfield, and Jack Becker, 208–15. Newcastle upon Tyne: Cambridge Scholars Publishing.

Parker, Matthew. 2014. *Goldeneye. Where James Bond Was Born: Ian Fleming's Jamaica.* London: Windmill Books.

Rodríguez Beruff, Jorge, and Gerardo Cordero. 2005. "The Caribbean: The 'Third Border' and the War on Drugs." In *Drugs and Democracy in Latin America: The Impact of U.S. Policy,* edited by Coletta A. Youngers, and Eileen Rosin, 303–37. Boulder: Lynne Rienner Publishers.

Rogers, Lois. 2002. "Bond Licensed to Light Up Again." *The Sunday Times,* November 17. https://www.thetimes.co.uk/article/bond-licensed-to-light-up-again-8pjc80qml8b.

Salinas, Eros, Lluís Mundet, and Eduardo Salinas. 2018. "Historical Evolution and Spatial Development of Tourism in Cuba, 1919–2017: What Is Next?" *Tourism Planning & Development* 15 (3): 216–38. https://doi.org/10.1080/21568316.2018.1427142.

Scott, Cord A. 2020. "Cold War Politics, Cuba, and Spy vs. Spy." *Journal of Graphic Novels and Comics* 11 (3): 315–24.

Simons, Geoff. 1996. *Cuba: From Conquistador to Castro*. Houndmills: Macmillan Press.

Sweig, Julia E. 2012. *Cuba: What Everybody Needs to Know*. Second edition. Oxford: Oxford University Press.

Van Der Borght, Kim, and John Strawson. 2002. "Cuba and the Axis of Evil: An Old Outlaw in the New Order." In *Law after Ground Zero*, edited by John Strawson, 59–70. London: The GlassHouse Press.

Willman, Skip. 2005. "The Kennedys, Fleming, and Cuba: Bond's Foreign Policy." In *Ian Fleming & James Bond: The Cultural Politics of 007*, edited by Edward P. Comentale, Stephen Watt, and Skip Willman, 178–201. Bloomington: Indiana University Press.

Chapter 6

Bond in Japan

International Pride, National Disgrace, and Glo/Cal Intricacies

Rea Amit

On December 11, 1965, the fourth installment of the James Bond franchise, *Thunderball* (Young), premiered in Tokyo, Japan. This was the first and still only time that a film pertaining to the series received an initial release outside the United States or the United Kingdom. Local commentators celebrated this fact, and some, such as Yōichi Kiriyama, who wrote for the film aficionado magazine *Sukurīn*, enthusiastically contextualized it in national terms as a "new year present to our country" (wagakuni e wa oshogatsu no purezento) (Kiriyama 1965, 147). Previous Bond films were also distributed in Japan, but months after their Western premieres, and yet the first three were not critically well-received. *Thunderball*, on the other hand, has markedly become a major Japanese blockbuster.[1] To be sure, the film was the most successful Bond production up to that point worldwide, and a global box-office hit. However, its success in Japan is remarkable given that domestic productions dominated the local film market at the time.

Despite its unprecedented box-office reception, Japanese critics and observers often expressed reservations about not only *Thunderball*, but the entire Bond trademark. One example in this regard is writer Momo Iida, who published his debut novel *Monomi yo, yoru wa nagakiya* (Take Point, The Night Is Long, 1961) based on the real-life adventures in Japan of wartime spy Richard Sorge, a notable contribution to the burgeoning popularity of spy fiction in postwar Japan. In a long review, Iida warns that *Thunderball* is part of a larger scheme that he mocks as "Bond-ism," which aims at the gentle bosom (*futokoro*) of the common Japanese in the guise of a new year gift (*toshidama*). In fact, he notes, Bond is simply a brand tightly associated with the series' star, Sean Connery, whereas the titular 1965 Tokyo premiere is only a publicity stunt for the next film that was already in early production stages on location in Japan (Iida 1966, 184–88). Indeed, unlike the celebration in Japan of being the first to screen *Thunderball*, the following film, *You Only Live Twice* (Gilbert, 1967),[2] which was set in Japan, opened in London first; distribution in Japan began days after its North American release, and many soon decried this as a Japanese national disgrace (*kokujoku eiga*).

This chapter traces the fluctuation in the reception of the 1960s Bond franchise in Japan and highlights its effect on local film discourses. However, rather than identifying the phenomenon along the lines of David Bordwell's notion of the "significant space" that global films open in local markets (Bordwell 2000, 82–83.), I argue that Bond's influence in Japan stems mostly from domestic factors such as television broadcasts and locally produced film series. *Thunderball* was released not long after Japan hosted the international Olympic Games in 1964, and the Japanese film market similarly "hosted" the global Bond installment, allowing it to compete against local productions such as Nikkatsu's branded *mukokuseki* (stateless) action films, and Toho's *Kokkusai himitsu keisatsu* (International Secret Police) series, among many other local productions such as television programs and even literature. Thus, rather than internationality, the Japanese reception of *Thunderball* and in a different sense that of *You Only Live Twice* is ultimately indicative of what Roland Robertson terms "glocalism" (Robertson 1995, 25–44), and the prevailing tensions between global, local, and even national factors within the often too hastily labeled "transnational"[3] film market structure.[4]

Internationalism: The Geopolitics of Bond in Japan

Bond is famously and distinctively British, and the world he perceives, particularly in Ian Fleming's original novels, is seen from this national perspective. However, during the 1960s, international power dynamics dramatically changed, giving rise to new global forces amid Britain's decline in influence. This shift, as Jeremy Black asserts, is echoed in Bond's own transformation from a literary figure into a wider-reaching cinematic one that is largely achieved by North American producers and investment. On the one hand, as Lisa Funnell and Klaus Dodds illustrate, Bond is portrayed as a dominant player within an overblown image of the "special relationship" between Britain and the United States (Funnell and Dodds 2017, 71–74). On the other hand, however, as Black points out, James Bond films throughout the 1960s unmistakably depict a world where the United States takes a more central role than the United Kingdom, as both faced together heightened tensions with the Soviet bloc during the Cold War (Black 2004, 293–94).

Yet the depiction of international vectors is not only a matter of representation in the early James Bond films. As the series gained worldwide attention, it even, as Klaus Dodds argues, actively "helped define the Cold War zeitgeist" (Dodds 2005, 278). That is, the perception of the most powerful players in the new international equilibrium were shaped by images the series popularized throughout the world including not just in North America and Europe, but as Dodds emphasizes, even in Africa, and most importantly in the context of this chapter, in Asia.

Japan was devastated in 1945 as a result of its defeat in World War II. This was not only due to the horrific consequences of the atomic bombings of Hiroshima and Nagasaki; nearly every major city—including and most profoundly, the capital Tokyo—sustained massive damage from frequent American air raids that left the entire country's industrial infrastructure in shambles. However, under the new American-imposed constitution and permanent American military presence, Japan soon experienced an unprecedented rapid growth, and in terms of GNP, by the late 1960s it became the second-largest economy in the world.[5] While the country did acknowledge itself as a *keizai taikoku* (an economical "big country"), it was not ready to harness its status to exert influence in the international arena, or at least not before the 1970s, when, as Chris Oliver points out, the term *kokusaika* (internationalization) became more widely used in Japanese public discourses (Oliver 2009, 47–54). Rather than international geopolitics, public opinion in Japan was ostensibly shaped more by the opposition to the US-Japan Security Treaty known as Anpo, which led to frequent violent protests around the country (*Anpo tōsō* or Anpo protests).

Despite the anti-American mass demonstrations, surveys from the time explicitly show positive attitude toward the United States and a much higher degree of animosity toward the Soviet Union (Yoshimi 2007, 11–12). Thus, the country closely aligned itself with the West that was led by the United States. Although the globally recognized forms of Japanese soft power driven by cultural products that Koichi Iwabuchi calls "pop-culture diplomacy" began in earnest only in the 1980s, at least two of Japan's most popular global icons were introduced during this time frame (Iwabuchi 2015, 419–43). The first is the monster-turned- cinematic-franchise Gojira, which became known outside of Japan as Godzilla following the success of the 1954 monster film (*kaijū eiga*). The global and domestic popularity of the Japanese monster, as Barak Kushner argues, was Japan's first postwar media event, one that signals the country's return to the international stage (Kushner 2006, 41–60).

The second cultural icon emerging during this period was the TV character Tetsuwan Atomu, who became known in the West as Astro Boy. Although less widely known today, as Marc Steinberg argues, its creation gave rise to a phenomenon that is Japan's most famous international brand: Japanese animation or *anime* (Steinberg 2012, 1–36). Yet, unlike the Bond series, the two Japanese franchises seem politically ambivalent, and do not explicitly reflect the Cold War or the role Japan plays in it. In a way, these two Japanese series mirror the nation's hesitancy in engaging with other nations and its propensity to abstain from international tensions, which is not a surprising stance considering Japan's actions during World War II. Hence, despite its alignments with the United States and the West, Japan positioned itself in a uniquely ambivalent national position in relation to other nations.

Michael Raine exemplifies Japan's peculiar national position in his discussion of the *Wataridori* action film series (Wondering Bird) of nearly fifteen installments produced by the studio Nikkatsu between 1959 and 1962. The series is representative of the studio's *mukokuseki* (nationless) theme whereby films lightly assume a stereotypically non-Japanese air—mainly by filming in rural locations around the country. In the case of this series, as Raine points out, films borrow features or aspects associated with the American western genre to form an "absurdist mélange of desirable Americana" that he conceptualizes as a "Cold War cultural infrastructure" (Raine 2020, 129). That is, by associating themselves with the archetypical American genre, these unmistakably Japanese films portray an inward-looking nationally ambiguous cultural position from which to reimagine the Japanese nation state.

The reception of the Bond series in Japan is indicative of similar tendencies to that projected by the *Wataridori* films, at least initially, to disassociate the country from its real geopolitical position beyond its physical borders. Local audiences were invited to imagine not themselves, but their national interests, as shared with James Bond. Moreover, the local press repeatedly emphasized the North American aspects of the production as well as Sean Connery's Scottishness playing a character who serves British "Queen and country," thereby showcasing an ambivalent nationality, and enhancing a sense of alignment with the amorphous American-led "West." Notwithstanding this position, *You Only Live Twice*'s Tanaka (played by Tetsurō Tamba) and Bond have a close respectful relationship hailing from two island-states in the US geopolitical orbit.

Japanese producers had previously worked to project an ambivalent national identification for local viewers. Most tellingly, this was the case with the 1954 Southeast Asian festival, with which, as Erica Ka-yan Poon argues, Japan did not only intend to assert influence in Asia, but also to respond to a sense of inferiority vis-à-vis the West (Poon 2019, 76–92). Japan's peculiar position as an Asian nation that is not in fact located in the southeastern part of the continent was manifested by the way Takejirō Ōtani, the chairman of the executive committee of the festival, presented Japanese films not as representative of their country of origin, but rather as products of local major studios. The peculiar order of the nations included, after Thailand and the Philippines, Japan's Tōei as the third "nation," Shintōhō the sixth, Daiei the eleventh, Tōhō the twelfth, and Shōchiku thirteenth.[6]

Beyond any cinematic production, the 1964 Olympic Games was the media event that ultimately necessitated Japan's reckoning with the international community. However, like the Southeast Film Festival, the host role allowed Japan to facilitate international engagements on local terms. This was undoubtedly a watershed moment for the country on the global stage insofar as it was being recognized as a new rising force. Yet, rather than a chance to project outward ambitions, the mega-sport event served more to project to local viewers a domestic image of an international Japan, and to do so in real time through national television (Chun 2009, 223–26). Predictably, unlike global satellite broadcasting, local telecasting of the international games in Japan underscored the national team's place among leading nations, as a domestic affair.

Although less pronounced before the Olympic games, reception of the global Bond franchise in Japan follows a similar logic. Until around 1964, the Japanese major film studios maintained a firm grip on the local market, mainly by directly or indirectly controlling most film theaters in the country, whereas independent and foreign production had only limited visibility, confined mainly to the largest urban areas. That films pertaining to the Bond series before *Thunderball* gained much revenue in Japan is therefore remarkable, but the 1965 Bond premiere in the country was a matter of an epistemological break from the previous media system, as it was arguably the first non-Japanese film to displace local studios at the box office. The reasons for this achievement, however, are still mostly local rather than international. As I argue elsewhere, the Japanese major studios held a nearly complete domination of the domestic film market until around 1965 by their binding contracts with cinemas throughout the country.[7] The loosening of the studios' monopoly during and after this year was gradual, but they still exerted control over the local mediascape in the years that followed even as Hollywood, other foreign, and independent productions gained more visibility.

Bond Turns "Japanese"

In one relatively short scene in *You Only Live Twice*—the 1967 film that proceeded *Thunderball*, and that was shot on location in Japan—Bond goes through a special treatment to make him appear "Japanese." This is a peculiar and highly sexualized pseudo-surgical procedure conducted by five Japanese women, four of whom in minimal clothing, who operate on Bond's eyes, and mainly his androgenic hair.[8]

The scene, and the subsequent sequences featuring Bond passing as "Japanese," are the main aspect of contestation for Seiji Fukunaga's review of the relatively recent reissue of the film with Japanese subtitles on Blu-ray (Fukunaga 2000, 158–61). For commentators at the time of the film's theatrical release in Japan, however, other aspects were not just more noteworthy, but perhaps more telling with the regard to what makes Bond a national phenomenon. For example, reviewing the film for *Kinema junpō*, Japan's longest-running film journal, Shinbi Ogura writes (without recounting the abovementioned contentious scenes) that references in the film to Japanese culture portray it as either extremely laughable (*bakusho*), or simply too poorly executed (*heta*). The overall assessment in the review, however, is that the film exceeds the one preceding it in the series in incorporating *kamishibai*-like elements (*zensaku o uemawaru kamishibai teki na yōso*) (Ogura 1967, 61–62).

By *kamishibai*, Ogura refers to the medium that Sharalyn Orbaugh succinctly defines as comprised of "a set of pictures used by a performer to tell a story to an audience, usually of children aged four to twelve" (Orbaugh 2012, 78). Although Orbaugh discusses it as a multisensory art form, and as an affective medium that should not necessarily be regarded as children's entertainment, it was and still is chiefly seen as catering to younger viewers. In the context of James Bond films, Japanese critics often used local terms and references like *kamishibai* to either single out inferior traits or as means to domesticate them. For instance, actor Jō Shishido, who appears in several *Wataridori* films mentioned before, contributed a tongue-in-cheek critique of *Goldfinger* (1964) to the cinephile magazine *Shinario* (Shishido 1965, 67). In contrast, Ogura, who mainly agrees with Shishido, argues nonetheless that the film is at least better than adult's *kamishibai* (Ogura 1965, 81). Thus, it appears as if, at least for some critics, the uniquely local pictorial storytelling

Figure 6.1.   Bond "becoming Japanese" in *You Only Live Twice*.
Source: EON Productions et al. 1967. Screenshot by author.

medium served as a conceptual litmus test for the quality of domestically circulating foreign content.

Critic Hiroshi Isoyama also evokes the term in his critique of *Thunderball*, claiming that despite the overall thrill, especially with the use of gadgets, the film becomes a childish *kamishibai* (Isoyama 1966, 44–45). By conjuring local terms, critics did not aim to facilitate better understanding of foreign images or sounds, but rather to resituate films within an inherently Japanese media ecosystem that, like the Olympics broadcasts, prioritizes or highlights Japanese aspects, even when they are otherwise considered secondary by international viewers. Isoyama, for instance, emphasizes as particularly powerful the use of underwater filming, an aspect that was achieved, as several other journals underscored, by a Japan-made device.

In contrast to Isoyama's critique, Oki Ichikawa praised the film's use of humor, calling it a magnificent success (migoto na seikō), and celebrating it as a "manga for grown-ups" (otona no manga) (Ichikawa 1966, 74). Other enthusiastic commentators introduced more specific Japanese references in their discussion of Bond films, especially in the case of the most popular among them, *Thunderball*. Tellingly in this regard is Toshio Oka's inquiry (kōsatsu), in which he lays out the reasons why he became a fan of the franchise and what makes it particularly appealing to Japanese. He associates the series with Fūtarō Yamada's ninja novels, before moving on to more specifically to identify Bond himself with Myōbudani, a sumo wrestler who became famous for winning fights against the top-ranking Yokozuna (Oka 1966, 98–99).

While the analogy between Bond and any popular sumo wrestler may seem fanciful, the reference to Yamada and to popular fiction featuring the famous (or infamous) premodern Japanese shadow warriors is indicative of how the art of spying was conceived, and to some extent, also mythologized, in the country. Although ninjas were a premodern phenomenon, they continued to inundate popular imagination, and Yamada's fiction featuring them was at its peak in the late 1950s and throughout the 1960s. At the same time, the Japanese modern spy novel was also becoming more popular with novels such as the aforementioned one by Momo Iida, and more so with Jōji Yūki's 1962 *Gomesu no na wa Gomesu* (Gomez's Name is Gomez), Michio Tsuzuki's 1964 *Sanjū roshutsu* (Triple Exposure), as well as a series of novels by Tōru Miyoshi. Some of these novels were also adapted into films. Literature, including translations of Ian Fleming's novels,[9] thereby played a significant role in fueling interest in spying and spies, a fact that bolstered a readily receptive viewership for Bond films in Japan.

In addition to literature, youth magazines featured spy comic strips and even graphic novelizations of Bond tales catering to younger readership.[10] To the wider public, the early release of Tom Jones's single of the film's theme song was another major factor that helped promote the film. Most important, however, was television. Of special importance in this regard was the December 9, 1965, airing of the hour-long documentary *007: Jemuzu Bondo no subete* (Everything About James Bond, 007), which received high ratings and was Bond's first appearance on small screens in Japan. Furthermore, while not directly related to the Bond series—although nonetheless of even greater importance—was the popular American spy television series *The Man from U.N.C.L.E.* (1964–1968) that was aired in Japan as *0011 Naporeon Soro*. These non-cinematic media products prepared local viewership to welcoming the global franchise's first premiere in the Far East nation. Lastly, emblematic of television's role in domesticating Bond is a scene in *You Only Live Twice* where the international spy uncovers the villains' illegal import of liquefied oxygen. The warehouse where the chemical is stored, and where Bond himself is soon knocked to the ground, also stashes boxes labeled "Nihon Sanyō Terebi" or "Japan Sanyo TV."

Susceptibility to spy fiction in 1960s Japan is also seen directly in the local film market. One notable example is director Setsuo Yamamoto's 1965 film *Supai* (Spy), which as critic Rikiya Tayama points out, was itself also fed by the popularity of Seichō Matsumoto's *Kuroi kiri* (Black Mist) nonfiction book series that covered shadowy or underreported events throughout Japan's history (Tayama 1965, 71). A case that directly demonstrates the Bond franchise's influence on the local film market is Tōhō's *Kokkusai himitsu keisatsu* (International Secret Police) series. As critic Teruaki Hirai writes in his review of *Kayaku no taru* (A Barrel of Gunpowder, 1964), the series' third installment, it was a clear imitation of the James Bond 007 series (Hirai 1965, 148). The film, as do all other ones pertaining to the series, indeed follows a Bond-like plotline: A witty, philanderer spy (played by Tatsuya Mihashi) is

Figure 6.2.   Boxes labeled "Japanese Sanyo Television" near chemical containers in *You Only Live Twice*.
Source: EON Productions et al., 1967. Screenshot by author.

sent on missions around the world to thwart operations by overtly malicious nation-like crime organizations. Although Hirai laments in his review that the series is not cinematic (eigateki ga nai), he asserts that this is true about Bond films as well.

From Grace to Disgrace

Beyond similarities between the international Bond franchise and its local imitation, the Japanese *International Secret Police* series played a crucial role in the—eventually failed—process of appropriating Bond in Japan. It was sensible for *You Only Live Twice* producers to recruit their cast from a series that may have been seen as the Japanese Bond, as they did with the two "Bond girls" Akiko Wakabayashi and Mie Hama, who had previously starred as the two leading women in the fourth *International Secret Police* film *Kagi no kagi* (Key of Keys, 1967). Unexpectedly, however, despite incorporating Japanese elements into the production as well as recruiting local star power, *You Only Live Twice* was ultimately discussed in Japan ignominiously as a national disgrace (*kokujoku eiga*).

Although no critic has raised this issue directly, some in the industry have anticipated condemnation against the film and especially the Japanese who participated in its production. While the source of the "national disgrace" label remains opaque, it seems to have been well-known around film circles, even before production has commenced. Attesting to this sense of trepidation around the film is producer Kikumaru Okuda, who was involved in the film's preproduction stages, and who is acknowledged with thanks in the film's credits. Okuda writes in an article for the magazine *Bungeishunjū* that he met Bond's producers during the production of *None but the Brave* (1965), based on a story he himself had written, starting Frank Sinatra and *International Secret Police* series' lead actor Tatsuya Mihashi. Soon after he recalls a warning by internationally acclaimed Japanese star Toshirō Mifune to reject cooperation on a national disgrace film (Okuda 1967, 284–92).

Okuda moves on to refute this and other vague critiques of the film along the line of national disgrace by other unnamed commentators. Yet he concludes without directly identifying the problem for which the film was or might be seen in such terms, by suggesting that the only solution is the production of two versions, one for domestic and the other for international viewers. Okuda does not specify how the versions would differ, and where should the already existing version be released. One might surmise that— given its local critique— *You Only Live Twice* was too "international," and that the demand was to replace it with a Japanese-tailored version. However, the label *kokujoku eiga* had a significant precedent prior to *You Only Live Twice*'s release that suggests otherwise. The case was Kōji Wakamatsu's 1965 "pink film" (softcore pornographic film) *Kabe no naka no himegoto* (Affairs within Walls). The film was not an anomaly within the director's—at the time already rather prolific—oeuvre, with its exploration of sex and violence. Yet, the film was declared, as Alexander Zahlten points out, following *Mainichi Shinbun* critic Kyūshirō Kusakabe as a "national disgrace film" due to its selection to be screened at the Fifteenth Berlin International Film Festival (Zahlten 2017, 48–50).

The two cases seem utterly different, mainly because *You Only Live Twice* has never been regarded as representative of Japan. Moreover, the Bond installation joins a long list of international productions that previously misrepresented aspects of Japanese culture.[11] Yet, while several non-Japanese films shot on location in Japan had, too, depicted Japanese women in an overtly sexualized fashion, the James Bond series is notorious for its misogynistic tendencies, and perhaps even more so regarding Asian femininity.[12] Thus, the fall from grace of the Bond series in Japan was likely not the result of the way it misrepresented Japan as a country, but due to the exploitive images of Japanese female bodies it distributed. This is not an ethical concern, as problematic images of exploited women were, and still are, ubiquitous in the local film market. Rather, Japanese critics seem to have wanted to preserve the impression that such images are for Japanese eyes only. Much like with the case of the fast-expanding local soft-core film industry in the mid-1960s, which raised little concern as long as it was a domestic affair, it became an issue of national shame when presented to non-Japanese viewers. The problem, it seems, was less the content of the films and more the prospective viewership. The international Bond franchise, despite lesser degree of images exploiting Japanese women than many local productions, was seen as shameful because it exposes Japanese female bodies to non-Japanese male viewers.

Similar to Okuda's review (albeit from an entirely different perspective), Hiroshi Minami, one of Japan's leading social psychologists at the time, also dismissed the notion of national shame associated in Japan with *You Only Live Twice* in a *Kinema junpō* article. Like Okuda, he too simply acknowledges the local critique attributed to the film without properly presenting it. Unlike him, however, Minami argues that the film has an important lesson to teach "us, Japanese citizens" (wareware nihon kokumin ni totte taihen kyōkun eiga). He recognizes the film's similarities with ninja fiction (*ninja mono*), and while generally equating the film with manga for young boys, he also underscores the depiction of Japan in the film as a nation positioned between two superpowers amid an international space race (Minami 1967, 72).

While the review veers from his areas of expertise to explore issues bound up with international politics, Minami's academic writings can shed light on the sense of shame with which the film was received in Japan. In one of his manuscripts, Minami distinguishes between the concept of shame in the West and in Japan. In principle, he claims that in the West the notion of disgrace can be alleviated by a process of public revelation or confession that often concludes with forgiveness, or conciliation. In Japan, on the other hand, Minami argues that shameful consciousness (*haji ishiki*) is intrinsically interwoven with the notions of duty (*giri*) and honor (*meiyo*), and it is therefore much more difficult for shame to be reprieved.[13] Although Minami does not discuss national or shared forms of disgrace, following this logic it can be deducted that such notions arise precisely by the process welcomed in the West of public dissemination of what is seen as harmful to an individual's or as a country's failure to maintain its duty and to defend its reputation.

A case that further illustrates Bond's idiosyncratic disposition within the Japanese public sphere is Woody Allen's 1966 *What's Up, Tiger Lily?*. The film is a reedited version of *Key of Keys* accompanied with an added comical voice-over and commentary. Allen's creative treatment of the film, as Ryan Fraser points out, assumes a North American (of European descent) ethnocentric and condescending point of view from which Allen presents a stereotypically racial or ethnical portrayal of an inherently inferior foreign culture (Fraser 2010, 28–29). Why then has the non-Japanese James Bond production been seen as shameful by some, while the more explicitly parodied image of Japan has not? One explanation is simply that *You Only Live Twice* has been more widely watched than Allen's film. However, according to Minami's theorization, the problem is rooted in factors of agency and responsibility. While Akiko Wakabayashi and Mie Hama, among other Japanese cast and staff actively participated in the international projection of Japan through the Bond franchise, this was not the case in *What's Up, Tiger Lily?*, which projected a North American image of Japan detached from intentional Japanese involvement. In other words, the distinction between the global and the local in Japan stands not for a stable condition in the world, but rather for a disengaging or disorienting perspective.

It is therefore not surprising that, as Victor Roudometof shows, the concept of "glocal" has probably originated from the Japanese term *dochakuka* (Roudometof 2015, 775). According to this conception, no phenomenon is considered global or local, but one has to be "indigenized" and aptly "infused" as such. Both global Bond instalments *Thunderball* and *You Only Live Twice* were "glocalized" in this way, even though only in the case of the former film the process has deemed successful.

Conclusion

In the 1960s, Japan experienced rapid economic expansion, as well as trailblazing medial transformations in areas such as television and film. The

Bond franchise, mainly through *Thunderball,* gained a rare introduction into the country under the guise of an international cultural product that caters to Western viewers with specific attentiveness to Japanese sensitivities. Once that impression came into question, local commentators quickly rejected the "local" label associated with *You Only Live Twice* and acknowledged it as a film that globalized Japan for international viewership. While the two Bond films this chapter discusses were both popular in Japan, and while local critics were equality harsh on them, the "glocalized" or *dochakuka* phenomenon Bond in Japan ushered in is still limited to these two installments of the franchise.

It is arguable that Bond films and novels inspired Japanese artists such as *Gorugo 13*'s creator Takao Saito, and that they bolstered the already growing local interest in media content featuring spies. More than influencing the creation of any cultural product, however, the perceived honor of being the first to screen a film from the international series—which was then followed by a domestically produced Bond film that projected to the world images of the country—reignited a national discourse largely suppressed since the end of World War II. The domestic reaction to the possibility of international attention to Japan lead to an overblown polarization between national pride and disgrace. While the discourse was largely limited to individuals associated with the local media industry, it is emblematic of Japan's ambivalent stand in the world stage. Like the misleading image of an Imperial Great Britain that James Bond is predicated on, Japan was no longer an empire in the same sense it had been until the war. Yet, as a close American allied nation, it imagined itself as more influential than it actually was. Its claims for global fame were therefore a matter of an unrealizable fantasy: a glo/cal media phenomenon bifurcated by a desire for greater assimilation within the international community as well as, at the same time, a conservative wish for (at least some degree of) cultural isolation.

Notes

1. Japan's 1970 Film Year Book lists the film as the second most profitable foreign film in the country of all time until this point, a remarkable achievement given that the top film *Ben-Hur* (Wyler 1959), as well as the films ranked below *Thunderball, Gone with the Wind* (Fleming, 1939), *The Longest Day* (Annakin, Marton, and Wicki 1962), *West Side Story* (Wise 1961), and *The Ten Commandments* (DeMille 1956), received multiple releases. The 1960s Bond films received only a single release, and still *You Only Live Twice* and *Goldfinger* too are listed among the top ten best grossing foreign films. The first two films, *Dr. No* (Young, 1962), and *From Russia with Love* (Young 1963), as well as the last instalment of the decade *On Her Majesty's Secret Service* (Hunt, 1969), are not registered as blockbusters (*Eiga nenkan* 1970, 56).

2. The title is said to have been inspired by a Basho haiku poem. See: Gardiner, 2021.

3. For a compelling discussion on transnationalism in the Japanese cinematic context see: Miyao 2019, 109–116.

4. For a detailed critique of the transnational label in global film markets see: Reyes, Ian and Wyatt, Justin 2019, 1–13.

5. See, for example: Taira 1971, 225–230.

6. *Shūkan eiga puresu*, 330, May 18, 1954, 1.

7. See: Amit, Rea. 2019. "Programming a Public Mediascape: Distribution and the Japanese Motion Pictures Experience." *On_Culture: The Open Journal for the Study of Culture* 8.

8. Obviously, the sequence presents the women in an overtly sexualized fashion. Yet, after the removal of a piece of cloth covering Bond's naked body, Aki (played by Akiko Kobayashi) says laughing to her fellow coworkers in Japanese: "atashi tachi no himitsu yo) or "this is our secret," insinuating perhaps an unflattering feature in Bond's otherwise unquestioned masculinity (he himself asks before why they bother working on unshown parts of the body).

9. The first Japanese translation was of *Live and Let Die*, three years after the original publication, in 1957 by Kazuo Inoue, whose translation of *Dr. No* appeared in 1959. He also translated *Goldfinger*, *From Russia With Love*, and *Diamonds Are Forever* in 1960. Inoue was also the translator of *Thunderball* in 1962, and of *You Only Live Twice* in 1964, within months after it first appeared in English.

10. Most notably, Shōgakukan Manga Label released such graphic novelizations of *Thunderball* by famed manga-ka Takao Saito. The artist started serializing Bond comic strips for the boys' magazine *Bōizuraifu* in 1963 before establishing his reputation as the creator of one of Japan's most successful manga series *Gorugo 13* in the latter half of the decade. The series' protagonist was highly likely influenced by James Bond, and the two share some characteristics, including, most explicitly, the tendency toward womanizing (although Gorugo is far less delicate).

11. Such films include: *House of Bamboo* (dir. Fuller, 1955), *The Teahouse of the August Moon* (dir. Mann, 1956), *The Geisha Boy* (dir. Tashlin, 1958), *Cry for Happy* (dir. Marshall, 1961), and *My Geisha* (dir. Cardiff, 1962) among many other titles.

12. See, for example, Hiramoto and Pua, 2019.

13. Hiroshi Minami, Nihonjinron no keifu (Genealogy of Japanese-ness Theories) (Tokyo: Kodansha, 1980), 185–87.

Bibliography

Amit, Rea. 2019. "Programming a Public Mediascape: Distribution and the Japanese Motion Pictures Experience." *On_Culture: The Open Journal for the Study of Culture* 8. https://doi.org/10.22029/oc.2019.1166.

Black, Jeremy. 2004. "The Geopolitics of James Bond," *National Security* 19 (2): 290–303.

Bordwell, David. 2000. *Planet Hong Kong: Popular Cinema and the Art of Entertainment*. Cambridge, MA: Harvard University Press.

Chun, Jayson Makoto. 2009. *"A Nation of a Hundred Million Idiots"? A Social History of Japanese Television, 1953–1973*. New York: Routledge.

Dodds, Klaus. 2005. "Screening Geopolitics: James Bond and the Early Cold War films (1962–1967)," *Geopolitics* 10 (2): 266–89.

Eiga nenkan [Film Yearbook]. 1970. Tokyo: Jiji Eiga Tsūshinsha.

Fraser, Ryan. 2010. *"What's Up, Tiger Lily?* On Woody Allen and the Screen Translator's Trojan Horse." *TTR: traduction, terminologie, rédaction* 3(1): 17–39.

Fukunaga, Seiji. 2020. "Hariuddo eiga no naka no okashi na Nippon: Nihonjin ni narimashita Jēmuzu Bondo" [An Odd Japan in a Hollywood Film: The James Bond Who Became Japanese], *Yomiuri kuōtarī* 53: 158–61.

Funnell, Lisa, and Klaus Dodds. 2017. *Geographies, Genders and Geopolitics of James Bond*. London: Palgrave Macmillan.

Gardiner, Tim. 2021. "'Ku Only Live Twice': Ian Fleming's Use of Haiku Poetry." *International Journal of James Bond Studies* 4(1): 1–10.

Hirai, Teruaki. 1965. "Kokusai himitsukeisatsu: Kayaku no teru" (Review of: International Secret Police: A Barrel of Gunpowder), *Kinema junpō* 384 (1199): 148.

Hiramoto, Mie, and Phoebe Pua. 2019. "Racializing Heterosexuality: Non-Normativity and East Asian Characters in James Bond Films," *Language in Society* 48(4): 541–63.

Ichikawa, Oki. 1966. "007/Sandāboru sakusenn"[Operation Thunderball], *Kinema junpō* 409 (1224): 74.

Iida, Momo. 1966. "Bondoizumu no ryūkō" [The Bondism Craze], *Sekai* 3 (244): 184–88.

Isoyama, Hiroshi. 1966. "Suriru manten, kyōi no suichū satsuei" [Full Thrill, Amazing Underwater Filming], *Kinema junpō* 407 (1222): 44–45.

Iwabuchi, Koichi. 2015. "Pop-culture Diplomacy in Japan: Soft Power, Nation Branding and the Question of 'International Cultural Exchange.'" *International Journal of Cultural Policy* 21(4): 419–43.

Kushner, Barak. 2006. "Gojira as Japan's First Postwar Media Event." In *In Godzilla's Footsteps: Japanese Pop Culture Icons on the Global Stage*, edited by William Tsutsui and Michiko Ito, 10–50. New York: Palgrave Macmillan.

Minami, Hiroshi. 1967. "007 wa nido shinu" (Review of *You Only Live Twice*) *Kinema junpō* 444 (1260): 72.

———. 1980. *Nihonjinron no keifu* [A Genealogy of Japanese-ness Theories]. Tokyo: Kodansha.

Miyao, Daisuke. 2019. "How Can We Talk About 'Transnational' When We Talk About Japanese Cinema?" *Journal of Japanese and Korean Cinema* 11 (2): 109–16.

Ogura, Shinbi. 1965. "007: Gōrudo fingā" [007: Goldfinger], *Kinema junpō* 390 (1205): 81–82.

———. 1967. "007 wa nido shinu" [007: You Only Live Twice (literally: 007 Dies Twice)], *Kinema junpō* 443 (1259): 61–62.

Oka, Toshio. 1966. "007 shirīzu no dokusōteki na omoshirosa ni tsuite no kōsatsu" (A Consideration of the 007 Series' Fascinating Originality), *Sukurīn* 21 (2): 98–99.

Okuda, Kikumaru. 1967. "Igai! 007 wa shinshi datta" [Unexpected! 007 Was a Gentleman], *Bungeishunjū* 45 (3): 284–92.

Oliver, Chris. 2009. "Kokusaika, Revisited: Reinventing 'Internationalization' in Late 1960s Japan," *Sophia Junior College Faculty Journal* 29: 47–54.

Orbaugh, Sharalyn. 2012. "'Kamishibai' and the Art of the Interval," *Mechademia* 7: 78–100.

Poon, Erica Ka-yan. 2019. "Southeast Asian Film Festival: The Site of the Cold War Cultural Struggle," *Journal of Chinese Cinemas* 13(1): 76–92.

Raine, Michael. 2020. "The Cold War as Media Environment in 1960s Japanese Cinema," in *The Cold War and Asian Cinemas*, edited by Poshek Fu and Man-Fung Yip, 119–38. New York: Routledge.

Reyes, Ian, and Wyatt, Justin. 2019. "On the Banality of Transnational Film" *Markets, Globalization & Development Review* 4(3): 1–13.

Robertson, Roland. 1995. "Glocalization: Time-space and Homogeneity-Heterogeneity," in *Global Modernities*, edited by Mike Featherstone, Scott Lash, and Roland Robertson, 25–44. London: Sage.

Roudometof, Victor. 2015. "The Glocal and Global Studies," *Globalizations* 12(5): 774–87.

Shishido, Jō. 1965. "077: Gōrudo fingā" [007: Goldfinger], *Shinario* 21 (4): 57.

*Shū*kan eiga puresu [Weekly Film Press], May 18, 1954.

Steinberg, Marc. 2012. *Anime's Media Mix: Franchising Toys and Characters in Japan*. Minneapolis: University of Minnesota Press.

Taira, Koji. 1971. "Japan's Economic Relations with Asia," *Current History* 60 (356): 225–30.

Tayama, Rikiya. 1965. "*Supai*" (Review of the film *Spy*), *Kinema junpō* 401 (1216): 71.

Yoshimi, Shunya. 2007. *Shinbei to hanbei: Sengo Nihon no seijiteki muishiki* [Pro- and Anti- American: Postwar Japan's Political Unconsciousness]. Tokyo: Iwanamishinso.

Zahlten, Alexander. 2017. *The End of Japanese Cinema: Industrial Genres, National Times, and Media Ecologies*. Durham: Duke University Press.

Chapter 7

The Women Are Not Enough

Colonial Consumption, Universal Exports, and Family Lineage in OHMSS

Lisa Funnell[1]

James Bond is known for being a connoisseur with a refined palette, however his tastes extend beyond food and drink to include women (see Planka 2015, Strong 2018). In *You Only Live Twice* (Gilbert 1967), Bond asks his lover "Why do Chinese girls taste different from all other girls?" highlighting his experience with sampling the "flavors" of women from around the world. This linking of food with gender, sexuality, race, and nationality draws attention to the problematic consumptive practices of Bond, a white heteronormative Western Northern cis man, which are rooted in a long history of (bodily) conquest and occupation, and lie at the heart of imperial pursuits. This is evident across the series but is especially apparent in the Bond films of the 1960s.

While *On Her Majesty's Secret Service* (Hunt 1969) is often considered to be an outlier in the James Bond canon (see Verheul 2016), it has recently experienced somewhat of a renaissance among fans and critics, and was extensively referenced in the most recent *No Time to Die* (Fukanaga 2021). While the romance between Bond and Tracy DiVicenzo tends to be the focus of discussions, what is frequently overlooked is that *OHMSS* offers one of the most poignant depictions of colonial consumption—the act of exerting and/or enacting social, political, and/or economic dominance over a county and its people through cultural and specifically gastronomic discourses—both in terms of Bond's sexual conquests and displays of physical prowess. The film builds a narrative around the actions of megalomaniac Ernst Stavro Blofeld, who creates a network of twelve "Angels of Death," women from around "the world" who will (unknowingly) help to contaminate and sterilize the world's food supply in their respective homelands. However, Blofeld's skewed "global" representation betrays the film's European perspective and bias. This chapter will not only explore how Bond "samples" (or consumes) the "international buffet" of women but also how the nationalities of the "Angels of Death" relay a Eurocentric impression of "the world," one that overemphasizes whiteness, oversimplifies other racial identities, and completely overlooks the Global South and specifically the continents of South America and Africa. Paradoxically, this depiction has largely spared *OHMSS* from critiques of the Connery era films (1962–1967) that promoted racialized stereotypes particularly for Asian villains at the time (see Funnell and Dodds 2017).

Additionally, this paper will explore how Bond's consumptive practices are couched in a narrative that emphasizes the superiority of Britain, which Bond represents via MI6. The film sets Bond up as the colonial/universal expert/ export who bests Blofeld and his henchpeople in a series of physical feats inspired by the Winter Olympics (such as skiing, bobsledding, and curling), a global sports competition determining both individual and national corporeal dominance. It then challenges this professional identity through the emphasis on family histories and ancestral lineage whereby matriarchal/monarchal noble titles are given the strongest legitimacy. Ultimately, this chapter will show that Bond's choice to marry the countess, Tracy DiVicenzo, creates a direct threat to colonial order through a rejection of the queen, which can only be resolved through the killing of DiVicenzo and the return of Bond to service in the next film.

Colonial Consumption

OHMSS is an outlier in the Bond film canon with a formula that is reflective of the "women's film" from the Hollywood Golden Age (Santos 2015, 101). However, these thematic elements, which suggest that Bond will not only find love but also experience loss, bookend a different type of colonial engagement that centers on women, bodily conquest, and consumption. This is suggested in the credit sequence, which opens with a large martini glass located in the center of the screen into/onto which the union jack is being projected. In addition, a white crown is located on top of the glass. On either side are three women in silhouette who are kneeling or reclining from a seated position, all looking up at the crown. One of these women is wearing a headdress and holding a spear, an image that evokes colonial conquest in the Global South and presumed subjugation. Thus, in the first thirty seconds, the opening credits visualize the hierarchy of colonial power that structures and defines the narrative of the film.

The notion of colonial consumption is most strongly pronounced at the forty-five-second mark, when images of naked women in silhouette begin to slide down through the martini glass and into the stem. Importantly, there is a distinction being made here between the images of Bond girls and other established figures featured in previous (Sean Connery) films being projected (in color) into the glass and the anonymous women in black shadow flowing through them—figures who will be consumed while their names, identities, and stories remain unknown. The credits end with a shot of six women in silhouette either kneeling or reclining while looking up at a white crown. The choice of color to differentiate the monarchy (white) from the women who are literally presented under colonial rule (black) sends a powerful message about imperial conquest and particularly the historical (sexual) abuse of women across the Global South.

Thus, colonization is not simply about geographical expansion and the occupation of territory but also controlling and mobilizing (new) resources. This includes the bodies of women and especially racialized women, who are often claimed, possessed, and (mis)used without their consent by those in colonial power. Moreover, they remain "anonymous" with their identities never known and their stories rarely told. A somewhat similar line of argument can be applied to the twelve "Angels of Death" featured in *OHMSS*. These women believe that they are participating in an experimental program aimed at curing them of their food allergies; they have been told that they are undergoing a form of (hypnotic) therapy when in reality Blofeld is brainwashing them without their consent. These women are dehumanized and treated like vessels, rather than people, who will carry and infect crops around

Figure 7.1. Opening credits of *On Her Majesty's Secret Service*.
Source: EON Productions et al., 1969. Screenshot by author.

the world. While the assigned female at birth (AFAB) body has historically been described as a vessel of creation (due to its procreative potential), Blofeld transforms them into agents of death and strips them of their ability to act with autonomy.

While Blofeld claims and (mis)uses these women as resources for his dastardly plan, Bond also engages in the process of colonial consumption at Piz Gloria. He works undercover as Sir Hillary Bray, a man who supposedly has no sexual interest in women. When he is invited to share a meal with the twelve women and their guardian Irma Bunt, the film features overhead shots of women eating various dishes. These are intercut with medium close-up shots of women putting food into their mouth seductively and then chewing and enjoying their meals with a few of them moaning in pleasure. The dialogue at one point discusses "balls" and there is a direct connection being made here between sex and consumption. Bond capitalizes on this situation by sleeping with two women and presumably more had Bunt not put a halt to his late-night conquests. The film justifies Bond's sexual activity, which is done under false pretenses, by framing it as being necessary for mission success.

In Ian Fleming's 1963 source novel, the allergy patients were women exclusively from Britain and Ireland, and the villainous plot was decidedly insular. Blofeld was brainwashing these women into transmitting a biological agent that would destroy the agricultural economy on which postwar Britain strongly depended, thereby crippling their recovery efforts. By comparison, the film adaptation projects this plot outward by featuring allergy patients from around "the world." But a cursory look at the twelve women reveals that six of them are from Europe (Britain, Hungary, Scandinavia, Ireland, England, Germany), with two from the UK, three are from Asia (India, China, Israel), two from North America (the United States, Jamaica) and one from Australia. Moreover, all of the non-European countries have had at least one territory under British colonial rule: United States (until 1776), Australia (until 1901), India (until 1947), Israel (until 1948), Jamaica (until 1962), and China via Hong Kong (until 1997). The film presents a skewed Eurocentric, if not colonial, impression of "the world" and subsequently vilifies Blofeld for tracing his plot across the map of the (current and former) British Empire.

It is important to note that women from South America and Africa are not included in this worldview in spite of the long history of British occupation within and across both continents. Taken together, these continents accounted for 17 percent of the world's population in 1969, thereby rendering their exclusion a significant, although not surprising, oversight.[2] Moreover, this omission constitutes the erasure of women from the Global South in the depiction of places and people that "matter" in "the world." At the same time, the Eurocentric makeup of the twelve "Angels of Death" which privileges actors from the Global North is contradicted visually by the world map hanging in Blofeld's operation room with yellow dots suggesting that at least one "Angel" will be traveling to these unrepresented continents. Moreover, of the twelve patients, only white women are named and prominently featured in the film with speaking roles; they are given a voice and critical agency that is denied to the *Other* women. While 25 percent of the patients are racialized women, only the Black woman from Jamaica is hypersexualized when she eats a banana. The politics of representation in *OHMSS* are reflective of a colonial perspective about the (de)valuing and primacy of certain women over others.

Additionally, none of these women have surnames in the film, and this absence is presented as a house rule imposed by Irma Bunt (who has a surname herself). In a film where *lineage matters* for women on screen (see below), the depiction of characters without personal histories works to devalue and disassociate them from their ancestral/family roots. They become functions of Blofeld, working in servitude and subjugation to his plans without affirmative consent. During their time at Piz Gloria, they are dehumanized, reprogrammed, and transformed into Blofeld's biological weapons. The film vilifies Blofeld for claiming power outside of the colonial state but falls short on offering a critique of the British Empire and its historic claims on people, places, and resources.

This raises the question of how we interpret Bond's interactions with the women in/at Piz Gloria (and beyond in the canon) given that he was operating as an agent of the state. After sleeping with two patients and escaping from the facility, Bond becomes engaged to DiVicenzo and later returns to Piz Gloria in order to save her. His focus is on the contessa, a woman of high rank and established lineage (see below), rather than the twelve "Angels of Death" who were manipulated and victimized by Blofeld. In fact, there is no mention of the women once they leave the facility, and without knowledge of their surnames it would be very difficult to track them down. Instead, these unnamed women of "the world" are forgotten, their victimization overlooked, and their trauma rendered invisible and unimportant to the agents of colonial power/control.

Colonial/Universal Expert/Export

James Bond is a British MI6 agent who embarks on state-sanctioned missions around the world to help safeguard the geopolitical safety and resource security of the UK and its closest allies such as the United States (see Funnell and Dodds 2017). While debriefings often take place in London, the vast majority of the narrative, conflict, and action unfold in different and often "exotic" locations around the world. The films emphasize the continuing strength (via

Q and the development of technology) or perhaps the footprint and lingering legacy (via Bond's extraterritorial reach through partnership with the United States) of the British Empire (while overlooking its contemporaneous decline) by having Bond occupy spaces, mobilize resources, and lead people in various places worldwide including (newly) decolonized territories like Jamaica in *Dr. No* (Young 1962).[3] One way that MI6 has continued to represent their colonial-commercial power is by naming their front organization "Universal Exports," a term that suggests the postimperial power of Britain is actualized through operations within rather than occupation of territory.

In fact, *OHMSS* opens with a shot of the gold "Universal Exports (London)" sign, thereby signaling the global power and international standing of the UK via MI6 from the outset of the film (see Stock 2010). The term "universal" suggests the notion that British identity is (all too) often understood as a standard measurement in colonial engagements whereby the British self is defined in relation to the international/colonized other.[4] A good example of this is Orientalism, which dates back to the period of the Enlightenment (eighteenth century) and provided justifications for British/European colonialism and authority over "the Orient" (see Said 1978). Additionally, the word "exports" emphasizes the outward objectives and projections of the organization. This is signified through the state-sanctioned missions on which agents are sent; they travel out of the UK and "into the world" to meet their objectives, simultaneously operating and occupying space (physical and geopolitical) in other nations/territories.

The extent of Bond's global traveling is highlighted when Moneypenny is tasked with finding Bond early on in the film. She mentions putting out calls to Madrid (Spain), Cairo (Egypt), and Amsterdam (Germany). This presents the impression that Bond is not only a jet-setting spy when he is on the clock but he travels "the world" in his leisure time, vacationing in major European and North African cities. However, "the world" portrayed in *OHMSS* is decidedly Eurocentric, with Bond venturing no more than six thousand kilometers after earlier films that witnessed Sean Connery's Bond in Jamaica (*Dr. No* [1962]), Turkey (*From Russia with Love* [1963]), Bahamas (*Thunderball* [1965]), and Japan (*You Only Live Twice*, [1967]). The true geographical antipode of London is New Zealand, which is almost 19,000 km (or three times further) away, and Bond has never traveled there across the twenty-five-film history of the franchise.

The notion of "universal" is further emphasized by the location of Blofeld's lair on a mountain in Switzerland. As a nation, Switzerland has long maintained a policy of neutrality, and, since the Treaty of Paris in 1815, the country has not participated in a military conflict. However, neutrality does not translate into transparency. Swiss banks are notorious for maintaining secrecy laws that enable people and organizations to hide their assets, as noted in the film *Goldfinger* (1964). In 2016, it was estimated that Switzerland held "a 25% market share in global cross-border asset management business, making Switzerland a global leader in the field" ("The Swiss" 2016). This seems to be the perfect discreet location for a villain, like Blofeld, to hatch his plan for world domination without any external regulation, geopolitical oversight, and/or legal consequences. Additionally, given that Blofeld runs an international terrorist organization that lacks political affiliation, Switzerland seems like the ideal place to locate his headquarters and base of operations at Piz Gloria.[5]

On the one hand, by situating a large portion of the film in Switzerland, *OHMSS* presents a more personal and inward-facing narrative. In the climax of the film, for instance, Bond does not embark on a state-sanctioned mission to storm Piz Gloria and apprehend Blofeld. Instead, Bond circumvents the system by eliciting help from a Mafia leader, Marc-Ange Draco, and they enter the airspace around Piz Gloria under the guise of transporting medicine as part of a humanitarian mission. In the end, both Bond and Blofeld use Switzerland and broader notions of neutrality as a shield for their own personal benefit. Moreover, by stripping away the MI6 component, the film personalizes the conflict between the two men by focusing on the kidnapped Tracy DiVicenzo as the *object* of their mutual affections (see analysis below).

On the other hand, the location of Switzerland creates a neutral (and uncolonized) backdrop for competition, much like the Olympic Games, in which players compete against each other to highlight the superior athlete. In fact, the film features prominent sports in the Winter Olympics in two ways.[6] First, women play ice sports like curling ("Angels of Death") and go ice skating (DiVicenzo) to determine the ideal mate (i.e., winner) for Bond. DiVicenzo not only initiates her rescue of Bond by approaching him on an ice rink but she also drives them to safety through an ice car derby—which is not technically an Olympic sport but really should be!

Second, the men compete against each other in skiing and bobsled to determine who would be the ideal mate for DiVicenzo. For instance, when Bond escapes from Piz Gloria after uncovering Blofeld's plot, he travels down the mountain on skis, expertly avoiding both spotlights and machine gun fire. As the SPECTRE henchpeople, and even Blofeld himself, give chase, Bond deftly weaves between evergreens and the bullets to outpace his competition. The sequence, shot with camerapeople on skis and edited with quick cuts, takes on the look of a deadly alpine slalom race.[7] Even on one ski, Bond's physical dominance is evident, and his performance taps into the long-standing connection between sport, masculinity, and nationality in Great Britain and the Empire (see McDevitt 2004, Downes 2010); while Britain was unsuccessful in winning a medal at the recent X Olympic Winter Games

(1968) in France, Bond outperforms his international competition, proving his superiority and that of Britain in the following year.

Later, at the conclusion of the film's climatic raid on Piz Gloria, Bond chases a fleeing Blofeld in another way reminiscent of Olympic Winter Games: the single-person bobsled, made even deadlier with the exchange of gunfire, a hand grenade, and, when Bond manages to jump on Blofeld's bobsled, hand-to-hand combat.

Although Bond does not capture Blofeld, Bond completes the course and is met at the "finish line" by a friendly Saint Bernard, whom Bond instructs, "Go and get the brandy, huh? Five-star Hennessy, of course." With respect to the elemental, water factors prominently into Commander Bond's defeat of Blofeld; he bests his opponent in snow and ice, thereby "proving" both Bond and Britain reign supreme.[8] Thus, in *OHMSS*, it is winner takes all for the (colonial) white man, who is presented as the "universal expert." He defeats his opponent (to maintain geopolitical order) and demonstrates his fitness as the ideal mate (for love) thereby reaffirming/reestablishing a sense of British phallocentrism in "the world."

Lineage, Matriarchy, and Personal Identity

While the physical conflict between Bond and Blofeld[9] is positioned at the heart of the narrative, *OHMSS* also emphasizes lineage, pedigree, and family lines as well as the inherent privilege, social status, and access to resources (people, resources, information) that accompany family names, bloodlines, and/or (noble) titles. The film highlights the importance of having deep roots and intergenerational connections to an ancestral homeland and the subsequent authority they confer. It also centers on a contrast between external and internal conflict that is coded in terms of global performance and local

Figure 7.2. Bobsled chase in *On Her Majesty's Secret Service*.
Source: EON Productions et al., 1969. Screenshot by author.

identity respectively. This emphasis on history, tradition, and identity comes at the end of a decade of great social change in Britain.

In the 1960s, Britain saw the rise of social movements like second-wave feminism, changes in laws including decriminalization of homosexuality (1967), demographic shifts such as increasing immigration and the passing of the Race Relations Act (1968), and the rise of mass media and its impact on politics (see Negrine 1994). This resulted in a significant de-centering of the status quo and diminishment of their exclusive access to privilege through the rising social, legal, and cultural status of historically underrepresented and marginalized groups like women, racial minorities, immigrants, and individuals who identify as LGBTQ, among others. While *OHMSS* offers space for this change to be represented on-screen, particularly through Bond's cover as Sir Hillary Bray (with suggestions of homosexuality through the genealogist persona he takes on)[10] and his interactions with the "Angels of Death" (women who range in terms of their race and nationality who have been brought to Switzerland) at Piz Gloria, these encounters take place under false pretenses, and the figures are mobilized in service of two heteronormative white men seeking personal validation and competing against each other for superiority and the ideal mate.

Family trees and lineage are emphasized in the storylines of Bond and Blofeld. On the one hand, Blofeld is obsessed with having his (fraudulent) claim as Count Balthazar de Bleuchamp confirmed through quasi-legal/official channels. It is this quest for validation (and neediness) that opens the door for Bond to infiltrate Piz Gloria and uncover his plot. On the other hand, Bond has his own lineage discussed through the presentation of his family crest (dating back to 1387) and the discussion of his family motto, *orbis non sufficit* (the world is not enough). While this phrase can be interpreted in a variety of ways (see Funnell and Dodds 2017), it arguably highlights the insatiable appetite for Bond's colonial consumption especially as he works as an agent for MI6.

Prior to the Daniel Craig era (2006–2021), the background of Bond and his family history are rarely addressed in the series. Instead, the films of the 1960s suggest an upper- or upper-middle-class upbringing through the emphasis on his sophisticated and refined palate. Across the Sean Connery films, Bond is very particular in what he consumes (food, drinks, cigarettes), wears (clothing, watches), and drives (the Aston Martin DB5 being the most notable vehicle). This is carried over into the initial scenes of *OHMSS* with George Lazenby's Bond driving an Aston Martin DBS, staying in the best hotel suite, stating his preference for his own brand of cigarettes, ordering champagne and caviar, and golf being his choice of leisure activity. This presents the impression that Bond is a man of the world, a gastronome with refined tastes and extensive consumptive knowledge and practices.

This highly refined palate also extends to Bond's taste and appetite for women. As noted by Julia Wood, femininity can be devalued through the trivialization and deprecation of women (2011, 123). This includes equating women with food, which not only works to dehumanize them but also presupposes their consumption (particularly by the men making the comparison). In her analysis of the opening credit sequences in James Bond films, Sabine Planka argues that women are depicted "as appetizers—small dishes of food served before the main course of a meal in order to stimulate one's appetite" (2015, 141). This can be expanded into a broader consideration of women in the film proper with Bond even commenting in *You Only Live Twice* on the different flavors of women he has sampled. Through Bond's consumption of consumer goods and women, the film emphasizes (the bachelor) Bond's global reach, access, and touch.

Although Bond sleeps with various women in each film, only one woman becomes his Bond girl by the end of the movie (see Funnell 2018). What differentiates *OHMSS* is that Bond marries her and resigns from the service. DiVicenzo not only has the intelligence and physical capabilities (like driving skills and alpine skills) that make her an "ideal" match for Bond, but she also has a title and lineage that signal virtue (albeit in a classist/aristocratic way). The film sets up a contrast between Bond's profession/identity as the colonial/universal expert/export (i.e., agent) who has historically prioritized queen and country, and his desire for a more individualized and grounded identity with roots, a lineage, and eventually a family. Moreover, while Bond's conflict with Blofeld is corporeal/athletic, outward-facing, and global in nature, his internal conflict over identity is internal, inward-facing, and more localized. This is notable in Bond selecting the contessa for his wife (i.e., true/local identity) after sampling the "international buffet" of women as part of his job/duty (i.e., global identity).

Unlike the "Angels of Death" who were selected for their allergies, and national ties/affiliations, DiVicenzo is prioritized for her title: she is a contessa, from her mother's side, a position that brings with it notions of nobility and social respect. She will also inherit her father's wealth amassed from his criminal syndicate which is construed as one of the most powerful in the world. His office not only reflects his personal fortune but he appears to flaunt his wealth via the gold decor thereby suggesting he represents new money (see Littler 2019). The film appears to differentiate old from new money through its emphasis on titles and family lineage. DiVicenzo is arguably seen as being the ideal mate for men seeking to improve their individual social status because of her well-established (maternal) lineage rather than contemporaneous and self-made (paternal) wealth.

DiVicenzo is arguably pitted against Queen Elizabeth II, the matriarch of Britain, with the most noble British title and lineage. *OHMSS* is the first film in which a portrait of the queen plays a prominent and narrative function. On two occasions, Bond is shown looking at and addressing the portrait hung in his office. Early in the film, Bond tries to resign from the service after M refuses to sign off on him hunting down Blofeld. A dejected Bond sits at his desk, and his image is reflected in the portrait of the queen as he says "Sorry Mum"/ "Sorry Ma'am" and takes a sip from his flask.

This creates a direct (familial) link between the monarch and the agents who operate *on her majesty's secret service.* Later in the film, after M rejects Bond's request to lead a rescue mission to storm Piz Gloria and save DiVicenzo, he sits with his back to the portrait as he decides to go rogue and briefly looks over his shoulder at her when he calls up Draco with the plan. The difference in these bookending shots is the way that the image of Bond is (dis)connected from the portrait in the end thereby signaling a shift in his loyalty and *choice* of lineage and therefore identity from the queen (i.e., duty) to the contessa (i.e., love).

The film ends with the wedding between Bond and DiVicenzo, which not only signals the end of Bond's professional status as the global/universal expert/export and new identity as husband and potential patriarch of his own line. It also offers Bond the opportunity to gain social status outside of imperial directives and therefore serves as a challenge to colonial power. Moreover, as demonstrated across a handful of Bond films including *License to Kill* (Glen 1989) and *No Time To Die* (Fukanaga 2021), marriage is unsustainable in the world of Bond as it creates an underlying loyalty to partner/ family and the possibility of an agent turning their back on the queen, as

Figure 7.3. Drinking with the queen in *On Her Majesty's Secret Service.*
Source: EON Productions et al. 1969. Screenshot by author.

Bond (literally and figuratively) did in *OHMSS*, in order to save them; Bond must remain a global exporter and not a national importer which requires him to resist domestication of the self in order to focus on amplification of the global goals of the state. As a result, DiVicenzo has to die, an act which nullifies Bond's choice of wife over monarch and reverses his colonial rejection, thereby bringing him back into the fold as an agent working in service of the state rather than opportunistically for himself. While Bond might be defined by his state-sanctioned missions across the world in service of the empire, he is not granted an identity outside it.

Pardon Me

Although *OHMSS* is an outlier in the James Bond canon, it is the film most concerned with colonial consumption and family lineage. Unlike in other entries in the 1960s and 1970s, Blofeld is not motivated by hubris but rather self-preservation. Leading an unaffiliated international terrorist organization has left him vulnerable to the repercussions of his actions especially without a formidable (colonial) power (like the UK) to back him. He believes that by establishing himself within a prominent lineage and blackmailing the UK into pardoning his crimes, he will gain security and respect. For Blofeld, his (mis)treatment and (mis)use of other people and especially the "Angels of Death" is necessary for him to survive and thrive. While he uses tools and approaches associated with imperialism, he is ultimately vilified for staking personal claims and working outside (rather than for) British colonial state.

While Blofeld can (and should) be vilified for his (mis)treatment of women, it raises the question of whether Bond, who in many respects mirrors Blofeld in this film, is any different through his consumption of women, field tactics, and (re)allocation of resources for personal gain. He works as an agent of colonial power for as long as it benefits him and then replaces one (matriarchal) power for another in his quest for personal fulfillment. In the process, women are consumed, victimized, and discarded; their bodies serve as new colonies/territories to be claimed and controlled.[11] While the "Angels of Death" disappear from the narrative without a trace, Tracy DiVicenzo is murdered on her wedding day. These women are presented as collateral (or even colonial) damage in the struggle between two (white) men fighting to establish their own names and legacies during a time of great change in Britain.

Notes

1. Thank you to Michael Boyce for your thoughts on an earlier draft of this chapter.

2. According to the World Population Prospects produced by the United Nations, in 1969 the world had a population of 3.625 billion with Africa and South America accounting for 354 million and 279 million respectively

3. For a detailed discussion, see Ian Kinane's *Ian Fleming and the Politics of Ambivalence* (2021).

4. The use of such a generic font (with no distinguishing "brand") exemplifies the colonial pursuit in which differences are erased into a bland homogeneity.

5. In *Thunderball* (1965), the SPECTRE headquarters were located in Paris, and Emilio Largo is shown to arrive with the Eiffel Tower visible in the background. France and Switzerland are adjacent to each other, and Blofeld's shift to the latter maintains the Eurocentric positioning of his base of operations.

6. *OHMSS* began filming in late October 1968, eight months after the X Winter Olympics Games in France. Unlike their summer counterpart, the Winter Olympics hosted athletes from just under forty countries, mostly European. Despite their "global" aspirations, this sporting event relayed a Eurocentric perspective of "the world" similar to that of Blofeld. Importantly, Great Britain failed to win a single medal in this competition.

7. This is the first instance of James Bond skiing in a film and reflects the increased popularity of the sport following the 1968 Olympics. As Andreff shows, "skiing practice at the world level was expanding fast after the Grenoble Olympics—the number of skiers in the world multiplied 1.8 times from 1972 to 1980" (2019, 73), and ski holidays increased among the European middle class. Bond's expertise on the slopes further confirms his status as man of refinement and expensive tastes.

8. In *Thunderball*, while Bond leads the attack of Blofeld and his henchpeople underwater, he is actually saved by Domino Derval, who kills Blofeld on the boat. In *OHMSS*, both Bond and the audience are led to believe that Bond killed Blofeld, an incorrect assumption that led to deadly consequences.

9. While the "brother" relationship between Bond and Blofeld is made explicit in the Craig era, *OHMSS* implies a brotherly rivalry of equals through epic coding. The attention to Blofeld's earlobes, suggested to be surgically achieved in order to mimic a significant Bleuchamp genetic trait, recalls other "markings" as identification from literature: Odysseus's marked thigh, Cain's mark. Michael Atkinson's description of this phenomenon in the Arthur Conan Doyle story, "The Red-Headed League," could be referring to Bond and Blofeld: "They are like men of ancient myths, discovering at the heat of battle that that are [symbolically] brothers" (1996, 17).

10. See David Lowbridge-Ellis's "Queer Re-View: *On Her Majesty's Secret Service* (2021).

11. Even Marc-Ange Draco encourages Bond to use force with his daughter and even slaps her into unconsciousness when he cannot compel her with reason.

Bibliography

Andreff, Wladimir. 2019. "The Winter Sports Industry and Winter Olympics in Historical Perspective from Grenoble 1968 to Albertville 1992." In *Historical Perspectives on Sports Economics: Lessons From the Field,* edited by John K. Wilson and Richard Pomfert, 67–90. Cheltenham: Edward Elgar.

Atkinson, Michael. 1996. *The Secret Marriage of Sherlock Holmes and Other Eccentric Readings.* Ann Arbor: The University of Michigan Press.

Downes, Aviston. 2005. "From Boys to Men: Colonial Education, Cricket and Masculinity in the Caribbean, 1870–c.1920." *The International Journal of the History of Sport* 22 (1): 3–21.

Funnell, Lisa. 2018. "Reworking the Bond Girl Concept in the Craig Era Films." *Journal of Popular Film and Television* 20 (46): 11–21.

Funnell, Lisa, and Klaus Dodds. 2017. *Geographies, Genders and Geopolitics of James Bond.* London: Palgrave Macmillan.

Kinane, Ian. 2021. *Ian Fleming and the Politics of Ambivalence.* London: Bloomsbury.

Littler, Jo. 2019. "Normcore Plutocrats in Gold Elevators: Reading the Trump Tower Photographs." *Cultural Politics* 15 (1): 15–28.

Lowbridge-Ellis, David. 2021. "Queer Re-View: *On Her Majesty's Secret Service.*" *LicenceToQueer.com* May 30. https://www.licencetoqueer.com/blog/queer-re-view -on-her-majestys-secret-service.

Ludden, David, ed. 2003. *Reading Subaltern Studies: Critical History, Contested Meaning, and the Globalisation of South Asia.* Delhi: Permanent Black.

McDevitt, Patrick F. 2004. *"May the Best Man Win": Sport, Masculinity, and Nationalism in Great Britain and the Empire, 1880–1935.* London: Palgrave Macmillan.

Negrine, Ralph. 1994. *Politics and the Mass Media in Britain.* Second edition. London: Routledge.

Parris, LaRose T. 2011. "Franz Fanon: Existentialist, Dialectician, and Revolutionary." *Journal of Pan African Studies* 4 (7): 4–23.

Planka, Sabine. 2015. "Female Bodies in the James Bond Title Sequences." In *For His Eyes Only: The Women of James Bond*, edited by Lisa Funnell, 139–147. London: Wallflower Press.

Said, Edward W. 1978. *Orientalism.* New York: Pantheon Books.

Santos, Marlisa. 2015. "'This Never Happened to the Other Fellow': *On Her Majesty's Secret Service* as Bond Women's Film" In *For His Eyes Only: The Women of James Bond,* edited by Lisa Funnell, 101–18. London: Wallflower Press.

Stock, Paul. 2000. "Dial 'M' for Metonym: Universal Experts, M's Office Space, and Empire." *National Identities* 2: 35–47.

Strong, Jeremy. 2018. "James Bond: International Man of Gastronomy?" In *James Bond Uncovered*, edited by Jeremy Black, 61–85. London: Palgrave Macmillan.

Swiss Bankers Association. 2016. "The Swiss Banking Sector: Swiss Value to the UK." https://www.swissbanking.ch/_Resources/Persistent/1/9/3/1 /1931975d3eae560a669a9139b3d70c52e26a3923/SBA_The_Swiss_banking_sec-tor_EN.pdf.

United Nations. 2019. "Overall Total Population—Both Sexes." https://population.un .org/wpp/Download/Standard/Population/.

Verheul, Jaap. 2016. "This Never Happened to the Other Fellow: The Fluctuating Stardom of James Bond and George Lazenby." In *Lasting Screen Stars: Images That Fade and Personas That Endure*, edited by Lucy Bolton and Julie Lobalzo Wright, 217–30. London: Palgrave Macmillan.

Wood, Julia T. 2011. *Gendered Lives: Communication, Gender, and Culture*. 9th Edition. Boston: Wadsworth.

Chapter 8

The (Mediterranean) World Is Not Enough

Locating Europe's Global South in For Your Eyes Only

Paul Michael Johnson

One of the most abiding trademarks of the James Bond franchise is the global scope of diverse international settings it has portrayed. Whether shot on location or re-created through elaborate set design and special effects, each film of the series thrusts the globetrotting spy into remote, cosmopolitan, often exoticized, and sometimes outlandish locales around the world. In some sense, these efforts culminated with *Moonraker* (Gilbert 1979), which, in a bid to capitalize on the booming popularity of the first *Star Wars* (Lucas 1977) film, sent agent 007 into outer space in a script replete with shuttles, an orbital station, laser shoot-outs among the stars, and a sci-fi aesthetic. The next entry in the franchise, *For Your Eyes Only* (Glen 1981; hereafter *FYEO*), would represent an attempt to ground the series, as it were, through a soberer tone, less extravagant story, fewer gadgets, and a tighter budget (Giammarco 2002, 128, 172; Glen 1981; Wilson 1981; "Box Office History" 2022). To a degree, it is true that the grittier realism and vengeance-driven plot of *FYEO* stands out among the megalomaniacal villains, campy vibe, and parodic humor that have become synonymous with the Roger Moore era of 1973–1985 (Bennett and Woollacott 2003, 29). What few critics have observed, however, is the rather more straightforward fact that the 1981 film takes place almost entirely within a southern European milieu, making it only one of two in the canon in which Bond and his fellow characters never abandon the confines of continental Europe.[1]

What implications does this geographical circumscription hold for a franchise that has come to define itself by the exceptionally transnational breadth of its cinematic scenes, shooting locations, and audiences? The question becomes more pointed when we consider that the geographies of *FYEO* are substantially more limited than those of the short stories by Ian Fleming on which it is loosely based, even though the cinematic medium arguably offers a greater range of geographical movement than the generic constraints of the short story. The reasons why, I want to suggest, have less to do with aesthetics—the need to return the franchise to its roots after the galactic scale of *Moonraker*—than they do with politics. *FYEO*, anchored almost exclusively in Greece, Spain, and Italy, summons a much longer, richer history that serves to reinforce intra-European colonialism, casting the Mediterranean region as a parochial site of either leisurely escape or lawlessness at a time when these countries had only recently emerged as attractive destinations for international mass tourism (Obrador Pons et al. 2009, 2). Even if the Mediterranean region has long constituted a "world" in and of itself (Braudel 1996),[2] in what follows I want to suggest that the overt Eurocentrism of *FYEO* is precisely what makes it a prime object of analysis for the series as a whole. True to its title, the film offers a singular vantage from which to scrutinize Bond's worldview: peering from within Europe at once reveals dynamics that operate internally as well as beyond the continent, in addition to a latent Eurocentrism in other films of the storied franchise.

In particular, *FYEO* offers a stark contrast between the spy's native Great Britain and what the cultural theorist Roberto Dainotto has called Europe's "Global South," figured through the film's portrayal of Spain and Greece as agricultural economies with dilapidated infrastructure, antiquated yet charming traditions, ineffective legal systems, and impassioned citizens.[3] While scholars have recently shown how the Bond films assemble "global representational hierarchies" in places like Latin America (Korpisaari and Hakola 2021, 2), few have noted their existence internal to the agent's native Europe. Yet such tropes are neither new nor unique to cinema. The French philosopher Montesquieu, for example, asserted as early as the eighteenth century that "as you move toward the [European] countries of the south, you will believe you have moved away from morality itself: the liveliest passions will increase crime; each will seek to take from others all the advantages that can favor these same passions" (Montesquieu 1989, 234). Much more recent, though in many cases no less problematic, studies have sought to prove that people of the Mediterranean are more emotional than rational (Pennebaker et al. 1996), are plagued by a cult of male virility (Gilmore 1987, 16), or have been governed for centuries by a primitive obsession with honor and shame (Peristiany 1966). More generally, such latitudinal stereotypes are often expressed diachronically, with Southern Europe assumed to represent a more ancient past, to be lagging "behind" the modern, developed, and future-oriented Europe of the North.[4] Rather than simply rehashing these clichés, my analysis will chart a tension between the local and global that in turn reveals deeper cultural, historical, and economic anxieties on the part of the James Bond franchise and its viewers.

Typecasting Spain and Greece

FYEO relays a preview of these clichés within the first quarter-hour of the film, in a scene set aboard the *Triana*, anchored off the Greek island of Corfu. It is there that Melina Havelock arrives to visit her parents, who are covertly using their ship to aid the British government in locating the ATAC, a ballistic missile control system it fears could fall into Soviet hands after sinking off the Albanian coast. Just after she greets her mother and father, however, the pilot who had delivered her to the *Triana*, later identified as the contract killer Hector Gonzalez, doubles back to brutally gun them down. As Havelock turns her head to survey the carnage strewn across the boat's deck, the soundtrack cues a short and melodramatic chorus of strings, tambourines, and cymbals, music which, as she leans over her parents' bloody bodies, gives way to the arpeggiation, tremolo, and *rasgueado* of a classical guitar. These sounds crescendo as Havelock looks up toward the camera and it zooms into an extreme close-up of her eyes, red and afflicted with sudden grief. Much the same musical riff will play when Bond comes face-to-face with her for the first time, shortly after she kills Gonzalez in Spain, thus reinforcing the link between her anguish and unrelenting desire for revenge. Equally significant is how these melodies, rhythms, and choices of instrumentation are meant to evoke the provincial attraction of Southern Europe, its vaguely Old World, folkloric traditions captured in song. Such aural cues likewise signal a tacit link between the fiery nature of the Greek Melina Havelock and that of the Mediterranean enclaves in which she and Bond will circulate throughout the film. Most notable is the degree to which Spain and Greece become subsumed to an overarching Mediterranean representational regime and, in the process, become interchangeable stand-ins for one another. This effect is patent on-screen—the *rasgueado* technique of classical guitar is a decidedly flamenco style from Iberia, despite its playing when the camera focuses on Havelock—as well as behind it: despite the film's extended scene outside Madrid, shooting never took place in Spain, with studio lots and, especially, the Greek landscape serving instead as a proxy. Conflation of this sort confirms that the writers and director sought to leverage common tropes that would be received by audiences with a remotely archaic, Mediterranean feel.

Indeed, in contrast with the staid aura of MI6 headquarters in the previous scene, Bond's arrival in Spain is heralded by the spirited sounds of Spanish guitar, the rhythmic percussion of tambourines and castanets, and blaring trumpets. This stereotypically local flair (which, if anything, is more representative of Southern Spain rather than Madrid) is complemented by subtle yet unmistakable visual cues that emerge as Bond's Lotus Esprit rounds the turn of a winding rural road. These include livestock and people in the roadway, peasants wearing straw hats and traditional attire, and farmers manually harvesting olives. Appearing lost, Bond consults a road map before making a U-turn, suggesting a labyrinthine system of byways lacking proper signage and order. He eventually locates the villa harboring Gonzalez, who, before Bond can investigate further, is summarily killed by Havelock. A chase ensues, which allows for a barrage of additional details that reinforce the Spanish setting as charmingly antiquated. As the speeding vehicles struggle to traverse a small village, viewers are afforded a glimpse of workers repairing crumbling stucco facades and dilapidated walls while propped up on rickety wooden ladders; old women in bonnets hanging their laundry on clotheslines among flowers and wicker baskets; and more peasants in straw hats selling produce along the narrow streets. After the sudden appearance of an aging regional bus causes Bond and Havelock's escape vehicle to overturn, a congregation of local villagers rallies to their aid, managing to flip it back over and restart it with a push, a triumph they swiftly celebrate by cheering, howling, and waving their arms in the air (Figure 8.1). The fleeting scene is almost evocative of a crowd at a bullfight, their gleeful vigor tinged by a hint of machismo. The pursuit resumes outside of town on the same maze-like roads foreshadowed earlier and teeming with decrepit old trucks and peasants. Bond and Havelock finally escape their pursuers by crisscrossing through the rough, mountainous terrain of the olive groves, maneuvers that allow Bond to jest, "I love a drive in the country, don't you?"

His quip underscores how the film relays the impression of a simultaneous backwardness yet romantic allure of Spain, rendering it an appealing foil for

Figure 8.1. Still from *For Your Eyes Only*.
Source: EON Productions et al., 1981. Screenshot by author.

modern, metropolitan London. Greece, too, partakes of these dynamics with what are often nearly identical visual and aural cues. Near the end of the film, in a brief scene set in a village called St. Cyril's, Bond must make his way across a plaza thronged with celebrants of a traditional Greek wedding. After dodging the costumed, clapping, singing, and dancing revelers, he enters the confessional booth of a quaint Greek Orthodox church to meet with Q and ascertain the whereabouts of the villain's lair. Disguised as a bearded priest, the quartermaster remarks to Bond that "so far we've managed to locate 439 St. Cyrils in Greece. Heaven only knows to which one Kristatos took the ATAC." While echoing the depiction of Spain as a homogenous, parochial backwater in need of greater order, the befuddled Q's statement conveys the sense of a country beset by the cult of sainthood, an inordinate religiosity that is reinforced by the visual imagery of the setting at large. In like fashion, the site of the final action scene and Kristatos's secret hideout is an ancient monastery adorned with stained glass and Byzantine religious art, to which Columbo and his entourage travel in the guise of monks or religious pilgrims. Despite noting in passing that the monastery has been abandoned, that reality for Columbo apparently does not diminish the effectiveness of the disguise. Rather uncannily, these details accentuate the already heightened artifice of the film's representation of Southern Europe, its primitive local color contrasting with the global, cosmopolitan aura of Bond and his native Britain.

Similar tropes emerge earlier in the film, such as when Bond accompanies Havelock on a walk through the center of Corfu Town. Throughout their stroll, viewers are treated to elegant yet crumbling facades and narrow pedestrian streets lined with Greek-speaking fruit sellers hawking their wares. In one crowded square, the main characters happen upon two men dancing a folkloric jig, accompanied by guitar and mandolin or bouzouki players, seemingly meant to reflect a famous scene in the popular film *Zorba the Greek* (Cacoyannis 1964) (Figure 8.2). While the locals and tourists alike clap along with the music, Bond cracks an expression somewhere between bemused and supercilious, and in general remains stiffly aloof from the festive atmosphere while bantering with Havelock, who is shown to feel blissfully at ease. After cutting swiftly to an evening tableau with a vista of the sea, she breaks down crying at the thought of her father, whom she remarks "loved the view from here." Significantly, the beloved view in question was filmed at the Maitland monument, erected to honor an English military officer who served as commissioner of the Ionian islands, a British possession throughout much of the nineteenth century. Though it would be lost on many viewers of the film, this colonially freighted detail, like the monument itself, stands as a potent reminder of Britain's imperial past, while more subtly signaling its ongoing ambitions for extraterritorial influence. As James Chapman has noted, Fleming's Bond novels "represent a nationalist fantasy

Figure 8.2. Still from *For Your Eyes Only*.
Source: EON Productions et al. 1981. Screenshot by author.

in which Britain's decline as a world power did not really take place. One of the ideological functions of the Bond narrative is to construct an imaginary world in which the *Pax Britannica* still operates" (Chapman 2000, 38–39). One of the primary means by which this "nationalist fantasy" remains intact on the silver screen, I would suggest, is by setting the films in former British colonies, where, though its absolute sovereignty has been revoked, the United Kingdom may at least boast some lingering cultural clout and symbolic capital. This is the case with India, Pakistan, Jamaica, the Bahamas, Hong Kong, and South Africa, locales featured in other Bond films and which are either members of the Commonwealth or, at one time or another, have formed part of Britain's overseas domains.

In the Mediterranean, this same dynamic obtains with Egypt (included extensively in *The Spy Who Loved Me* [Gilbert 1977]), Gibraltar (a British possession to this day that opens *The Living Daylights* [Glen 1987]), and Malta. This latter island nation, historically the base of the Royal Navy's Mediterranean Fleet and Allied Forces Mediterranean, a NATO command that the UK held in the 1950s and 1960s, receives its own nod in *FYEO*, as the ship carrying the ATAC weighs anchor out of Malta's capital of La Valletta. That Britain is operating a top secret ballistic missile tracking system on a ship disguised as a fishing boat sailing from Malta, in fact, originates the conflict central to the premise of Bond's mission and the film at large. Though set in a sufficiently vague Cold War–era milieu, it is perhaps telling that, when *FYEO* premiered in 1981, Britain had relinquished control of its last Maltese territories scarcely two years earlier. Like the decision to locate several scenes of the film on Corfu, whose historical ties to the UK exceed those of any other region in Greece, such details thus not only render the storyline more credible and realistic, but also telegraph the notion of a Great Britain still looming large in the Mediterranean even after its official exit from the arena. More than the overtly geopolitical stakes of these details, what I wish to underscore is their cultural symbolism, which has tended to be overlooked in geopolitical analyses of the film (for instance, McMorrow 2011, 422–26). To cite merely one example, the sequence at a palatial Corfiot casino, where Bond plays high-stakes baccarat with British expats and global jetsetters in his midst, advances a telling opposition between the wealth and economic power of foreign visitors and the far more meager subsistence of the vendors, peddlers, and service workers portrayed in the city center of the previous scene. In this sense, the underwater Hellenic archaeological ruins being excavated by the *Triana*, highlighted in several camera shots, serve as a compelling metaphor for a once illustrious yet now decrepit Greek civilization in need of charitable rescue.

Melina Havelock's Mediterranean Embodiment

Yet nowhere is the contrast between Northern and Southern Europe more patent, perhaps, than in the main characters' cars: Bond's white Lotus Esprit Turbo, a sleek, fast, and aerodynamic luxury sports coupe, versus Havelock's banana-yellow Citroën 2CV, a bare-bones, budget-friendly hatchback with meager horsepower and speed, a veritable jalopy and proverbial clown car if ever there was one. Whereas the Lotus was manufactured in Britain, one of the highest-volume assembly plants of the French marque of Citroën was in Vigo, Spain, where the 2CV proved practical and popular for a growing domestic market in the 1950s and 1960s. Bond's Lotus could not appear more out of place among the Spanish olive groves, and in fact it proves completely useless, since it promptly explodes when one of the villains tries to break into it—demonstrating that Q's security system for the car was, so to speak, overkill. Its fate leaves Havelock's 2CV as an unlikely yet highly effective savior. Though it is hopelessly sluggish alongside the villains' full-sized sedans, its lighter weight, higher ground clearance, and beefier suspension are ideally suited for the topography of the narrow, winding roads and plantations. Though the question is moot after the Lotus self-detonates, one wonders whether all its speed and presumably high-tech gadgets and weaponry would have been superfluous anyway.

But just as the two vehicles figure the symbolic capital of their respective national origins—the United Kingdom as modern, urban, and refined, and Spain as underdeveloped, rural, and utilitarian—so too are they emblematic, in a sense, of their drivers. Havelock reconnoiters the villa outside Madrid in a dark khaki ensemble complete with wide-brimmed hat and mosquito net; Bond, while leaving behind the iconic tuxedo, sports a more formal white button-down oxford, brown jacket, slacks, and penny loafers. It may be that this choice of attire is what allows the guards to quickly capture Bond, while Havelock manages to avoid falling into their hands despite being Gonzalez's true assassin. Having grown up on the *Triana*, the young Havelock encountered all sides of the Mediterranean, including the Greek islands, Turkey, and North Africa. In addition to the vengeful spirit she will ascribe to her Greek heritage, it is that background that seems to have endowed her with a strong sense of self-reliance, survival, practical knowledge, and ease in passing in and out of different geographical spaces. Because she does not fully escape the sexism and patriarchal structures that have more typically attended the franchise, I cannot agree that the "often overlooked heroine" of Havelock necessarily "represents the values of radical feminism" (Pagnoni Berns 2015, 122), though it is true that very few of the franchise's women characters approach her decisiveness and ongoing resolve. What interests me, in any case, is how the deceptively complex Havelock becomes a material and symbolic stand-in for the Mediterranean itself, and how her regional, national, and ethnic heritage becomes another intersectional vector, alongside gender, for subverting the more dominant narrative of the film. Although gender stereotypes since antiquity have cast women as hysterical, susceptible to emotion, and incapable of reason, a similar chauvinism, as I have already noted, attended inhabitants of the Mediterranean basin. If Havelock at once conforms to some of the franchise's more troubling gender norms yet also stands out for challenging them, she likewise embodies yet simultaneously resists the conventional boilerplates of Mediterranean identity.[5]

After Bond and Havelock escape to safety in Spain, he attempts to help her find a departing flight, but she informs him of her intention to continue pursuing those responsible for her parents' murder. With no small dosage of paternalism, he then admonishes her about seeking vengeance, quoting an ostensibly Chinese proverb that "before setting out on revenge, you first dig two graves." Reacting defiantly, she replies, "I don't expect you to understand. You're English. But I'm half-Greek. And Greek women, like Electra, always avenge their loved ones." The film then immediately cues in the same dramatic, recurring musical jingle infused with vaguely Spanish guitar, reinforcing once again the association between Southern Europe and the impassioned, impulsive, and lawless nature of its inhabitants, as though they were governed not by a modern, centralized judicial system but by antiquated clan- and kinship-based norms of popular retribution. By ascribing her duty to avenge her parents to a distant ethnic origin, moreover, the contrast between the British/Northern and the Greek/Southern is rendered even more explicit. In other words, Havelock draws her motivation as much from her gender identity as from a regional one. The Greek character of Columbo serves as a complementary example. When Bond first meets him, Columbo promptly returns the agent's gun to him, attributing the risky act of goodwill to his instinct for being "a good judge of men" and declaring that Bond appears to have "what the Greeks call *thrassos*," or "guts." As a swarthy, swashbuck-ling smuggler of "gold, diamonds, cigarettes, [and] pistachio nuts," it is as though the character of Columbo were meant to embody an updated, 1980s version of the Mediterranean's longstanding reputation for piracy. Though he develops an affinity for Bond through a local idiom of masculinity, he is, like Havelock, charming in his mettle and irrational courage. More generally, both Columbo and Kristatos derive their livelihood from the illegal trafficking of goods, and, in a significant metafictional moment, Bond uses as a cover the pretense that he is a novelist writing a book about Greek smugglers.[6]

This focus on vengeance and illegality, which recalls Montesquieu's tendentious pronouncements on Southern Europe's supposed inclination toward criminality, is ironic because a case can be made that Havelock's behavior is not just more prudent but also more ethical than Bond's. At the casino, Kristatos advises Bond that "the odds favor standing pat," to which the gambling spy responds, "if you play the odds," a mantra he will repeat moments later when warned that pursuing the forsaken Countess Lisl von Schlaf, Columbo's lover, may be a trap. Such conduct is anything but rational and, of course, very much in keeping with the character's ethos. Yet if Bond and Havelock both behave somewhat impulsively, the difference is that the former does so with all the privileges of his profession—legal, financial, and physical protections—that allow him to confront adverse situations with characteristic nonchalance. For Havelock, the stakes are in many ways much higher, for she must navigate the dangers of her personal vendetta alone, with almost none of the resources readily available to an agent of her Majesty's government, all while grieving the death of her parents. Even though her bereavement is only rarely, if ever, shown to hinder her ability to cope with the circumstances at hand, the script casts her as a vengeful, emotional, rather ingenuous, and unpredictable individual in need of (Northern European) men's control. Even her acts of compassion—such as when she mercifully tends to the wound of a guard she has shot at the monastery—are treated less as an ethical stance than as a naive sentimentality that could put her comrades at risk. Bond's actions, in contrast, are necessarily unquestioned, as if they were the only natural, logical response to a given scenario, even when they too are motivated at least partly by revenge. The most patent example of this is when Bond kicks Locque's vehicle off a cliff, making him careen to his death. This is, in fact, one of the most ruthless moments of the Roger Moore films, in which the character almost never kills an unarmed assailant or reacts in cold blood.

Othering Southern Europe, in Theory and History

Though these ironies work to subvert or at least disrupt certain dominant hierarchies of the franchise, *FYEO* represents Southern Europe as largely stagnant, as though suspended in a premodern era. As my analysis has shown, the film leverages visual scenery, the musical soundtrack, the personality and actions of supporting characters, and other subtle details to forward a largely stereotypical depiction of the Mediterranean, marked by underdeveloped infrastructure, lawlessness, and passionate, irrational individuals. I would like to conclude by returning to the question posed at the outset as to why the film declined to include action outside the bounds of Europe, and what this more limited setting might mean for our understanding of the global phenomenon that is the James Bond franchise. First, from a theoretical perspective, the very existence of a primitivist sketch of Southern Europe in the film suggests, in a sense, a rather simple reason for why its action never ventures elsewhere: it didn't need to. In his philosophical and historical analysis of the phenomenon of Eurocentrism, Roberto Dainotto demonstrates how, around the eighteenth century, Europe begins to curtail its long-standing tendency to hold Asia as an Other against which to define itself, as a foil to perpetuate its self-deluded identity of moral and civilizational superiority. "A modern European identity," he explains, "begins when the non-Europe is internalized—when the south, indeed, becomes the sufficient and indispensable *internal* Other: Europe, but also the negative part of it" (Dainotto 2007, 4). Negative representations of Europe's "global South," then, became necessary for the continent to curb its dependence on those beyond its borders and, therefore, for the proliferation of Eurocentric theories about Europe: "Eurocentrism *needs* a figure of antithesis internal to Europe itself—it *needs* to posit a 'south' as the negative moment in the dialectical progress of the Spirit of Europe" (Dainotto 2011, 39). Interpreted in this light, by emphasizing Spain and Greece as unruly yet attractive backwaters, as internal others, *FYEO* could re-create the global, and often colonial, dynamic of the franchise, all without breaking the bank.[7] Bond no longer needed to gallivant around the world to annihilate threats to British assets and civilized order when those threats were already lurking in his own backyard.

Second, on a more practical plane, that *FYEO* takes place almost exclusively in the UK, Spain, Italy, and Greece may respond to the historical material conditions at play in these countries around the time of the film's development and premiere. Both Greece and Spain had only recently regained democratic governments, with the former having emerged from a military junta (1967–1974) and the latter, from the long dictatorship of Francisco Franco (1939–1975). After intermittent periods of international isolation, economic recession, and civil unrest, both nations were by the early

1980s reclaiming their place on the European and global stages while building on their reputations as seductive international tourist destinations. The UK, meanwhile, was only beginning to recover from an economic downturn of its own, which began in the late sixties and culminated with the Winter of Discontent of 1978–1979. Ironically, these events led the country to be diagnosed as the "sick man of Europe," an epithet which had more often been applied to those same Southern European countries that, due to their recurrent financial woes, would during later efforts at continental integration be branded with the derogatory acronym of PIGS (Portugal, Italy, Greece, and Spain). Regardless, in the wake of the mounting losses of Britain's few remaining colonial possessions, Southern Europe had become an even more enticing playground for expats and snowbirds in search of foreign leisure, sunny beaches, and cheap goods. Some countries like Spain even capitalized on these associations, drawing on long-standing commonplaces to develop the slogan "Passion for Life" for its tourist industry, all while emphasizing its old-world charm.[8] Anachronistic as they often were, such tropes were thus in the early eighties also opportune for a budding domestic hospitality industry in the Mediterranean. If on the one hand *FYEO* can best be understood within this evolving, intra-European landscape of competing economies, geopolitical rivalries, and mutual allure, then, on the other, the film served as a timely reminder to viewers that, despite a newly ascendant Southern Europe, Great Britain was still superior in terms of modernization and refinement. Amid a changing Europe and the national anxieties and fantasies it generated, what better avatar to stake a claim for the ongoing cultural and political authority of England than James Bond?

Though *FYEO* would be the first and last Bond movie to date to feature Greece, Spain would serve as the opening setting of 1999's *The World Is Not Enough* (Apted). By then a fully integrated member of the European Union, Spain's representation in the film differs radically from that of the early eighties. Immediately after the iconic gun barrel sequence, viewers see Bond walking through the urban center of Bilbao, an industrial city in the northern Basque Country. Though the soundtrack cannot resist a fleeting flourish of Spanish guitar as the camera pans to spotlight the city's newly opened Guggenheim Museum, a visually stunning, avant-garde architectural masterpiece designed by Frank Gehry, the scene is otherwise free of the commonplaces that had typecast Spain as a provincial backwater some two decades earlier. Instead, with the action centering on a financial transaction gone awry, Spain is portrayed as the modern, economically vibrant EU member state that it was—despite the fact that the banker character central to the scene, conspicuously, is not Spanish but Swiss. The evolving depiction of Southern Europe in the Bond movies reminds us that, to an extent, they are subject to international geopolitical forces that operate behind the screen and, in some cases, beyond a more limited fictional setting. To meet the demands of the box office and a global audience, it appears the franchise attempts to balance the weight of tradition with the imperative of contemporary cultural relevance, echoing the historical conditions in which a given film was created. James Bond is a product of his time, even when it seems that some tropes never die.

Notes

1. Besides Bond's customary visits to MI6 headquarters in London, the only potential exception is a minor scene in Moscow, which lasts under a minute. *On Her Majesty's Secret Service* (Hunt 1969) is the only other film by Eon Productions to eschew other continents, since even the first two entries, *Dr. No* (Young 1962) and *From Russia with Love* (Young 1963), included British Jamaica and Turkey, respectively.

2. There is a long, troubling history of neglecting North Africa and the Near East in much purportedly Mediterranean scholarship, as I have noted elsewhere (Johnson 2020, 31–32). Because the present chapter will focus above all on stereotypes of the Mediterranean and their corollary Eurocentrism, however, I will refer to the Mediterranean as well as the more precise toponym of Southern Europe.

3. Italy is largely spared from this Mediterranean typecasting, as the action there centers on Cortina d'Ampezzo and revolves around the theme of winter Olympic sports.

4. These dynamics also materialize spatially through the vertical and horizontal, as Lisa Funnell and Klaus Dodds have elucidated with respect to the Bond franchise's depiction of East Asian versus South, Southeast, and Southwest Asian cities (Funnell and Dodds 2017, 109–34).

5. For a more thorough discussion of the gender politics of the Bond franchise than the cursory treatment I can offer here, see Funnell 2015.

6. Umberto Eco observed long ago that Bond villains often possess an ethnic heritage from Central or Southern Europe, and specifically noted the Mediterranean, along with other physical, sexual traits that marked them as villainous (Eco 2003, 40–41).

7. As noted above, *FYEO*'s budget was smaller than *Moonraker*'s, which was the most expensive film to produce of the Moore era ("Box Office History" 2022).

8. For more discussion of the Spanish tourist boom, its relationship to the dictatorship, and the more contentious and widely known slogan of "Spain Is Different," see Crumbaugh 2009, esp. 41–86.

Bibliography

Bennett, Tony, and Janet Woollacott. 2003. "The Moments of Bond." In *The James Bond Phenomenon: A Critical Reader,* edited by Christoph Lindner, 13–33. Manchester: Manchester University Press.

"Box Office History for James Bond Movies." 2022. *The Numbers*. Nash Information Services, 2022. https://www.the-numbers.com/movies/franchise/James-Bond#tab =summary.

Braudel, Fernand. 1996. *The Mediterranean and the Mediterranean World in the Age of Philip II*. Translated by Siân Reynolds. Berkeley: University of California Press.

Chapman, James. 2007. *Licence to Thrill: A Cultural History of the James Bond Films*. 2nd ed. London: I. B. Tauris.

Crumbaugh, Justin. 2009. *Destination Dictatorship: The Spectacle of Spain's Tourist Boom and the Reinvention of Difference*. Albany: SUNY Press.

Dainotto, Roberto M. 2007. *Europe (in Theory)*. Durham, NC: Duke University Press.

———. 2011. "Does Europe Have a South?: An Essay on Borders." *The Global South* 5 (1): 37–50.

Eco, Umberto. 2003. "Narrative Structures in Fleming." In *The James Bond Phenomenon: A Critical Reader*, edited by Christoph Lindner, 34–55. Manchester: Manchester University Press.

Fernandez, James W. 1983. "Consciousness and Class in Southern Spain." *American Ethnologist* 10: 165–73.

Fleming, Ian. (1960) 2006. *For Your Eyes Only*. London: Penguin Books.

Funnell, Lisa, ed. 2015. *For His Eyes Only: The Women of James Bond*. London: Wallflower Press.

Funnell, Lisa, and Klaus Dodds. 2017. *Geographies, Genders and Geopolitics of James Bond*. London: Palgrave Macmillan.

Giammarco, David. 2002. *For Your Eyes Only: Behind the Scenes of the James Bond Films*. Toronto: ECW Press.

Gilmore, David D. 1987. "Introduction: The Shame of Dishonor." In *Honor and Shame and the Unity of the Mediterranean*, edited by Gilmore, 2–21. Washington, DC: American Anthropological Association.

Glen, John. 1981. Audio Commentary. *For Your Eyes Only*. United Artists.

Johnson, Paul Michael. 2020. *Affective Geographies: Cervantes, Emotion, and the Literary Mediterranean*. Toronto: University of Toronto Press.

Korpisaari, Antti, and Outi J. Hakola. 2021. "The Portrayal of Continental Latin America in the James Bond Films." *The International Journal of James Bond Studies* 4 (1): 1–19. http://doi.org/10.24877/jbs.66.

McMorrow, Jack. 2011. "'Mr. Kiss Kiss, Bang Bang': The Effects of Geo Politics in the 1980s, 1990s and 2000 on the James Bond Movies *For Your Eyes Only*, *Goldeneye*, and *Casino Royale*." In *James Bond in World and Popular Culture, Second Edition*, edited by Robert G. Weiner, B. Lynn Whitfield, and Jack Becker, 422–37. Newcastle upon Tyne: Cambridge Scholars Publishing.

Montesquieu. 1989. *The Spirit of the Laws*. Edited and translated by Anne M. Cohler, Basia Carolyn Miller, and Harold Samuel Stone. Cambridge: Cambridge University Press.

Obrador Pons, Pau, Mike Crang, and Penny Travlou, eds. 2009. *Cultures of Mass Tourism: Doing the Mediterranean in the Age of Banal Mobilities*. Farnham: Ashgate.

Pagnoni Berns, Fernando Gabriel. 2015. "Sisterhood as Resistance in *For Your Eyes Only* and *Octopussy*." In *For His Eyes Only: The Women of James Bond*, edited by Lisa Funnell, 119–27. London: Wallflower Press.

Pennebaker, James W., Bernard Rimé, and Virginia E. Blankenship. 1996. "Stereotypes of Emotional Expressiveness of Northerners and Southerners: A Cross-Cultural Test of Montesquieu's Hypotheses." *Journal of Personality and Social Psychology* 70 (2): 372–80.

Peristiany, J. G., ed. 1966. *Honour and Shame: The Values of Mediterranean Society*. Chicago: University of Chicago Press.

Wilson, Michael G. 1981. Audio Commentary. *For Your Eyes Only*. United Artists.

Afterword

"Take Me Around the World One More Time"

James Page

The mystery of James Bond's enduring popularity has been puzzling studio executives for decades. Like *Thunderball*, their fight for answers goes on, and on, and on. Is it fortune or foresight that propels Bond through decade after decade? The real challenge though for rivals to the Bond franchise, and increasingly itself, is Hollywood's hesitancy for risk.

As one of the key voices behind the delay of *No Time To Die* (Fukunaga 2021) when COVID-19 was about to hit pandemic status in early 2020 (see MI6 2020), I spent a lot of time analyzing the box office performance of the Daniel Craig era in over eighty countries around the world to project what the film's earnings could be if various territories were open or closed for business. We were convinced at the time that MGM and Universal were working from a similar spreadsheet, but it turned out that decisions were being made more by gut instinct than mathematics, with a sprinkling of wishful thinking (i.e., "It sounds like the Chinese authorities are doing everything they can to contain it"—Barbara Broccoli) (Siegel 2021).

Beyond the dismal outlook for its ill-fated April 2020 release, a picture emerged of a shift in power of box office territories. Whilst the early era of Bond was dominated by UK and US takings, with a healthy boost from Western Europe and Japan, modern-day Bond fortunes were steered by countries hitherto unreachable by 007 such as Russia and China. Both of these countries are now in the top ten territories for a Bond release.

When China started to open its cinemas to foreign-made films in the 2000s, only one or two Western blockbusters were permitted per year. *Casino Royale* (Campbell 2006) was the first James Bond film to open there, and in 2006 brought in $11.8 million (all figures are given in USD)—a new market that 007 had not earned from before. Although the studios only see 50 percent of the money, the potential for China could not be ignored, and the gold rush was on. Takings would grow film by film for Craig's run: $20.6 million for *Quantum of Solace* (Forster 2008), $59 million for *Skyfall* (Mendes 2012), and $84 million for *Spectre* (Mendes 2016). When the gigantic production budget of $290 million was set for *No Time To Die*, the break-even point for profitability was set to be around $950 million through its theatrical release. Part of the calculation was an expectation of $100 million from China. Even when social-distancing restrictions were eased in China and cinemas started to return to normal in late 2021, the box-office for *No Time To Die* came in at half of that estimated pre-pandemic: just $49.2 million. It was a big blow to a film that the exhibition industry was hoping would save their post-pandemic fortunes (see Johnson and Funnell 2022) and proof that nothing in this world is guaranteed.

It is perhaps counterintuitive, then, that although Bond has found new audiences around the world and the markets for his adventures have expanded, the profitability of the films have plummeted. When considering return on investment (ROI) calculations, all five of the Daniel Craig era films rank in the bottom third, and that is without taking into account marketing costs. The overriding factor in this? Spiraling production budgets.

The two most financially successful films of the Craig era in terms of ROI—*Casino Royale* and *Skyfall*—share one thing in common beyond their critical success: a reduced budget with crafty use of location work and a back-to-basics production ethic. Both use cheaper production bases to double for more expensive locales, but still manage to ground the viewer in a sense of the real world. Craig never set foot in Miami International Airport or a Macau casino, but audiences believed he did. Compare that to the overblown expense of shoots in the African desert for *Spectre* or Gravina di Puglia in *No Time To Die* that used CGI to augment the real-world locations so much so that it corrupted the authentic sense of space with artificial overproduced sheen, defeating the purpose of the location work (if you want a homework assignment, analyze how much of the natural beauty of the Italian landscape behind Bond's jump off the bridge in *No Time To Die* is augmented and later wiped out by CGI from early sneak peak, through various trailers and then TV spots, to the final film). Earlier films in the series that did not have the crutch or luxury of CGI enamored their audiences with location work, whether it was the ski slopes of Cortina in *For Your Eyes Only* (Glen 1981) or the Junkanoo in the Bahamas in *Thunderball* (Young 1965)—these were places that felt real. The latter is a great example of how modern productions have diluted the authenticity of locations. Whereas the Junkanoo was a real festival (see if you can spot local residents with fourth-wall-breaking "007" signs in the parade), the attempt to re-create a similar festival for *Spectre* was the opposite: it was entirely concocted for the film with the art department controlling every costume, every float, and every makeup design. It did not feel real because it wasn't. Ironically, the Day of the Dead festival in Mexico City has now become a real annual event due to demand from the tourism industry.

As these examples demonstrate, authenticity has waxed and waned throughout the sixty years of the franchise, as have cinema trends and fashions. Whilst the early films invented new cinematic language and raised the bar for action adventure, by the late 1970s after the departure of coproducer Harry Saltzman, the franchise started to follow rather than lead. Bold bets slipped away in favor of safe calculations. Which other filmmakers would take their hero to Japan in 1967 when postwar prejudices in large portions of the US audience were still rampant? Or cast an unknown nonactor to take over the lead role in 1969 at the height of "Bondmania"? (see Chapman 2007) Or feature an interracial love scene in 1973? Or consider packing Roger Moore off to civil-war-torn communist Cambodia for location work? The Hollywood decision-by-spreadsheet mentality now rules out such endeavors. One such whiff of an at-bat was the rising popularity of Bollywood with Western markets in the 2000s, with stars such as Aishwarya Rai grabbing headlines as Bond girl rumors swirled around Pierce Brosnan's fourth film. Producers passed on the idea, but reconsidered India as a possibility for *Skyfall*, only for the number crunchers to dictate that location work for the pre-title sequence would be more favorable and less risky in Istanbul. India will overtake China as the world's most populist country this year, but the Western film industry couldn't be less interested as the box-office takings can't leave the country easily.

Tough decisions are ahead for the next incarnation of James Bond, but if the way it has been produced for the past fifteen years is anything to go by, we can expect safe bets that are designed to mitigate risk with global audiences: location work in tax-break countries regardless of story, overbearing CGI touch-ups of anything out of place, plots that don't have any agendas, and no more Chinese bad guys.

An alternate future is a return to the roots of the franchise: cutting-edge geopolitical threats; bold casting choices that push against societal norms; audience-challenging themes; smaller budgets that stoke creativity; and authentic location work.

Long after you know the plot and can quote the lines of dialogue verbatim, we come back to these films for a sense of place and time. We don't just want to be James Bond. We want to be James Bond *when* and *where* he is. I may have cashed in my Big Ask coupon with producers already, but if I had another it would be, in the words of Holly Goodhead, "take me around the world one more time."

Bibliography

Chapman, James. 2007. *Licence to Thrill: A Cultural History of the James Bond Films.* 2nd ed. London: I. B. Tauris.

Johnson, Tyler, and Lisa Funnell. 2022. "No Time To Die, Literally: Risk, Fandom, and Theatergoing during the COVID-19 Pandemic." *Popular Culture Review* 33 (2): 41–76.

MI6 Staff. 2020. "No Time for Indecision." MI6-HQ.com March 2. https://www.mi6-hq.com/sections/articles/opinion-delay-no-time-to-die-release-corona-virus-pandemic?id=04666.

Siegel, Tatiana. 2021. "No Time To Lose: Hollywood Pins Its Hopes on Bond Director Cary Fukunaga." *The Hollywood Reporter*, September 22. https://www.hollywoodreporter.com/movies/movie-features/bond-director-cary-fukunaga-no-time-to-die-1235017724/.

Index

Page numbers in italic indicate figures and tables

About the Contributors

Rea Amit is assistant professor in the Department of Modern Languages, Literatures and Linguistics at the University of Oklahoma. He has published mainly on Asian media, aesthetics, and theory in journals such as Philosophy East and West, Positions: Asia Critique, Participations: International Journal of Audience Research, Animation Studies, and On_Culture—The Open Journal for the Study of Culture, as well as several book chapters in edited volumes.

Klaus Dodds is executive dean of the School of Life Sciences and Environment and professor of geopolitics at Royal Holloway, University of London, as well as a fellow of the Academy of Social Sciences. He has published many books and articles concerned with the geopolitics of James Bond and popular geopolitics including *Border Wars* (Penguin 2022) which has been translated into many languages.

Swarnavel Eswaran is associate professor in the Department of English and the School of Journalism at Michigan State University. His documentaries include *Nagapattinam: Waves from the Deep* (2018), *Hmong Memories at the Crossroad* (2016), and *Migrations of Islam* (2014). His research focuses on Tamil cinema's history, aesthetics, and politics, the contemporary digital era, and concomitant changes in film production, distribution, and reception. His books include *Tamil Cinema Reviews: 1931–1960* (Nizhal 2020) and *Madras Studios: Narrative, Genre, and Ideology in Tamil Cinema* (Sage 2015). His fiction feature *Kattumaram* (Catamaran 2019) has been screened in over fifty film festivals, including the prestigious Frameline, InsideOut, and Kashish.

Lisa Funnell is associate dean of creative industries at Mohawk College in Canada. She specializes in gender and geopolitics in the James Bond franchise and other action films. She is the author of *Geographies, Genders, and Geopolitics of James Bond* (Palgrave Macmillan 2017) with Klaus Dodds, editor of *For His Eyes Only: The Women of James Bond* (Wallflower Press 2015), and editor of *Resisting James Bond: Power and Privilege in the Daniel Craig Era* (Bloomsbury 2023) with Christoph Lindner, among other award-winning monographs, anthologies, and articles.

Monica Germanà is reader in gothic and contemporary studies at the University of Westminster. Her most recent publications include *The Scottish Gothic: An Edinburgh Companion* (2018), coedited with Carol Davison and short-listed for the Allan Lloyd Prize, *Bond Girls: Body, Fashion, Gender* (Bloomsbury 2019), short-listed for the Emily Toth Award, and a special issue of *Gothic Studies* on haunted Scotlands (March 2022). She has also published articles and chapters on various aspects of the Bond franchise and (global) gothic popular culture.

Aaron D. Horton is professor of history at Alabama State University and specializes in modern Japanese and German cultural history. He is the author of *POWs,* Der Ruf, *and the Genesis of Group 47: The Political Journey of Alfred Andersch and Hans Werner Richter* (Fairleigh Dickenson University Press 2014). His recent publications, including several book chapters and the edited volume *Identity in Professional Wrestling: Essays on Nationality, Race and Gender* (McFarland 2018), deal with the confluences of identity and popular culture in film, music, and sports.

Paul Michael Johnson is associate professor of Hispanic studies at DePauw University and a 2023–2024 visiting fellow at Harvard's Houghton Library. Trained as a specialist in early modern Spanish literature, his research has encompassed such topics as the history of emotion, visual and sound studies, oceanic studies, public monuments, and translation. In addition to his book *Affective Geographies: Cervantes, Emotion, and the Literary Mediterranean* (University of Toronto Press 2020), his work has appeared in venues such as *PMLA, Bulletin of Spanish Studies, MLN,* and the *Norton Critical Edition of "Don Quijote."*

Antti Korpisaari holds a PhD in Latin American studies and an MA in archaeology. He is university lecturer of Latin American studies at the University of Helsinki, Finland. Korpisaari's key publications include the monographs *Death in the Bolivian High Plateau: Burials and Tiwanaku Society* (Archaeopress 2006) and *Pariti: The Ceremonial Tiwanaku Pottery of an Island in Lake Titicaca* (Academia Scientiarum Fennica 2011), the edited *volume El Horizonte Medio: Nuevos aportes para el sur de Perú, norte de Chile y Bolivia* (Institut Français d'Etudes Andines 2015), and, in the field of

James Bond studies, the article "The Portrayal of Continental Latin America in the James Bond Films" (2021).

James Page is cofounder of the most visited James Bond website MI6-HQ.com, the print magazine *MI6 Confidential*, and the podcast *James Bond & Friends*. Over the past twenty-five years, he has journaled the franchise's twists and turns on a daily basis, interviewed hundreds of cast and crew, written thousands of articles, and consulted on the history of 007 with product licensees, documentary makers, comic book publishers, video game studios, and mainstream media outlets.

Jessica Siu-yin Yeung is research assistant professor at the Centre for Film and Creative Industries of Lingnan University. Her essays have appeared in *Cultural History, Archiv orientální, Journal of World Literature, Humans at Work in the Digital Age*, and *Cultural Conflict in Hong Kong*. She coedited a special issue on *Comedies in East Asian Media* of *Archiv orientální* with Ta-wei Chi and Elaine Chung. She is working on a few essays on Hong Kong and Taiwan literature and cinema during the Cold War and writing a book on semiotics, queerness, and allegory in Taiwan and Hong Kong novels and cinema.

David Wilt, PhD, is a film historian, writer, and professorial lecturer in film studies at the George Washington University. In addition to Mexican cinema, his research interests include popular culture and society, and propaganda. He has authored and coauthored books including *The Mexican Filmography 1916–2001* (McFarland 2004), *Hollywood War Films: 1939–1945* (McFarland 1996), *Hard-Boiled in Hollywood* (BGSU Popular Press 1991), and *Doing Their Bit: Wartime American Animated Films, 1939–1945* (McFarland 1987), as well as contributed to *The 10 Cent War* (University Press of Mississippi 2017), *Companion to Film Noir* (Blackwell 2013), and *Latsploitation, Exploitation Cinemas, and Latin America* (Routledge 2009), among other collections.

Milton Keynes UK
Ingram Content Group UK Ltd.
UKHW011414211223
434786UK00006B/71